The Politics of Energy Crises

The Politics of Energy Crises

JULIET E. CARLISLE,
JESSICA T. FEEZELL,
KRISTY E. H. MICHAUD,
and
ERIC R. A. N. SMITH

OXFORD
UNIVERSITY PRESS

OXFORD
UNIVERSITY PRESS

Oxford University Press is a department of the University of Oxford. It furthers
the University's objective of excellence in research, scholarship, and education
by publishing worldwide. Oxford is a registered trade mark of Oxford University
Press in the UK and certain other countries.

Published in the United States of America by Oxford University Press
198 Madison Avenue, New York, NY 10016, United States of America.

Library of Congress Cataloging-in-Publication Data
Names: Carlisle, Juliet E., author.
Title: The politics of energy crises / Juliet E. Carlisle, Jessica T. Feezell,
Kristy E.H. Michaud, and Eric R.A.N. Smith.
Description: New York, NY : Oxford University Press, 2017. | Includes bibliographical
references and index. | Description based on print version record and CIP data provided
by publisher; resource not viewed.
Identifiers: LCCN 2016019524 (print) | LCCN 2016012501 (ebook) |
ISBN 9780190264659 (Updf) | ISBN 9780190635923 (Epub) |
ISBN 9780190264635 (hardcover : alk. paper) | ISBN 9780190264642 (pbk. : alk. paper)
Subjects: LCSH: Energy policy—United States | Petroleum products—Prices—United States. |
Petroleum reserves—Political aspects—United States. | Petroleum industry and trade—
Political aspects—United States. | Energy consumption—United States.
Classification: LCC HD9502.U52 (print) | LCC HD9502.U52 S585 2017 (ebook) |
DDC 333.790973—dc23
LC record available at https://lccn.loc.gov/2016019524

1 3 5 7 9 8 6 4 2

Paperback printed by Webcom Inc., Canada
Hardback printed by Bridgeport National Bindery, Inc., United States of America

To the memory of
Christine Piper and Martha Smith
And to Rob, Finn, and Wells,
Danny and Miles,
Thomas, Jameson, Everett, and Rowan,
and Elizabeth, Katharine and Stephanie—
who are all renewable sources of energy in our lives

CONTENTS

ACKNOWLEDGMENTS

We suspect that we are not the first group of authors to open their book by acknowledging that the final product was a long time in the making. This certainly was, and I suspect at least once along the way each of us wondered if it would ever be finished. When we began this endeavor, in 2006, we were a group of four graduate students and our advisor. Our first meeting occurred in late spring of 2006 in a conference room on the campus of UC Santa Barbara where we excitedly sketched out the book, assigned tasks, and created a listserv for future email correspondence titled, "energy divas." Since that meeting, much has changed, and many of these changes forced delays in finishing our book. In particular, we have collectively experienced the completion of three dissertations, three weddings, one wedding officiated, four births (but five babies!) that added to a toddler and two teenagers, and four new jobs with four moves, one tenure, and, ironically enough, one energy crisis. We also set and missed innumerable deadlines. During that first meeting we never anticipated we would take so long to finish this project, but we are certainly indebted to the patience and persistence of each of us and the sometimes authoritative task-management of one of us, to have finished what we all affectionately refer to as "the [damn] book."

It would be a terrible oversight not to acknowledge Leeanna Smith. Leanna was with us at that first meeting as a co-author, and she had a significant role in early chapter drafts. However, as the years passed, Leeanna heard a calling outside of academia and therefore left to pursue a different career path. So while she left us and this project, she surely contributed to it and later cheered us on. We are immensely grateful for her contributions and camaraderie during this project.

In acting they say there are no small roles, only small actors. We honor this sentiment as we thank our research assistants: Rizwan Ashgar, Mia Livaudais, Dan May, Christoph Mergerson, Walter Radovich, Jamie Silverstein, and Chelsea Turner. Every effort they made helped us inch closer to this book's completion.

Gerhard Peters deserves special thanks for his work helping us collect data from the American Presidency Project (http://www.presidency.ucsb.edu/), a comprehensive online library of documents related to the presidency and a wonderful resource. Sarah A. Binder was very generous and shared with us her data of major energy-related legislation both attempted and passed. Additionally, we are appreciative of Elizabeth Coggins of the Policy Agendas Project (http://policyagendas.org/) who estimated policy mood trends for us from survey items regarding energy development.

The anonymous reviewers for Oxford University Press provided extremely useful suggestions and guidance, which we believe made our book far better than it would have been otherwise.

The staff at the US Energy Information Administration (EIA) are also owed our gratitude. Without the important work they do, this project would not have been possible.

This project received support from the California State University, Northridge College of Social and Behavioral Sciences Research Fellowship, and for that we are grateful. Furthermore, some of the data used in chapters 3 and 4 were collected in other projects funded by grants from the University of California Toxic Substances Research and Teaching Program, the University of California Energy Institute's California Energy Studies Program, and the US Minerals Management Service of the US Department of the Interior.

Finally, all of us wish to thank those special ones in our lives who served as the proverbial shoulder, sounding board, and distraction along this journey—our families: Rob Patton, Finn and Wells Carlisle-Patton, Danny and Miles Feezell, Thomas, Jameson, Everett and Rowan Michaud-Hartman, and Elizabeth, Steffi, and Katie Newman-Smith.

The Politics of Energy Crises

1

Introduction

"Gas Dealers Say They Aren't Guzzling Profits

Service station owners deny making more money because of price surges, but many motorists aren't buying it."[1]

"Davis Orders State Agencies to Probe Soaring Cost of Gas"[2]

Headlines such as these regularly appear when energy crises strike and gasoline or electricity prices rise sharply. The public reacts with annoyance and suspicion when prices shoot up, they call on politicians to do something, and politicians respond. Energy crises instantly put energy issues on the nation's agenda, sometimes with dramatic consequences for public policy. Yet despite the fact that the United States has been hit with a series of energy crises since the Arab-Israeli War triggered the first OPEC boycott in 1973, a great deal remains unknown about them. Much has been written about each individual energy crisis, but the patterns that repeat themselves across all energy crises have largely been ignored. In this book, we investigate the political battles during energy crises and seek to discover what they have in common.

Energy crises, or energy price shocks as many economists call them, are rapid, large increases in energy prices—especially in oil prices. When faced with sharp price hikes, voters get angry and demand that politicians do something about the problem. That puts energy policy on the nation's agenda. Voters, journalists, policy advocates, lobbyists, and elected officials all start talking about what to do. A window of opportunity for policy change opens up, and new laws and government regulations are often the result.

These energy crises are important first and foremost because energy prices are critically important to the United States economy. We live in what historian David Nye calls the "high-energy economy."[3] Although the United States has a bit less than 5 percent of the world's population, we use 20 percent of the world's oil and 18 percent of its total energy.[4] Our transportation system—which not only lets us drive to work, but fills our stores with goods from around the world and gives us opportunities to vacation in exotic foreign climes—consumes 28 percent of the nation's energy.[5] Ninety-four percent of that—from automobiles and airplanes to ships and trains—is fueled by oil.[6] In addition to being the primary source for our transportation fuels, petroleum is also the primary feedstock for most of the chemicals and polymers that we consume.[7] A great deal of our clothing, cars, computers, furniture, and other goods are made from petroleum byproducts. Our modern world is made possible by energy, and especially by petroleum.

The health of our economy depends on energy prices. Past energy crises have triggered economic recessions. During the 1973–74 OPEC boycott, for example, gasoline prices shot up from three dollars a barrel to $11.65 in three months.[8] The price increase had the same effect as a huge tax increase. Exactly as Keynesian economists would predict, it pulled money out of the US economy and drove the country into a recession. Whether energy price shocks cause recessions—as one did in 1973—or worsen a recession sparked by other causes—as the energy price shock of 2007–8 did—they are clearly important economic events. On the flip side, low energy prices have helped fuel economic booms. Historians and economists point to our relatively low energy prices as a major boon to our economy.[9]

Energy crises are also important because they push energy policy to the top of the nation's political agenda. Most of the major policy shifts on energy issues have come in response to energy crises. Automobile fuel efficiency (CAFE) standards, the Strategic Petroleum Reserve, and the establishment of the Department of Energy were all products of past energy crises. Many other laws and regulations governing the oil and gas industry, transportation, and other petroleum-dependent industries were passed in response to high energy prices as well.

Energy crises are important to the environment as well because energy policies have consequences for the environment. The regulation of the price of oil in 1971 kept gasoline prices low and effectively encouraged more gasoline consumption and greenhouse gas emissions; the deregulation of the price of oil a decade later reversed that policy.[10] CAFE standards not only reduce the amount of gasoline we use; they reduce greenhouse gas emissions as well. Allowing oil drilling in the ultra-deep waters of the Gulf of Mexico with inadequate safety regulations eventually led to the Deepwater Horizon blowout in 2010.[11]

Many proposed policy choices also pose environmental risks or benefits. Drilling oil wells in the Arctic National Wildlife Refuge, using coal-to-liquid technology to produce synthetic diesel fuel, cutting back on regulations of the oil and gas industry, or shifting to electric cars all could have profound effects on our environment. Moreover, there is growing evidence that hydrofracking for oil and gas poses risks as well.

In short, oil prices have a critical impact on the economy and the environment. When oil prices rise or fall, America responds. The responses are most obvious in the aftermath of energy crises.

The Energy Crises

Since 1973, the United States has been hit with five energy crises. We will take each one up in detail in later chapters. Here we offer only a brief review to set the stage for our discussion.

The first energy crisis began with the October 1973 invasion of Israel by Egypt and Syria. At first, the invasion seemed to be succeeding. Israel's armies were forced to retreat and to call on Washington for additional supplies and aid. When President Nixon announced an emergency military aid package for Israel and American supply planes began arriving in Israel, Arab leaders struck back with the oil weapon. The Arab members of OPEC stopped oil shipments to the United States. The result of the embargo was a wave of price hikes and gasoline shortages across America. In the following weeks, the sight of lines at gasoline stations became commonplace. In some cities, police had to be stationed at gasoline stations to prevent violence. In the midst of this crisis, oil company profits shot up 52 percent. Consumer advocates and some politicians suggested that the oil companies were manipulating prices to make money. The public largely believed them. Polls showed that as many as three-quarters of the public believed that the oil industry was conspiring to fix prices.[12] Congress responded with hearings to investigate the charges, and eventually with laws to address the crisis.

The next energy crisis began with the Iranian revolution. Throughout 1978, the Ayatollah Ruhollah Khomeini, a fundamentalist Islamic opponent of the Shah of Iran, had been calling for demonstrations against the Shah in an effort to topple him. In December, those efforts peaked in a month of violence and a complete shutdown of Iranian oil exports. The demonstrations worked. In January, the Shah abandoned his country to the Ayatollah Khomeini and his followers.

Few observers foresaw the consequences of the Shah's fall. Iran supplied only 5 percent of the world's oil. Nevertheless, an oil panic set in. Between hoarding and speculative buying, prices climbed sharply throughout 1979 and into 1980. In the fall of 1980, Iraq worsened the situation by invading Iran. The Iraq-Iran War continued to keep Iranian oil off the market and caused a 70 percent cutback in Iraqi oil exports as well. The results for America included higher prices, shortages, and the by-then familiar and infuriating lines at gas stations. Prices eventually peaked in 1981 and then began sliding down as demand fell during a worldwide recession, which was partly triggered by the high oil prices.

In August 1990, Iraqi dictator Saddam Hussein ordered his army to invade Kuwait. The invasion shut off the flow of Kuwait's oil to world markets. Moreover, the ideas that Iraq now controlled 20 percent of OPEC production and 20 percent of the world's known oil reserves and that Saddam Hussein was a major influence on world oil markets worried Western nations. The result was an immediate jump in world oil prices.

The United States and its allies launched their counterattack in January 1991. The Persian Gulf War was short, brutal, and completely dominated by the US military. Iraq's army collapsed before the combined might of the United States and its allies, but before they fled from Kuwait, Iraqi troops set over 730 oil wells on fire, leaving an environmental and economic disaster behind them.

The 1990s ended with another price blow to the United States, albeit one that crept up more quietly. The cause was not the 2001 attack on the World Trade Center and the Pentagon, but a series of OPEC price hikes starting in 1999. In December 1998, oil prices had fallen to $8.03 a barrel because of overproduction and sharp declines in demand from weak Asian markets. In inflation-adjusted dollars, that was the cheapest oil had ever been. Those rock-bottom prices were causing serious economic problems for Saudi Arabia and other oil-producing countries. In response to the situation, OPEC started reducing the flow of oil in order to drive up prices. With a series of production cuts, OPEC managed to drive the price of oil to $30.36 a barrel by November 2000 and make the price of oil one of the most critical issues in the 2000 presidential election.

The second wave of the price shock began in early 2004. The Iraqi insurgency was growing, and America seemed incapable of stopping it. Prices edged up, reaching just under $50 a barrel in the summer of 2005, immediately before Hurricanes Katrina and Rita roared into the Gulf of Mexico. In the aftermath, oil briefly rose over $70 a barrel before dipping. But then oil prices began rising again. Year after year, prices moved up until the recession struck in 2008. By then it was no longer clear whether the expression "energy price shock" was appropriate. Rising oil prices had become a chronic condition, a trend that was broken only when the high prices helped drive the United States into recession and demand for oil fell.

In every energy crisis the United States has faced, we have seen a common sequence of events—what we call the "energy crisis cycle."[13] The steps in the cycle are (1) When foreign oil production is sharply cut, energy prices rise quickly—starting the cycle. (2) Along with increases in energy prices come large increases in the profits of energy producers. The news media inform the public about the soaring profits. (3) Politicians and interest group advocates criticize the energy industry for their greed in profiting at other people's misfortune, and accuse them of manipulating prices to increase profits. Some critics even claim that the energy industry fabricated the energy crisis to increase profits. (4) Most of the public believes the industry critics. They do not accept claims that the energy crisis is real, and so they feel justified in demanding that the government fix the problem without any cost to the public. (5) Business interests join the debate with demands to relax environmental regulations in order to produce more energy. For them, the energy crisis presents a window of opportunity to weaken environmental protections and increase their profits. (6) Environmental groups resist business demands and propose their own green solutions to the energy crisis. (7) Congress and the president attempt to respond with legislation and executive action to address the crisis and the competing political demands.

In most respects, the energy-crisis cycle is no different from what Anthony Downs, John Kingdon, or Frank Baumgartner and Bryan Jones have described when they discuss the agenda setting and policymaking process.[14] What makes energy crises a special case is that several aspects of the process are predictable. When world energy production quickly slows down because of wars or OPEC pricing decisions, oil prices rise because of the laws of supply and demand, the profits of energy producing companies always shoot up, politicians and policy advocates always accuse the energy companies of manipulating energy prices, the public always believes them, and a window of opportunity for policy change opens. That makes energy crises different from most other policymaking cases. We know that people will get angry and we know who will get the blame.

Theoretical Approach

Our study of agenda setting and policymaking builds on the theory of punctuated equilibrium in agenda setting and policymaking developed by Baumgartner and Jones and others.[15] Their basic argument is that the American political system is designed so that policy is fairly steady and unchanging most of the time, but occasionally there are "punctuations" of large, rapid policy change. The punctuations are initiated by what Roger W. Cobb and Charles D. Elder, Thomas Birkland, and others refer to as "triggering events" or "focusing events," which are exogenous shocks to the prevailing policy system and yield sharp policy change.[16]

We go beyond previous work by giving more attention to the role of public opinion than do other studies. We see public opinion as one of the driving forces behind policy changes regarding energy. Moreover, we see public opinion as having a role throughout the policymaking process, not just at the time when a focusing event initiates the process. Public opinion is important because almost all Americans own cars and drive. They see gasoline prices posted on huge signs at gas stations everywhere. When they buy gas, they see how much it costs and how much it has changed. And when they answer public opinion polls, politicians see how upset voters can become about gasoline prices.

Jones and Baumgartner write that agenda setting and policymaking are so complicated that no grand theory will ever be developed to explain them adequately.[17] They are probably right. However, we can learn a good deal about agenda setting and policymaking in the narrow area of energy policy. Energy issues are important, so this is worth doing. Moreover, there are bound to be more energy crises as oil supplies dwindle and as Middle Eastern wars continue to occur.

Plan of the Book

We begin our examination of the politics of energy policy in chapter 2 with a look at energy crises through the lens of Baumgartner and Jones's punctuated equilibrium theory. We use the methods they developed to explore the impact of energy crises (e.g., media content analysis and congressional hearing counts). We use some of the data they have collected in their Policy Agendas Project supplemented with our own data from other sources. Unlike most work on policy agendas, we focus on explaining substantive policies passed by Congress, rather than on budgets.

Chapter 3 examines how public opinion on energy policy changes over time, especially during energy crises. We look at general environmentalism and specific opinions about energy policy because the two parallel one another in important ways. We then move from general environmentalism to look at the public's support for offshore oil drilling and other energy development policies. We show that support for energy development rises and falls with the price of gasoline in the same way that environmentalism fluctuates with general economic health. This fluctuation creates windows of opportunity for policy change. When energy crises strike and prices are high, people want change— which opens opportunities for both energy industries and environmentalists to push their proposals onto the nation's political agenda.

The chapter continues with an examination of who gets blamed for high prices during energy crises. Blame plays a critical role in energy crises. When energy prices spike, people react angrily. Rising gasoline prices hurt people financially. Even people who can afford to spend fifty dollars to fill their gas tanks do not like it. So they look for explanations. Who or what caused the prices to rise? Who is to blame? That search involves sorting the competing politicians and policy advocates into good guys and bad guys, and has repercussions for policymaking.

Chapter 4 looks at the critical role that trust plays during energy crises. Trust is important because competing factions are seeking public support for their proposals. Environmentalists, oil companies, and other participants attempt to persuade the public to accept their versions of the truth and their policy recommendations because they believe that winning public support will increase their chances of winning their policy battles.

The remaining chapters look at what happened in each one of our energy crises. Chapter 5 looks at the crisis of 1973–74. Chapter 6 looks at the crisis that was sparked by the fall of Iran and the Iran-Iraq war in 1979–80. Chapter 7 looks at energy issues at the time of the Persian Gulf War in 1990–91. Chapter 8 is an examination of the energy price spikes in 1999–2001 and 2008, which vary in nature and from the previous crises.

Following the presentation of the core theory and the historical examination of each crisis, our concluding Chapter 9 revisits the theory of agenda setting and punctuated equilibrium, discussing some limits to Birkland's definition of focusing events. In our conclusion, we also offer our commentary on the implications of these limits and possible extensions and how we can understand theory in the dynamic environment of policymaking.

PART I

THE ROLES OF AGENDA SETTING, PUBLIC OPINION, AND TRUST DURING ENERGY CRISES

Energy Crises and Agenda Setting

"Never let a good crisis go to waste."[1]

Energy crises change the nation's political agenda. Surging prices draw attention to energy policy. Voters' anger about rising prices attracts media attention. Interest groups, recognizing that they have a window of opportunity, call for policy reforms. And politicians respond. The goal of this chapter is to put these crises in a theoretical framework.

Since the 1973–74 energy crisis, the United Staes has experienced a series of similar crises. During each one, the public called on politicians to step in and help. In this chapter, we will use the theory of punctuated equilibrium[2] (PE) to set the foundation for our analysis of energy policy. Punctuated equilibrium, as we discuss in more detail below, unites two literatures that were once disjointed—public policy and agenda setting. As Frank Baumgartner has said, "A punctuated equilibrium (PE) perspective on the study of public policy reminds us to pay attention equally to the forces in politics that create stability in public policy as well as those that occasionally conspire to allow dramatic changes . . . punctuations may come only rarely. . . [but] can have long-lasting consequences."[3] We believe that this perspective can reveal a great deal about the politics of energy crises.

To set the stage for our investigation of energy crises, we begin with a review of agenda setting and the theory of punctuated equilibrium. We discuss how the theory should be modified to address cases such as energy crises. We then use the tools of punctuated equilibrium theory to examine the history of energy crises starting with the 1973–74 crisis.

Agenda-Setting Theory

Agenda setting has been the topic of much empirical research stretching back to the 1960s. While Walter Lippmann's *Public Opinion*[4] might very well be the first to describe the mass media's link between "the world outside and the world inside our heads," it was Maxwell McCombs and Donald L. Shaw who, in their "Chapel Hill Study," offered the first important empirical analyses of public agenda setting. In their work, McCombs and Shaw present the theory of agenda setting that describes a direct relationship between the media's attention (amount and prominence of coverage) to a particular issue and the public's ranking of the perceived importance of that issue. According to McCombs and Shaw,

> In choosing and displaying news, editors, newsroom staff, and broad-casters play an important part in shaping political reality. Readers learn not only about a given issue, but how much importance to attach to that issue from the amount of information in a news story and its position. The mass media may well determine the important issues—that is, the media may set the "agenda" of the campaign.[5]

Related to McCombs and Shaw, Anthony Downs describes the "issue-attention cycle."[6] In his analysis of environmental policy, Downs traces five stages through which an issue rises and falls on the public agenda, beginning with the pre-problem (stage one), where the issue exists and experts are aware of it, but there has been little media attention. In stage two, there is "alarmed discovery and euphoric enthusiasm,"[7] followed by stage three, where there is public rec-ognition of the dimensions and costs associated with solving the problem. Stage four is characterized by a general decline in the public's interest in the problem, and finally, the fifth and last "post-problem stage,"[8] occurs when the public's attention stabilizes and does so at a point lower than it was at peak interest, but higher than at the beginning of the process.

Downs's cyclical theory argues that external shocks provide opportunities for substantive policy change. The policy issue moves through a process in which public attention peaks and then gradually declines. Over time public policy con-cerns shift elsewhere, and the original policy area is left somewhat changed but outside the public setting. The residual changes often alter the policy in a sub-stantial way, and will most likely play a key role when faced with a subsequent shock.[9]

Roger W. Cobb and Charles D. Elder's work deals directly with the process of policy agenda-building. They seek to explain from where policy issues derive. More precisely they ask, "How is an agenda built, (i.e., how is an issue placed on it), and who participates in the process of building it?"[10] In the spirit of E. E. Schattschneider's earlier work,[11] Cobb and Elder assume bias in the system insofar as there are "social forces" that influence and control the agenda and those that do not. Elites, in their perspective, have a strong hand in deciding what issues make it to the agenda. In their explication, Cobb and Elder argue, however, that major social change is possible: "Once a grievance reaches this system agenda, formal consideration on a governmental agenda is likely, if not inevitable."[12]

In later work, Cobb and Elder[13] consider "circumstantial reactors" or "triggering events," which are described as unanticipated events that spur issue initiation. Natural disasters such as the 1969 oil rig blowout in the Santa Barbara channel, events such as riots and assassinations, and even more general ecological change such as population growth, technological change, or economic change, such as an energy crisis, are all considered "circumstantial reactors" or "focusing events," as John Kingdon,[14] and later Thomas Birkland,[15] refer to them. Again, as a result of some focusing event, issues become elevated on the agenda and can push open a "window of opportunity" for policy change. "Sometimes crises come along that simply bowl over everything standing in the way of prominence on the agenda."[16]

In, *Agendas, Alternatives, and Public Policies*[17], John Kingdon laid out his agenda-setting theory, which defines three streams: problems, policy, and politics. The *problem stream* is composed of focusing events (i.e., crises, disasters), indicators, and feedback. The *political stream* is composed of public mood, interest group campaigns, electoral changes, congressional party division, and administrative changes. The *policy stream* consists of a "gradual accumulation of knowledge and perspective among specialists in a given policy area, and the generation of policy proposals by such specialists."[18]

The three streams are "largely independent of each other and each develops according to its own dynamics and rules."[19] Nevertheless, according to Kingdon's theory, "at some critical junctures the three streams are joined, and the greatest policy changes grow out of the coupling of problems, policy proposals, and politics."[20] These critical junctures or "policy windows" are usually the result of a change in the political stream (e.g., a new administration). A *problem* that commands attention, such as an energy crisis, is coupled with *policy* proposals as a solution to the crisis. Additionally, the energy crisis shifts the *political* stream by altering public opinion. This is what Kingdon refers to as a "complete linkage," when all three streams are joined together and this "enhances the odds that a subject will become firmly fixed on a decision agenda."[21] A further significant contribution that Kingdon makes is his distinction between those *inside* the government (e.g., president, the president's staff, appointees, bureaucrats, civil servants, members of Congress, etc.) and those *outside* the government (e.g., interest groups, political parties, academic researchers, media, consultants, and public opinion, etc.).

Baumgartner and Jones borrowed the concept of punctuated equilibrium in policy making from Stephen Gould and Niles Eldredge's findings about punctuated equilibria in evolutionary biology.[22] Gould and Eldredge's work showed paleontologists that evolution is mostly gradual and continuous with little change for long periods of time, punctuated by brief moments of considerable change. That is, the theory of punctuated equilibrium asserts that change occurs in relatively rapid spurts, rather than in a slow and gradual process.

In this spirit, Baumgartner and Jones explain the agenda-setting process by drawing a parallel between punctuated equilibrium and policy change.[23] The dynamics associated with the agenda lead to abrupt shifts in policymaking because of a change in the attention that a particular issue is paid. So, while there exist extended periods where issues receive little attention, the stability is "punctuated" by an upheaval or change: "The American political system, built as it is on a conservative constitutional base designed to limit radical action, is nevertheless continually swept by policy change, change that alternates between incremental drifts and rapid alternations of existing arrangements."[24] The punctuations, as described by Baumgartner and Jones, are initiated by what Cobb and Elder refer to as "triggering events" or "circumstantial reactors," and by others[25] as "focusing events," which are exogenous shocks to the prevailing policy system and yield explosive and sharp policy change.

According to Baumgartner and Jones's theory, the policy process is both dynamic and complex. There exist long periods of relative stability during which a policy receives little attention. However, when a particular issue receives attention, there is a rapid expansion of the issue. During the period of stable subsystem politics, the dominant actors within the subsystem control the policy image and support the status quo of limited participation—the policy monopolies "systematically dampen pressures for change."[26] As a result of the limited participation, we see limited and predictable policy change. In order to redefine a policy image, the expansion of conflict works to destroy the former subsystem, thereby leading to increased attention and the involvement of new actors.

Fundamental to the theory of punctuated equilibrium and the policymaking process are positive and negative feedback—forces that push policy change further along (positive), or restrain it and pull policy back toward the status quo. During periods of stability or incremental policy change, the process of negative feedback is dominant. This is not to say, however, that change never results from negative feedback. Change can indeed occur, but as Baumgartner and Jones explain, the change in a negative feedback system is akin to a homeostatic device insofar as change that occurs produces a force in the opposite direction, which thereby promotes a degree of stability.[27] In contrast, rapid bursts of disruption are often associated with positive feedback. What might be an initial and small change thus can give way to a sudden burst of cascading events that work quickly to alter the status quo. That is, "ideas of momentum, bandwagon effects, thresholds, and cascades play critical roles."[28] As Baumgartner and Jones note, the end of positive feedback does not necessarily return to the status quo, but perhaps settles into a new period of stability, perhaps radically different from the original.

Birkland[29] provides a comprehensive analysis of disasters—earthquakes, hurricanes, oil spills, and nuclear accidents—as focusing events. Birkland's refinement of Kingdon's notion of focusing events makes an important contribution to the agenda-setting literature with his theoretical treatment of events in terms of attention and policy impacts—essentially, why some events yield governmental responses and others do not. Specifically, Birkland defines "a potential focusing event as an event that is sudden, relatively rare, can be reasonably defined as harmful or revealing the possibility of potentially greater future harms, inflicts harms or suggests potential harms that are or could be concentrated on a definable geographical area or community of interest, and that is known to policy makers and the public virtually simultaneously."[30] We are keen to note as well that Birkland stresses that events are focal in terms of degree (more or less focal) rather than dichotomously (is or is not focal). In terms of our analysis, this distinction is important.

Birkland also argues that in order to understand the impact of a potential focal event, one must examine the political situation in the policy domain, which is best explained by Paul A. Sabatier's advocacy coalition framework.[31] According to Sabatier, within each policy domain several advocacy coalitions typically form around their shared core values and beliefs. The coalitions consist of stakeholders, government officials, experts, and other activists in the policy community. How well organized they are and how well they are able to respond to potential focusing events has a substantial impact on whether the focal events lead to policy changes. Birkland argues that focusing events highlight policy deficiencies and therefore potentially lead to grand policy changes, but do so when policy actors are organized and exploit the event. "Focusing events are much more likely to be important where the policy community that reacts to the event is relatively well organized and is able to use focusing events to dramatize the need for improved policy."[32]

The media's role in the policymaking process is integral, especially in terms of a focusing event. Media attention can spur rapid change by focusing the public's attention on particular issues. The agenda-setting literature demonstrates the relationship between the media's success at casting a light on an issue and the corresponding importance the public gives the issue. As a result of the attention that the media give to a particular issue, the issue becomes salient in the minds of the public, and, consequently, the public declares these issues to be most important. As Baumgartner and Jones's own work has demonstrated, the degree of attention the media have given to nuclear energy, tobacco, and pesticides, for example, corresponds with both public attention and congressional action on those issues.[33] Therefore, the influence of a focusing event on policy actors can be significant. Once the media and public begin to pay greater attention to an issue, that attention can then push the once-dormant problem to a top-spot on the political agenda in light of the recent and probable policy failure brought to bear by the focusing event.

Focusing Events and Focusing Episodes

The key elements of focusing events, according to Birkland, are that they (1) occur suddenly, (2) are relatively rare, (3) are large in scale, with real or potential harm, and (4) become known to both the public and policymakers nearly simultaneously. These elements certainly fit the cases that he examined in *After Disaster*—hurricanes, earthquakes, oil spills, and the Three Mile Island nuclear power plant disaster. However, they do not fit energy crises particularly well. Energy crises develop over weeks and months, not hours or days. Moreover, in some cases, experts have seen them coming, so they do not become known to policymakers and the public at the same time.

In the 1973 energy crisis, for example, the price of a barrel of oil rose from $3.00 to $11.65, but it took three months.[34] When OPEC leaders declared an embargo on Israel and the United States and said that they would reduce overall production in a series of monthly 5 percent cuts, the American public may not have seen what was coming, but energy experts certainly did. The lag between the time at which a barrel of crude oil is put on a tanker at a higher price and the eventual hike in prices at the gasoline pump is well understood by economists. So, too, did oil economists understand the implications of OPEC reductions in production.

Another twist is that some energy crises had long-term impacts on oil prices. After the first energy crisis in 1973–74, prices did not return to their original level. They dropped from their peak, but the overall level had changed for years to come. This is quite unlike the situations following natural disasters, oil spills, and nuclear accidents. People clean up and the world returns to normal.

One might be tempted to argue that Birkland's definition should be revised and stretched to allow energy crises to fit, but his decision to separate out sudden events that have dramatic impacts makes sense. The politics of focusing events are not the same as the more drawn-out developments that we call "focusing episodes."

Our definition of focusing episodes is similar to that of Birkland. Focusing episodes (1) occur rapidly, but can spread out over weeks or even months, (2) are relatively rare, (3) are large in scale, with real or potential harm, and (4) generally become known to policymakers before the public, although the lag time may only be weeks or months. The differences in time are not large, but they open opportunities for different types of political maneuvers and strategies. They are crises, but crises that play out over weeks and months, not days, so that policymakers and policy advocates can take stock of the situation and make careful decisions about their moves. Moreover, because they have more time, they have more policy options at their disposal. With hurricanes, earthquakes, and nuclear power plant disasters, Congress can only act after the crisis passes. With a focusing episode such as an energy crisis, Congress has time to act while the crisis is continuing.

Birkland makes the point that focusing events should not be conceptualized as being dichotomous. There is a continuum with some focal events being huge and others less so. Similarly, we argue that there is a continuum between focal events and what Birkland describes as "routine politics."[35] Focusing events are the hurricanes, oil spills, nuclear power plant accidents, and other sudden events that Birkland examines. In contrast, one might think of routine politics as issues such as the fights over immigration reform, Social Security, minimum wage levels, appropriate estate taxes, and the set of issues that fuel the debates over inequality in wealth and income.[36] Focusing episodes fall in between the two extremes, but are closer to focusing events. They spread out over weeks or months, drawing attention from the public, the news media, policy advocates, and politicians. They are not sudden, but they have many characteristics in common with focusing events.

Birkland also argues that issues are socially constructed. As he puts it, "Problems and events are not simply objective, obvious problems that automatically gain attention simply because they are compelling issues. Rather, there are usually many different, plausible ways to conceive of issues, of which only a few dominant interpretations emerge."[37]

Energy crises are not the only examples of focal episodes. Other examples include the California drought, Love Canal, the spread of Ebola, and the recognition that hydrofracking for oil and natural gas, along with the attendant reinjection wells, were causing earthquakes. All of these examples started slowly, played out over months or longer, got a great deal of media attention, and resulted in congressional or state legislation. By way of illustration, droughts in California have occurred before, but the most recent drought (from late 2001 to 2015) has been exceptional mostly due to its compounded effect, with each subsequent "wet period" (between December and March) becoming drier and drier. In 2011–12 minor effects of the drought were evident, but with even drier conditions the following year (2012–13 being the driest year in the 100-year record), the effects grew more severe and expanded geographically.[38] To exacerbate the problem, in 2014 California experienced the warmest year on record.[39] The California drought, like other droughts, exemplifies these slow-moving disasters because of their "creeping" nature, which makes it difficult to clearly identify a beginning and an end. Consequently, the disastrous effects of droughts and other slow-moving disasters can sometimes take months or years to appear. Moreover, one extreme weather event does not end the drought. The media attention toward the drought has been great, especially since 2014,[40] and policy proposals and government regulations were adopted to help mitigate the effects of the drought, including low-flow regulations and mandatory water use reductions, the latter via Executive Order signed by Jerry Brown on April 1, 2015. Brown's executive order also included guidelines that will help save water, increase enforcement against wasteful water use, invest in new technologies that will help California deal with water management, and streamline the state's response to droughts.[41]

Love Canal also serves as a good example of the more slowly occurring focal episode. Love Canal was land originally excavated by William T. Love as a canal that would connect the upper and lower Niagara River. Facing financial challenges, Love abandoned the project, and the City of Niagara Falls began using the land as a municipal waste disposal site, where between 1942 and 1953 the Hooker Chemical Corporation dumped tens of thousands of tons of chemical waste. In 1953, the Niagara Falls School Board purchased the land for $1 and built a school on the dumpsite. A middle-class community known as Love Canal was built nearby, and, eventually, residents began to complain of health problems, such as birth defects, children experiencing chemical burns after playing outside, and unusually high number of miscarriages. In addition to unexplained illnesses, residents noticed strange odors, dying vegetation, and an unusual black sludge that filled their basements. However, nothing was done for more than twenty years, when in the late 1970s the state of New York began to investigate the complaints. The length of time for the disaster to be realized was largely the result of the lag in recognizing the threat. The most likely delay in addressing the complaints was the lack of information about the low-level, long-term exposure to hazards, which made it difficult establish a direct causal link between the dumping and the negative impact on environmental and human health.[42] Moreover, once such toxins were identified and determined as the cause of such ill effects, it took some time for experts and policy makers to develop a strategy to remedy the problem. Furthermore, in the 1970s there was greater attention by activists and media to the perils of toxic pollution on the environment and human health. And, due to the enhanced attention, policies were adopted to deal with liability in cases of contamination. Specifically, the Comprehensive Environmental Response Compensation and Liability Act (CERCLA), commonly known as Superfund, was passed by Congress on December 11, 1980.

As these examples illustrate, focus episodes share similarities with Birkland's notion of focusing events, in that both involve the unfolding of events that garner the attention of the public and policymakers. They differ in the length of time during which they unfold, and in the order in which policymakers and the public learn about the issue. Because energy crises generally unfold over weeks or months, cause a great deal of harm, and are a discovered by policymakers before the public learns about them, they are better described as focusing episodes.

Focusing Events and Episodes as Causal Triggering Mechanisms and the Role of Public Opinion

Potential focusing events and episodes are important because they can become the proximate causes of agenda change and eventually policy change. If Kingdon's three streams converge—that is, if there is a problem that is widely recognized, there are appropriate policy solutions, and the political situation is ripe for change (which means that one of Sabatier's advocacy collations is strong and prepared to act)—then the focusing event or episode draws attention to the problem and a sequence that leads to change is initiated.

Why does the focusing event or episode have this effect? The answer is public opinion. Politicians have reason to fear the public and respond to it when the public wants something, and the news media have reason to cover what the public wants to read and see. Underlying focusing events and episodes are public desires and demands.

Elected officials respond to what they perceive to be the public's beliefs and preferences because of their desire to win reelection. There are many influences on what elected officials do in office, but public opinion is an important one. Even congressional incumbents who hold objectively safe seats feel the need to satisfy the public's demands because they feel that they are actually in marginal seats and may lose unexpectedly. Thomas E. Mann shows this in his classic 1978 study, *Unsafe at Any Margin*, and subsequent investigators have come to the same conclusion.[43] Legislators are perpetually concerned with reelection. As a result, they want their constituents to believe that the legislators are paying attention and doing the public's bidding. When an issue suddenly appears all over the news, their concerns are increased, and they try to show that they are responding to their voters.

The news media also want to please the public, although to editors and report-ers, members of the public are consumers. In order to sell more newspapers and get more viewers and readers, journalists go after the stories that will be most interesting and attractive to the public. As Birkland observes, "News impera-tives make sudden, novel, and injurious events particularly attractive for news coverage. Environmental catastrophes and natural disasters often provide much more photogenic stories than do problems that rely on changes in indicators for their purported urgency."[44] To that, we can add that spiking energy prices, spreading Ebola epidemics, withering droughts, and other slow-motion disas-ters also make good news subjects because people want to learn about them. These episodes may affect people more slowly than disasters, but they spark in-terest and concern, even fear.

That public opinion provides the foundation for focus events and episodes is clear, but the nature of the influence of public opinion is complicated. First, as researchers starting with McCombs and Shaw have shown, the news media can persuade people how important a problem is.[45] When the news media cover topics, the public decides that they must be important. There is a clear "cause and effect" relationship. For example, studies have shown that when the news media start covering crime or environmental pollution, an increased number of people tell pollsters that they are concerned with crime or pollu-tion.[46] There is a clear temporal sequence here. First come the news stories, then the increase in the public's sense that a problem is important. Second, in some cases, the public ignores the news media and decides on its own what is important. When people have direct experience with an issue, which they do with inflation or rising gasoline prices, the evidence shows that they can make up their own minds about the importance of the issues without regard to what the news media say.[47] These are "obtrusive" issues as opposed to issues with which people have no direct experience, which are "unobtrusive" issues. From the point of view of elected officials, of course, it does not make any difference why the public finds something important. If the public cares, politicians will generally respond.

A third way in which the influence of public opinion is complicated is that the content of what people think, not just whether they think an issue is im-portant, has an impact on focusing events and episodes. The stockpiling of oil and gasoline during the 1973–74 energy crisis provides an example. During the crisis, individuals and firms in both the United States and Germany increased their stockpiles of oil and gasoline. People saw indications of the energy crisis—higher prices, gas lines, and news coverage of the crisis—and they took action. Individual motorists responded by filling up their gasoline tanks more often and keeping the average level in their tanks higher. Firms responded by stockpiling oil and gasoline for business use. Overall, inventories of oil and gas increased during the crisis, which in turn pushed prices even higher. Ironically, this happened in both the United States, where oil imports dropped, and in Germany, where oil imports actually increased.[48] Peculiarities aside, feedback loops like these occur during focusing episodes. In this case, people acted themselves, but in other cases, people have been angry about high energy prices, and political leaders have responded with immediate steps, such as President Nixon's gasoline rationing during the 1973–74 crisis and California's price freeze on electricity during the 2000 electricity crisis.[49] Because focusing episodes take weeks or months to play out, the content of public opinion has ample opportunities to influence feedback loops and change the course of the crises.

A final point to make about public opinion is that it continues to be influential after the initial stage of focusing attention. Just as the desire for reelection makes elected officials pay attention to an issue when the public thinks that it is important, that same desire still matters when politicians are choosing among policy alternatives and eventually voting on legislation. Public opinion can limit the range of alternatives that are considered and push elected officials toward particular solutions.

Most studies of agenda setting only address public opinion in the initial start-up stage of the process. In Baumgartner and Jones's work, for example, Gallup's most important problem questions are discussed at the beginning of each case study, but then the analyses turn in a more institutional direction (e.g., congressional hearing counts, federal grants, budget allocations, etc.), and public opinion is dropped from discussion.[50] In short, most agenda-setting studies that consider public opinion connect it only to the initial start-up stage when the news media report about something and people find it important.

Previous scholars have warned against treating the policymaking process as if it were a series of stages.[51] Birkland writes, "Thinking of . . . the policy making process as being intertwined prevents us from succumbing to the analytical shortcomings of what became called the 'stages' model of policy making."[52] He was not speaking specifically of public opinion, but his caution bears weight. The content of what people think (i.e., beyond issue importance) continues to matter in the agenda-setting process because elected officials care about it.

California's anti-nuclear movement in the 1970s provides a useful example of the impact of public opinion.[53] Anti-nuclear sentiment was growing across the nation in the 1970s, motivated in part by a potentially catastrophic 1975 fire at Browns Ferry reactor in Alabama.[54] Leading anti-nuclear crusaders in California came together and wrote a ballot initiative, Proposition 15, which would have effectively killed the nuclear industry in California if it had passed. In response, just days before the June 1976 election, the California State legislature passed and Governor Brown signed three moderate bills that limited the nuclear industry. Proposition 15 lost, but the legislature's restrictions prevented any more nuclear power plants from being built. Public opinion mattered throughout the political process, not just at the beginning.

In many case studies, most important problem data have been analyzed and some time trend data on opinions on various issues considered, but a great deal remains untouched.[55] In energy policy, for example, does the public think a crisis is real or faked? Who is to blame for the high prices? Whom does the public trust to bring prices back down? In short, who are the good guys and bad guys? What immediate steps should be taken? In any given problem that captures the public's attention, there are important questions about public opinion that should be asked because they set the stage for the battle over the agenda and the public policy proposals that are eventually considered. But public opinion continues to matter as the agenda-setting process moves forward toward policy change.

Energy Policy and Agenda Setting

The theoretical framework of agenda setting has been widely used to explain a variety of issues and policies, especially those broadly categorized as environmental. Most notably, in his analysis of the annual changes in federal budgetary appropriations for a variety of environmental programs, Baumgartner shows periods of policy stability punctuated by sharp policy shifts.[56] Other efforts include Robert J. Duffy's broad assessment of the role that environmental groups play in agenda setting,[57] and Sarah B. Pralle's work on forest policies and on the politics of climate change policy, as well as work by other scholars.[58]

On energy-related issues, Birkland assesses the role of disasters—in particular the Exxon Valdez and Santa Barbara oil spills as well as nuclear accidents—as focusing events in altering the policy agenda.[59] Bradford H. Bishop considers the impact of the Deepwater Horizon blowout in the Gulf of Mexico as a focusing event for support toward oil drilling.[60] Finally, in Michael E. Kraft and Sheldon Kamienieki's[61] edited volume, the contributors consider the roles of open policy windows created by the aftermath of 9/11, energy blackouts, a spike in gas prices, and a Republican majority in Congress to expand oil drilling in the Alaskan National Wildlife Refuge. However, no study has yet conducted a thorough investigation of energy crises through the lens of the agenda-setting and punctuated equilibrium theory.

We now begin our exploration of energy crises via the theoretical perspective of agenda setting with energy crises as our focusing episodes. In doing so, we consider the trends and fluctuations in the price of imported oil, shifts in public opinion, media interest, and presidential and congressional attention from the initial 1973–74 energy crises through the three subsequent crises. More specifically, we explain what energy crises are and why they are important. We lay out a causal process that emphasizes the role that energy crises play in capturing the attention of the media and public. The focused attention of the public writ large (e.g., citizens, media, policy makers, policy coalitions) creates a window of opportunity for policy change. As a consequence of the sudden surge in the price of oil, some people become angry or upset about the rising prices and therefore make demands that government do something to remedy perceived policy failures. Policy makers respond to the public's demands and propose solutions that protect the public from high prices with price controls or subsidies.

Our explanatory variable is agenda activity, and therefore we include shifts in public opinion, media attention, and congressional and executive activity in response to the energy crises. Our independent variable (and focusing episode) is energy crises, or energy price shocks as many economists call them, which are rapid, large increases in energy prices—especially in oil prices. Again, our definition of focusing episodes is similar to that of Birkland. Focusing episodes (1) occur rapidly, but can spread out over weeks or even months, (2) are relatively rare, (3) are large in scale with real or potential harm, and (4) generally become known to policymakers before the public, although the lag time may only be weeks or months.

In terms of energy crises, it is important to note that we understand focusing episodes to be socially constructed and therefore dynamic. Consequently, "problems are not simply objectively big or small, benign or injurious, but instead are socially constructed through the use of symbols, beliefs, and facts to tell the story of how conditions became problems, who is benefited or harmed by the problem, whose fault it is, and how it can be solved."[62] As such, there is no magic percentage increase in prices that will trigger an energy crisis. The first energy crisis set the stage and prepared everyone to look for an energy crisis. If 1973 and 1979 had not happened, no one might have thought of it in 1990–91. The first one made observers hypersensitive to the possibility, and because the subsequent rises in prices resonated with the public, the issue was promoted to the agenda and therefore deemed a focusing episode. As our figures later in the chapter show, the nature of each of the price shocks vary, and so do the political effects of each. Some might argue,[63] for example, that the price shock of 1990–91 might not really have been a "shock," and that its effects on the agenda were minimal if existent at all. We, however, take the perspective that again, problems such as price shocks are constructed and part of a causal explanation,[64] and therefore "perceptions, not real world-indicators, count."[65] That is, "the impact of the event is proportional to the meaning that is assigned to it."[66] It is also important to note that Birkland's second point is that focusing events are rare and therefore unpredictable. As Birkland explains, "We can assume that an airplane will crash somewhere at some time in the future, but the wreck of a *particular* flight at a *particular* place and time is usually unexpected. Such an accident is unexpected because it is rare."[67] In some ways we can say the same thing about energy crises as plane crashes—in general we know that they will likely happen, but we cannot say exactly when and cannot predict the nature and scope.

By all accounts, the 1973–74 energy crisis falls in line with Birkland's definition of a focusing event. In 1973, several Arab nations, angered at US support of Israel in the 1973 Arab-Israeli War, launched an oil embargo against the United States and Holland. The embargo was accompanied by decreased OPEC production and with minimal global excess production capacity available outside OPEC. While the United States had faced energy shortages as far back as 1970, this was an altogether sudden, unpredictable, and widespread interruption of the supply of petroleum to the world, and became known to both public and policy makers simultaneously. For the United States, the embargo lead to short-term shortages and price increases after decades of abundant supplies and insatiable consumption. The results were alarming: citizens faced gas and energy rationing, and therefore long lines formed at the gas pumps across the nation. In some cases, violence at the gas pump erupted and gas shortages forced other stations to close altogether. Many have often identified the energy crisis as a significant factor in the subsequent economic recession that occurred in 1974 and 1975.

The 1979–80 oil shock is mostly consistent with Birkland's typology. In terms of how sudden the crisis was, it was not terribly sudden. Therefore, we see that with its slow approach it fits better within the definition of focusing episode than a focusing event. Initially, the oil shortage resulting from the fall of the Shah of Iran had little impact on the United States, mostly due to the scant 8 percent of oil Iran supplied to the United States. However, the ripple effect eventually hit American consumers, when in November 1978 premium gasoline grew short and the price of gas began to climb, rising 8 percent over the previous year. Again, while overall OPEC crude oil prices increased to unprecedented levels between 1979 and 1981, the price increase was not exactly sudden but rather occurred over a protracted length of time. Nevertheless, Americans faced gas rationing and presidential appeals for conservation to help buffer the gas shortage. Also, while political tension in the Middle East is not rare, the massive oil strikes in Iran in October of 1978 caused oil production to plummet by 40 percent, sending ripples of speculation and concern throughout the oil industry. Shortly after the strikes, and amid increasing political tensions, the Shah Mohammad Reza Pahlavi fled the country, which added political drama to an oil

shortage already underway. This shock was substantial; by November, oil production had dropped from 5.5 million bpd to less than 1 million bpd, which was
hardly enough to satisfy domestic demand and certainly not enough to allow
for export. Global concern grew in response to the massive drop in Iranian oil
production, and leaders started to call on reserves and public conservation. The
underlying and somewhat constant political unrest in the Middle East makes
oil shocks such as these both predictable and totally unpredictable, because it is
impossible to know just how a political event might lead to a strike or massive
shortage. In this case, the coupling of a large-scale oil shortage with dramatic
political events in Iran acutely focused both public and policymaker attention
on the crisis within the span of a couple months, and the Carter Administration
moved quickly in response.

When Iraq invaded Kuwait on August 2, 1990, crude oil prices rose suddenly and sharply for the third time in seventeen years. While the 1991 invasion
was increasingly probable, especially with threats from Iraq's dictator, Saddam
Hussein, that he could use the oil weapon again, it was not predictable.[68] In fact,
in the spring of 1990, amidst a turbulent energy market, US Senate hearings revealed that senators doubted the probability of a major oil disruption for the
next several years, possibly upward of ten.[69] Unlike previous crises, the United
States was sitting on a well-stocked Strategic Petroleum Reserve (SPR) that was
available to draw on in the presence of a shortage to alleviate supply interruption
and related price hikes. However, prices rose during this crisis without a real
shortage in oil; the "crisis" was perceived and socially constructed, resulting from
previous experience coupled with fear of future shortages based on the actions
of Saddam Hussein. As a result, the size and scope of the crisis and potential
consequences were unpredictable. The public and politicians became aware of
Hussein's actions simultaneously; however, the crisis that followed developed
differently for all actors. In this episode, Congress and the public were calling
for a drawdown of the SPR while President G. H. W. Bush was reluctant to do
so without a real shortage. Under substantial pressure, Bush eventually opened
up the SPR, gave it a test run to demonstrate its effectiveness, and helped to
alleviate public concern and shorten the crisis. An important result of the 1990–
91 crisis was that it enabled legislation that broadened the circumstances under
which the SPR could be used in future energy crises, an act that should temper
public concern in the face of a potential shortage.

The 1999–2000 and 2007–8 oil shocks differ from the earlier price shocks,
but they fit the criteria for a focusing episode. Neither of the price shocks were
associated with a sudden event that disrupted the physical supply of oil. In the
case of the 1999–2000 crisis, OPEC countries restricted production in response
to falling oil prices, which were the result of overproduction by OPEC, warm
winter weather, and stagnant Asian oil demand in the wake of the Asian economic

crisis. In the case of the 2007–8 crisis, stagnant production and increasing global demand drove up oil prices over the course of a year and a half.

With regard to the second of Birkland's criteria, the events leading up to oil shocks were not particularly rare, with the exception of the East Asian economic crisis that preceded the 1999–2000 energy crisis, and some would argue that they were not unexpected, either. In 1998, an article appearing in *Scientific American* warned that peak oil—the point at which we have pumped half the world's oil supply—would be reached no later than 2010.[70] Once we had reached that tipping point, the authors argued, oil prices would rise sharply and permanently unless demand for oil dropped. Although skeptics discounted this prediction when it was originally made, the steady increase in the price of oil and the two shocks that occurred within the first ten years of the twenty-first century provide support for the authors' expectations. Additionally, both crises occurred gradually, with a steady rise in oil prices taking place over the span of a year and a half.

While the most recent crises deviate from the first two of Birkland's criteria, they are consistent with the second two criteria. First, both crises were large in scale, affecting not just America, but the rest of the world. The oil shocks had dramatic effects on the United States and global economies. Second, although they were gradual and not entirely unexpected, they caught both policymakers and the public off-guard, placing the issue of energy policy at the center of the policy debate.

Therefore, to summarize our expectations, in accord with the basic arguments of agenda-setting theory and focusing events, or again *focusing episodes* as we call them, we hypothesize the following: (1) Energy price shocks occur, (2) the price shocks focus the attention of the media and public, (3) the increased attention by the public and media on the energy crisis affects the agenda activity of Congress and the president in terms of political activity related to energy. Energy price will be measured by the price of oil and oil imports as a percent of GDP. As we noted above, we view energy crises to be in part socially constructed, and as such there is no magic mathematical formula that indicates the existence of them. We measure public attention to energy issues with public opinion data that captures Americans who identify "energy" as the most important problem and a measure of policy mood regarding energy development. Media attention is indicated by energy-related articles in the *New York Times* and other major US newspapers. Finally, agenda activity is measured for both the president and Congress in terms of oral and written presidential statements regarding energy crises and petroleum, mentions of "energy" in presidential State of the Union speeches, the number of congressional hearings related to energy, and the number of major proposals, executive orders, and public laws relating to energy.

Energy Crises and Agenda Setting

Prior to the 1973 Arab-Israeli war and the subsequent embargo, the public had paid little attention to energy policy. In the years preceding the embargo, Americans had grown increasingly dependent on oil. From 1950 to 1970, oil consumption doubled, and while domestic oil helped fulfill that need, domestic supplies could not keep pace with demand. As a result, Americans had to rely increasingly on imported foreign oil. By 1970, the United States imported enough oil to satisfy 30 percent of its energy needs.[71] The Arab oil embargo came at a time when the United States was already suffering from energy shortages and rising prices.

The United States experienced its first significant spike in the price of oil in 1973, which coincided with the invasion of Israel by Egypt and Syria (see figure 2.1). As a result of America's airlifting supplies to Israel, Arab members of OPEC declared a partial embargo. Then, when President Nixon announced an emergency military aid package for Israel, the Arab oil-producing nations responded with a total embargo on oil shipments to the United States. The result of the embargo was a wave of price hikes and gasoline shortages across America, with prices jumping from about $13 per barrel in 1973 to $22 in 1974. The initial spike did not drop off afterward, but sat steady at about $22 per barrel for the

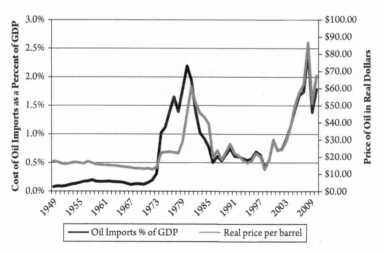

Figure 2.1 The Price of Oil and Oil Imports as Percent of GDP.
Value of Fossil Fuel Net Imports, 1949–2010 (table 3.9) and Crude Oil Domestic First Purchase Prices, Selected Years, 1949-2010 (table 5.18), EIA, 2010. Annual Energy Review 2010. Report DOE/ EIA-0384 (2010). Energy Information Administration, accessed May 13, 2016 https://www.eia.gov/ totalenergy/data/annual/archive/038410.pdf ; GDP: Bureau of Economic Analysis, http://www.bea. gov/national/—the data were on the main page under "Current-dollar and 'real' GDP (Excel)."

remainder of the decade. The spike in oil prices resulting from the embargo conforms to Birkland's definition of a focusing event. In fact, a Nixon aide describes the embargo as follows: "It was a shock to most of us. We had not anticipated the oil embargo and the gas shortages. The problem simply exploded, and we were engulfed."[72]

Coinciding with the Iranian revolution, the price per barrel of oil spiked again in 1979. While few foresaw the consequences of the Shah's fall as a result of the small proportion of the world's oil that Iran supplied (5 percent), an oil panic set in. Between hoarding and speculative buying, prices climbed sharply throughout 1979 and into 1980. In the fall of 1980, the situation was exacerbated by Iraq's invasion of Iran. The Iraq-Iran War continued to keep Iranian oil off the market and caused a 70 percent cutback in Iraqi oil exports as well. The results for America included higher prices, shortages, and the all-too-familiar lines at gas stations. Prices eventually peaked in 1981 and then began sliding down as demand fell during a worldwide recession, which was partly triggered by the high oil prices.

The third price spike occurred in August 1990, when Iraqi dictator Saddam Hussein ordered his army to invade Kuwait. The invasion shut off the flow of Kuwait's oil to world markets. Western nations grew concerned that Iraq now controlled 20 percent of OPEC production and 20 percent of the world's known oil reserves, and that Saddam Hussein was a major influence on world oil markets. As a result of the Iraqi invasion and the subsequent UN embargo of crude oil from both Iraq and Kuwait, plus fear that the conflict might spread into Saudi Arabia, crude oil prices spiked, increasing from about $13 per barrel in July to $22 in August, and then by mid-October hitting its peak at $31 per barrel.[73] Therefore, based on the US Energy Information Agency data, between July and October 1990, the price of crude oil rose 138 percent on world markets. In the days and months following the Iraqi invasion, with oil prices soaring upward, consumers eventually were forced to pay more for gasoline—up to an extra 29¢ per gallon for gasoline in October 1990 (the peak) compared with July, three months earlier.[74] After the United States and its allies launched their counterattack, Iraq's army quickly collapsed. Ultimately, the price spike was as short-lived as the war, and oil prices quickly fell back to $22 per barrel, not quite pre-war prices.

The final set of price increases we examine occurred between 1999 and 2008, and they mark the end of the era of cheap oil. The first price shock began in 1999, when OPEC members cut production in response to a drop in oil prices resulting from overproduction by OPEC, warm winter weather, and stagnant Asian oil demand resulting from the Asian economic crisis. The price of oil climbed from $11 per barrel in December 1998 to $37 per barrel in September 2000, making energy one of the most critical issues in the 2000 presidential election.

Although prices dropped after the peak in 2000, they never returned to their previous baseline, and they climbed steadily between 2002 and 2007, with occasional sharp increases in response to US military involvement in the Middle East and to hurricanes. Then, in 2007, the price of oil began a steep and steady climb as a result of stagnant global production and increased global demand, peaking at $145 per barrel in July 2008. Energy was once again an important campaign issue, this time in the 2008 presidential election. By the end of the year, prices had fallen to $41 per barrel, and the 2007–8 oil price shock was over.

Each of these oil price hikes since 1973 caused more than frustration and annoyance to consumers. They harmed the US economy as well. The second trend line in figure 2.1[75] is the cost of importing oil as a percentage of the gross domestic product. That cost acts as a tax. It takes money out of the US economy and transfers it elsewhere in the world. As a result, when oil prices rise, the economy falters. Ten of the eleven recessions since World War II and all of the recessions since the 1960s have been associated with oil price shocks. The causal role of the price shocks is still being sorted out by economists, but a good case can be made that sharp increases in world oil prices have contributed to US recessions.[76]

Let us turn to polling trends to better understand the influence that the oil price spikes had on the agenda. First, each of these oil price spikes are akin to what Kingdon and Birkland identify as a "focusing event" and demonstrate the beginning of the energy crisis cycle. As the energy crisis cycle predicts, the spike in oil and gas prices will jolt the public's attention to the issue.

The polling trends demonstrate that public concern turned toward energy issues during each of the energy crises. However, it is important to clarify that altogether public attention to energy issues is never very high, even during energy crises, especially when compared with the attention on the economy, which typically dominates the attention of the public. Nevertheless, in general the trend demonstrates how each energy crisis did focus American concern on the issue of energy. The proportion of Americans identifying energy as the most important problem ranges from a low of 0 percent in 1970 to a high of 20 percent in 1979. Furthermore, the ebb and flow of public attention seems to mostly correspond with price spikes and the energy crises.

Since the first energy crisis in 1973, national public opinion polls have asked Americans what they consider to be the most important problem facing the nation.[77] Figure 2.2 shows the percentage of the public who responded that energy prices were the leading problem. The data show that the first spike in public attention to energy issues coincided with the first major energy crisis in 1973–74. In 1974, at the height of the first energy crises, 10 percent of Americans cited energy as America's most important problem. In 1975 and 1976 the proportion declined to 6 percent and then 2 percent, respectively. Additionally, when the

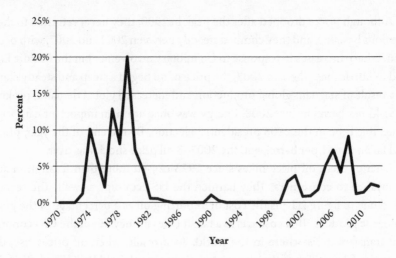

Figure 2.2 Proportion of Respondents Who Identify "Energy" as "Most Important Problem," 1970–2012.

The data used here were originally collected by Frank R. Baumgartner and Bryan D. Jones, with the support of National Science Foundation grant numbers SBR 9320922 and 0111611, and were distributed through the Department of Government at the University of Texas at Austin. Neither NSF nor the original collectors of the data bear any responsibility for the analysis reported here.

second energy crises began to appear in the late 1970s, we see a second wave of public attention with an uptick in the proportion identifying energy as the most important problem, reaching a high of 20 percent in 1979. A fairly steep decline of public attention followed, with energy falling off the radar for most Americans throughout the 1980s, presumably the result of the low price of oil over that period. In 1990–91, there is a very small jump in public attention, during the 1990 price shock, perhaps owing to the short duration and quick recovery of the Persian Gulf War. Throughout the rest of the decade again we see no concern about energy.

In December 1998, oil prices hit a low of $10.82 per barrel because of over-production, warm winter weather, and sharp declines in demand from weak Asian markets. This was the cheapest oil had ever been, adjusting for inflation. However, the low prices meant economic problems for oil-producing countries and, as a result, OPEC began cutting production, thereby driving the price of oil up, eventually to $33 a barrel by November 2000. The price of oil quickly became a major focal point of the 2000 presidential election and also once again registered as the most important problem on Gallup's poll.[78] Looking at figure 2.2, we see the uptick, albeit modest, in the proportion of Americans citing energy as the most important problem in 2000 and 2001. While this increase is slight relative to the increases during the other energy crises, we do see that generally public opinion ebbs and flows with the price of oil.

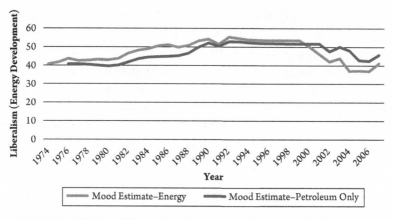

Figure 2.3 Policy Mood and Energy Development.

The policy mood was estimated for us by policyagendas.org however, the measures used to estimate the mood were collected from a variety of sources (these are listed in Appendix A).

In 2004, we again see Americans' concern turn toward energy as prices continued to press upward, reaching nearly $50 per barrel in 2004 and then spiking in the summer of 2005 to nearly $70 per barrel in the aftermath of hurricanes Katrina and Rita. The trend continues until 2008, when the economic recession forced energy prices back down. And, as we see, public concern about energy as the most important problem tracks with shifts in the price of oil.

Another indicator of shifting public attention toward energy prices is energy policy mood, presented in figure 2.3. Our energy policy measure is based on James Stimson's general policy mood.[79] Stimson compares *mood* to what Walter Lippmann called the "spirit of the age."[80] Stimson writes, "[Mood] connotes shared feelings that move over time and circumstance . . . of changing *general* dispositions."[81] Averaging across hundreds of political survey questions, policy mood is an aggregate measure of the public's preferences for more or less government, or "liberal" and "conservative" policy options, respectively. Policy mood is different from both partisanship and ideology insofar as it is not a long-standing disposition but a variable response to the changing political landscape.

Our measures of energy policy mood—estimated from eighty survey items regarding oil drilling (both offshore and in the Arctic National Wildlife Refuge, or ANWR)[82] between 1974 and 2007—present an aggregate measure of the public's policy preferences regarding energy development, broadly. We also include a mood trend for petroleum-only related development. Higher scores indicate a more pro-environment or liberal public, and lower scores a more pro-energy development or conservative public.

In the immediate aftermath of the 1973–74 energy crisis, the policy mood moves slightly up along the mood scale, showing a moderate shift toward less demand for energy production. In the rest of the 1970s, it remains fairly steady. In the 1980s, as the price of oil fell, both energy policy mood measures once again shift increasingly toward a liberal or pro-environment position. The upward trend ends in 1990, with a slight dip that corresponds to the Persian Gulf War and mini-oil price surge. Perhaps due to panic about a prolonged energy crisis, Americans turned toward increased American oil production and development. However, this is a rather quick blip, and in 1992, after the Persian Gulf War, the mood once again jumps slightly upward, in the pro-environmental direction to the pre-war level. Throughout the rest of the 1990s, the mood ever so slightly edges down, in the pro-development direction, and then begins to fall more quickly and significantly when oil prices start rising after 1998. This pro-development trend continues until 2006 and demonstrates that the demand for more energy production had returned. Although shifts in the policy mood are not sharp, policy mood does appear to be moving with the price of oil.

In terms of agenda setting and energy crises, energy policy mood should not be considered alone. It is important to consider how shifts in the public mood correspond to shifts in media attention as well as shifts in government activity and policy outputs, which we turn to now.

As two leading scholars of agenda setting point out, "A major source of instability in American politics is the shifting attention of the media."[83] Indeed, the media's role in the policymaking process cannot be ignored. Public attention to a particular issue can be radically affected by the amount of media coverage. In turn, such public attention can spur rapid policy change. For example, the degree of attention the media have given to nuclear energy, tobacco, and pesticides corresponds with both public attention and congressional action on those issues.[84]

With energy crises, our analysis provides evidence in accord with the theory of agenda setting. Like Michelle Wolfe, Bryan D. Jones, and Frank R. Baumgartner,[85] we are not so concerned with whether "the media lead (set agendas) or lag (index)," as the media and policy making are "intertwined in complex feedback systems."[86] As figure 2.4 shows, media coverage of oil issues, as indicated by counts of articles in the New York Times and major US papers[87] concerning energy crises and oil issues,[88] jumps during energy crises. Newspaper coverage of energy issues was very low in the years leading up to the 1973–74 energy crisis, with two stories in both the New York Times and in major US papers in 1970. However, those numbers jump in 1973 with approximately 200 stories for each of our two counts. The upticks are not nearly as significant for the energy crises in 1979–80 or 1990–91, but they are visible. In addition, there are significant increases in stories during the 1999–2001 and 2007–8 energy crises, according to both counts.

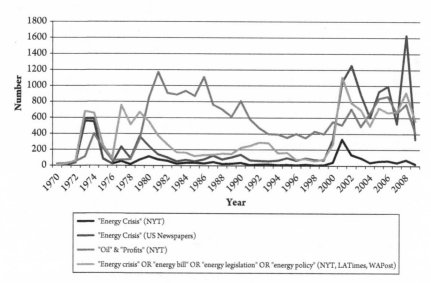

Figure 2.4 Articles Related to Energy Crisis in *New York Times* Index and US Newspapers, 1970–2008.
LexisNexis Academic

The formal political agenda includes matters of public policy that are brought before governmental decision makers for formal consideration. Punctuated equilibrium theory says that we should expect attention by public officials to energy prices to be minimal when oil prices are stable, but then be punctuated by bursts of attention from politicians when oil prices rise rapidly. Here we examine congressional and presidential activity related to the energy crises. Specifically, we consider the number of congressional hearings, the time-line for both major and non-major legislation that passed, major energy-related legislation that failed on the floor, oral and written statements by the president, including State of the Union addresses and executive orders.

For the most part, we are relying on measures pioneered by Baumgartner and Jones and others. However, our examination includes counts of oral and written statements from the president about energy issues, which we gathered from the American Presidency Project.[89] In addition, we consider legislation that has both passed and failed. Our reasoning is that all bills that have made their way onto the agenda should be considered, not just those that pass.

When public concern over energy prices spiked, politicians turned their attention toward energy issues. We look first at how presidents respond to energy crises. Using data from the American Presidency Project, we measure presidential attention with the number of mentions of "energy," "energy crisis," "oil," "petroleum," or "gas prices" in oral and written presidential statements from 1970 to 2012, shown in figure 2.5.[90] Figure 2.6 shows the number of statements related

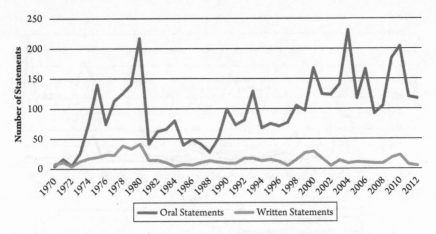

Figure 2.5 Oral and Written Presidential Statements Regarding Energy Crisis and Petroleum, 1970–2012.

The data used here were originally collected by Frank R. Baumgartner and Bryan D. Jones, with the support of National Science Foundation grant numbers SBR 9320922 and 0111611, and were distributed through the Department of Government at the University of Texas at Austin. Neither NSF nor the original collectors of the data bear any responsibility for the analysis reported here.

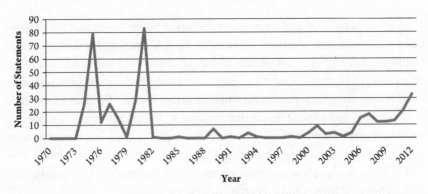

Figure 2.6 Number of Statements related to "Energy" in Presidential State of the Union Speeches by Year, 1970–2012.

The American Presidency Project (www.presidency.ucsb.edu)

to "energy" in presidential State of the Union speeches, which are derived from the Policy Agendas Project website.[91] Together, these data show that when the price of gas rises, the presidents respond.

In each energy crisis, presidents were called upon by the public to help alleviate the rising prices and shortages. While Nixon's efforts with regard to the 1973–74 energy crises are often considered piecemeal and the early years of his presidency are often characterized by his failure to enact a comprehensive energy program, he certainly talked about energy issues. In 1973, Nixon made thirty-seven statements concerning energy; in 1974, there were close to one hundred such statements between both Nixon, who resigned as president on August 9, 1974, and Ford. In 1975, Ford made over 150 oral and written statements concerning energy. We see similar patterns with our measure of presidential State of the Union speeches and for other presidents during the subsequent energy crises. In 1979 and 1980, President Carter made 140 written and over 200 oral statements regarding energy-related issues, respectively. From 1990 to 1991, G. H. W. Bush doubled the number of oral statements he made, which jumped from about fifty to one hundred. As well, presidential oral statements increased again from 2000 to 2001. In 1999, Clinton made nearly one hundred oral statements regarding energy related issues; in 2001 that grew to approximately 170, then dropped slightly in 2001 when G. W. Bush made approximately 150 oral statements. While written presidential statements are significantly lower overall, there are still noticeable upticks in response to the energy crises, most significantly in the 1970s.

Members of Congress respond to energy prices in the same way that the president does. When oil prices are stable, Congress gives little attention to energy policy, but when prices rise sharply—especially when the news media label it an "energy crisis"— Congress acts. Hearings are held and bills are introduced to give members of Congress something to show their constituents that they are working on the problem. In the three years leading up to the 1973–74 energy crisis (see figure 2.7), there were significantly fewer bills introduced in Congress and fewer hearings in Congress related to energy than there were during the energy crisis. From 1970 to 1972, lawmakers introduced a total of 442 bills related to energy; in 1973 alone, 686 bills were introduced. This increase in Congressional activity was sustained for the length of the energy crisis with 630 and 777 bills introduced in 1974 and 1975, respectively. As oil prices fell, the number dropped to 281 in 1976, only to rebound again in 1977 to 642 bills introduced. We see

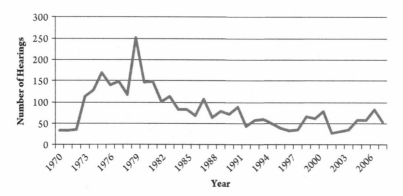

Figure 2.7 Number of Congressional Hearings Related to Energy, 1970–2008.
The data used here were originally collected by Frank R. Baumgartner and Bryan D. Jones, with the support of National Science Foundation grant numbers SBR 9320922 and 0111611, and were distributed through the Department of Government at the University of Texas at Austin. Neither NSF nor the original collectors of the data bear any responsibility for the analysis reported here.

similar trends in the volume of energy-related legislative proposals introduced
during subsequent energy crises as well, although increases in the 1990s are not
nearly as large as they were in the 1970s or in the most recent energy crises in
1999–2000 and 2007–8. Clearly, the policy windows created by the energy crises
provide opportunity for government officials to respond, and they do.

Our indicators of policy change, executive orders, congressional activity and
public laws (see Figures 2.8 to 2.10), also behave as agenda setting theory would
predict. That is, during the times of energy crises, we see a surge of congressional

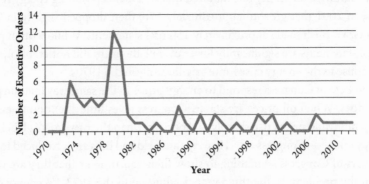

Figure 2.8 Executive Orders Related to Energy, 1970–2012.
The data used here were originally collected by Frank R. Baumgartner and Bryan D. Jones, with
the support of National Science Foundation grant numbers SBR 9320922 and 0111611, and were
distributed through the Department of Government at the University of Texas at Austin. Neither NSF
nor the original collectors of the data bear any responsibility for the analysis reported here.

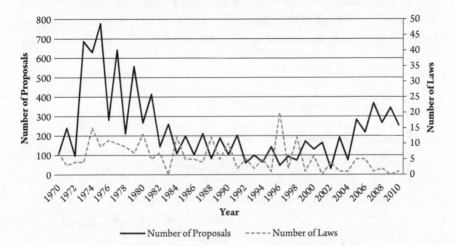

Figure 2.9 Number of Congressional Proposals and Public Laws Passed Related to
Energy, 1970–2010.
The data used here were originally collected by Frank R. Baumgartner and Bryan D. Jones, with
the support of National Science Foundation grant numbers SBR 9320922 and 0111611, and were
distributed through the Department of Government at the University of Texas at Austin. Neither NSF
nor the original collectors of the data bear any responsibility for the analysis reported here.

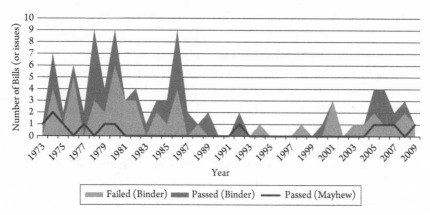

Figure 2.10 Major Energy Legislation Failed and Passed by Congress, 1973–2009 (Sarah A. Binder & David R. Mayhew).

activity and substantive changes in energy policy. We first consider the number of executive orders (figure 2.8). In the three years leading up to the 1973–74 energy crisis, there were no executive orders dealing with energy. However, in 1973 Nixon executed six and in 1974 he executed four. Similarly, in response to the energy crisis in 1979 and 1980, Carter signed twelve and ten executive orders, respectively. For the remaining energy crises, we really do not see significant increases in executive orders related to energy issues. Rather, it appears that the fluctuation from one year to the next is plus or minus one.

Beyond executive orders, there is also evidence of increases in both congressional activity related to energy as well as the number of bills passed by Congress and signed by the president, especially for the earlier crises. In 1973, of the 686 energy-related bills (figure 2.9) introduced in Congress, four were signed into law. The four laws, all considered major legislation,[92] include the Trans-Alaskan Pipeline Authorization Act of 1973 (PL 93-153), the Emergency Daylight Saving Time Energy Conservation Act (PL 93-182), the Emergency Highway Energy Conservation Act, setting the speed limit to 55 mph (PL 93-239), and the Mandatory Fuel Allocation Program (PL 93-159). Although never passed in 1973, both the House and Senate began work on what was considered the centerpiece of Nixon's Project Independence, the National Emergency Energy Act (NEEA). In 1974, altogether Congress passed and Nixon signed into law fifteen energy-related bills, both major and minor. That same year, on March 6, Nixon vetoed the NEEA.[93]

Policy change continued during the successive energy crises. In terms of *major* legislation related to energy (see figure 2.10),[94] the number of bills (or issues, in the case of Sarah A. Binder)[95] attempted and passed ebbs and flows in response to the four energy crises. Although the counts differ for Binder and David R. Mayhew because of how each one defines whether legislation is major or not but also because Binder's count is a count of "issues"—sometimes a single bill, often times collections of bills (in an omnibus or not), the counts certainly do move in similar patterns. According to Binder's count, in 1979 the 96th Congress passed and President Carter signed into law seven energy-related bills. Turning back to figure 2.9, we also see the number of public laws enacted by Congress and signed by Carter in 1980 nearly doubled from what was enacted and signed the previous year. These laws included the Energy Security Act, the US synthetic Fuels Corporation Act, the Biomass Energy and Alcohol Fuels Act, the Renewable Energy Resources Act, and the Solar Energy Resources Act. Similarly, in 1990 the number of energy-related bills signed into law doubled from the previous year, going from five to ten and then dropping to two laws in 1991. We also see 1996 as a historical moment with twenty energy-related bills signed into law, a significant increase from only one law the previous year. However, the majority of the bills signed into law in 1996 are not considered major legislation. Instead, many of these laws extended the deadlines of energy-related projects. Although not nearly as remarkable, we do see modest increases in the number of public laws as a result of the 1999–2000 and 2007–8 energy crises, few of which would be considered major legislation.

Conclusion

The policy process is both complex and dynamic. According to the theory of punctuated equilibrium, there are long periods of relative stability where an issue receives little or no attention. However, these periods of stability are punctuated by rapid and abrupt change, often sparked by an event or crisis. In this chapter, we discussed how the energy crises fit into the theoretical framework of punctuated equilibrium and agenda setting. In doing so, we considered the trends and fluctuations in the price of imported oil and how the rapid price shifts appear as focusing episodes. We considered how the focusing episodes then produce shifts in public opinion, media interest, and presidential and congressional attention from the initial 1973–74 energy crises through the three subsequent crises.

The concept of a window of opportunity has proven to be critical to our analysis. During the periods of stable subsystem politics, the dominant actors within the subsystem (oil companies) controlled the policy image and supported the status quo of limited participation. With limited participation, any energy-related policy change was limited and predictable. However, as the result of spikes in attention to the price of gas and energy shortages during the energy crises, the expansion of conflict worked to destroy the former subsystem, thereby leading to increased attention and involvement by new actors, most notably the public and interest groups, but also government officials in response to demands of the former. The highly salient punctuations produce high-profile policy changes. Indeed, as a Nixon energy expert notes, "The Alaska pipeline, the 55-mile speed limit, daylight-saving time, and the energy independence program were all products of OPEC action. We were not tuned into energy before 1972. For several reasons, we simply had not predicted the problem. The oil embargo changed the agenda dramatically."[96]

As our data and analysis demonstrate, the salience of energy-related issues varies over time. When oil prices surge upward in energy crises, energy issues appear on the public, media, and governmental agendas. Policy change as a result of these episodic shocks is also evident. In particular, we see large increases in the number of energy-related policy proposals attempted and passed in Congress. The nature of the policy change demonstrates that the opening of the policy window changed the types of actors involved, especially participation of public and environmental interest groups such as Common Cause, Sierra Club, and Friends of the Earth in the 1973–74 crisis.[97] As a result, energy policy began to align with the preferences of these groups and the policies they supported, such as the development of renewable energy and limiting windfall profits of oil companies. However, we also see pressures from other interests, such as the automobile industry and the oil companies, continue to play a significant role in shaping energy policy. We will examine these issues in more depth in coming chapters.

3

Public Opinion during
an Energy Crisis

When energy crises strike and oil prices surge upward, energy producers and their allies inevitably call for steps to increase production. They call for opening up Alaska's Arctic National Wildlife Refuge, ending the moratorium on offshore oil drilling, and other measures designed to increase domestic energy supplies. For their part, environmentalists resist the calls for more production, declaring that the public remains steadfastly opposed to sacrificing the environment for more oil or natural gas. Instead, they call for steps to reduce oil consumption such as improving the fuel efficiency of automobiles and investing in research on hybrid and all-electric cars. Advocacy coalitions on all sides appeal to the public for support, hoping that public pressure will force Congress to do as they want.

How does the public react when energy prices skyrocket? Do they reveal environmental principles and oppose oil and gas drilling, as environmentalists would have it? Or do they support more energy development in the belief that more domestic production will lower prices? When public opinion does change, which people change their views? Does everyone shift together, or do only a few, select groups account for movement in public opinion? Finally, who gets blamed for high prices during energy crises? When energy prices spike, people react angrily. Rising gasoline prices hurt people financially. Even people who can afford to spend fifty dollars to fill their gas tanks do not like it. So they look for explanations. Who or what caused the prices to rise? Who is to blame? That search for blame involves sorting the competing politicians and policy advocates into good guys and bad guys, and has repercussions for policy making.

The answers to these questions above matter because elected officials care about what their constituents think, especially on high-profile issues. Public opinion alone certainly does not determine how politicians will respond. They consider many factors when deciding on how to vote on legislation—the views of their party and committee leaders, their fellow legislators, interest group requests, donor opinions, their own personal preferences, as well as constituent preferences.[1] Yet public opinion, especially on issues that get lots of attention, is not a trivial concern. The overwhelming view among scholars who study the impact of public opinion on policy is that public opinion is a principal cause of policy on high-profile issues.[2]

In this chapter, we look at public opinion during times of crisis in energy markets. We will take a broad look at the public's environmentalism and at how public support for energy development changed over a thirty-year period, and then we will take a detailed look at how public opinion changed as energy prices rapidly moved up over a short period. We end with an examination of who gets blamed for energy prices.

Our goal in this chapter is to show how public opinion changes in response to changing energy prices, especially during energy crises when prices skyrocket. Changes in public opinion alone, of course, do not automatically lead to changes in public policy. Nevertheless, shifts in public opinion can create situations in which politicians and policy advocates can successfully push for new policies. In looking at public opinion, therefore, we are looking at the creation of windows of opportunity for policy change.

Environmentalism and the Economy

In a well-known paper published shortly after the first Earth Day, political scientist Anthony Downs predicted that public attention to environmental problems would fade away as other issues rose and drew attention.[3] As the environmental movement continued to grow in the following years and as polls showed sustained public interest in environmental problems, however, other scholars suggested that the state of the environment had become one of America's "enduring social concerns."[4] It was even suggested that environmental concern was impervious to energy crises and economic recessions.[5]

As it turns out, neither of these extreme claims is correct. Environmentalism was not a passing fad, but nor are people's environmental views fixed. Now that we have a record of over forty years of surveys asking what the public thinks about environmental issues, we can see that although there is a strong foundation of support for environmental protection, the public's environmentalism ebbs and flows in response to the economy and world events.

A good place to start looking at the public's environmentalism is with one of the most widely used measures of environmental concern, a question asked in every NORC General Social Survey of the US population since 1973:

> We are faced with many problems in this country, none of which can
> be solved easily or inexpensively. I'm going to name some of these

problems, and for each one I'd like you to tell me whether you think we're spending too much money on it, too little money, or about the right amount on it. . . . Improving and protecting the environment.[6]

We should note that in a recent prominent criticism of the environmental movement, Ted Nordhaus and Michael Shellenberger argue that data such as ours are superficial and misleading.[7] They point to surveys showing that people do not rank environmental problems among the most important issues facing the nation, citing a study that asked voters whether environmental issues played a major role in how they voted and found that only 22 percent said that they did. Leaving aside the fact that when an issue influences a fifth of the electorate, it may very well prove to be decisive, what Nordhaus and Shellenberger failed to realize is that asking people to explain their votes is a notoriously bad way to explain influences on voting decisions.[8] In fact, it is Nordhaus and Shellenberger's analysis that is superficial. The question they should have asked is whether people's environmental attitudes predict their voting choices. Using a more sophisticated approach to analyzing elections, Frank Davis and Albert Wurth found that people's opinions on environmental issues have a substantial impact on their presidential votes.[9] People who said that they wanted to spend more on environmental protection were significantly more likely to vote for Democratic candidates. In other words, the data we are presenting matter where it counts the most: in the voting booth.

Now let us see what the data have to tell us. The more concerned people are with environmental quality, the more tax dollars they are willing to invest protecting it, so the spending question is a good measure of environmentalism. Figure 3.1 shows how people have responded to the question since 1973. Support for more spending ranged from a low of 51 percent in 1980 to highs of 75 percent in 1989 and 1990. The 2008–10 recession dampened people's enthusiasm for spending on the environment, but even in those financially unstable times, a 57 percent majority wanted more spending, while only 13 percent wanted less.

To put spending data in a broader context, the next figure shows how environmental protection compares to other spending priorities—ranging from education to foreign aid. Separating out the nine time trends is a bit difficult, so we ordered the legend at the bottom of the figure to match the descending order of popularity of spending categories in 2014. That is, reading from left to right in the legend (or top down in 2014), we see that the area in which most people wanted increased spending was education. That is followed by fighting crime, healthcare, and protecting the environment—all of which are in a statistical tie in 2014. Less popular spending categories include cities, military defense, space exploration, welfare, and foreign aid.

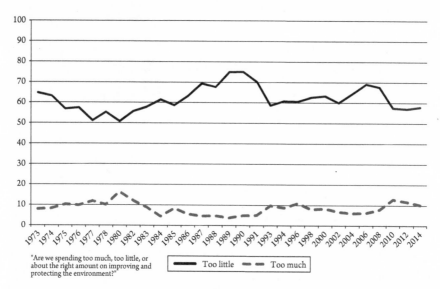

"Are we spending too much, too little, or about the right amount on improving and protecting the environment?"   ▬▬ Too little   ▬ ▬ Too much

Figure 3.1 Environmental Spending Preferences, 1973–2014.

We draw three conclusions from these data. First, people's spending preferences vary by topic. People do not just say "yes" to everything. They pick and choose. They pick the environment as a priority for spending, but not, for example, foreign aid. In 2010, 8 percent said that too little was being spent on foreign aid, but 63 percent said that too much was being spent, and the remaining 28 percent said that the spending level was about right. Those numbers contrast sharply with spending preferences on environmental protection.

Second, spending taxpayer money on the environment is fairly popular and has been ever since National Opinion Research Center (NORC) first began asking these questions over forty years ago. It has consistently ranked among the top four spending priorities, even beating crime for the last eight years before the 2008–10 recession. Contrary to what Nordhaus and Shellenberger claimed, Americans care about the environment very much—more so than they care about many other policy areas.

Third, the public's support for environmental protection is not constant. It varies over time. We could see this in figure 3.1, but the data in figure 3.2 show that the public's environmental spending preferences are not just moving with other opinion trends. There are other forces at work changing people's opinions. Our next step, therefore, is to ask what causes changes in support for environmental spending from year to year. We will start by reporting on Deborah Guber's work on this question.

In her study of American environmentalism, *The Grassroots of a Green Revolution*,[10] Guber uses regression analysis to show that the public's environmental spending preferences respond to a variety of changes in the economic

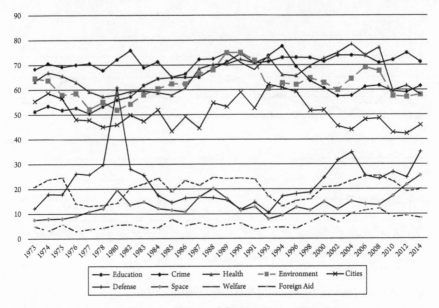

Figure 3.2 Spending Preferences: "Too Little" Being Spent, 1973–2014.

and political environment. She finds that both unemployment and inflation affect attitudes on spending. The better the state of the economy—that is, the lower the unemployment and inflation rates—the more people are willing to spend protecting the environment. Guber also reasons that the more the government spends on environmental protection, the less the public will demand even more spending. We might think of this as the Tea Party hypothesis. People want limits on government spending. To test this hypothesis, she includes federal budget spending on environmental protection as an independent variable in her models. As she suspected, as government spending on the environment increases, public demand for more spending declines.

Guber further reasons that the number of news media articles on environmental policy should influence environmental attitudes. Indeed, she finds that the more the media cover environmental issues, the more the public wants spending, a finding that is consistent with agenda-setting theory. Because younger Americans are more pro-environment than older Americans, Guber also predicts that as younger, post-war generations replaced older generations over time, the public would become more pro-environment. The data support that hypothesis as well. Finally, she includes in her analysis a variable measuring which party controlled the White House to see whether people are more likely to support environmental spending under a Democrat or Republican. Her hypothesis is that people would worry that Republicans would not support environmental protection enough, so under a Republican president, the public would want environmental spending increased. Again, the data supported her hypothesis, although our data analysis—reported below in table 3.1—raises doubts about the conclusion.

Overall, Guber's analysis shows that the public's environmental spending preferences respond to economic conditions and real-world events. Environmental attitudes do not exist in a vacuum. As Page and Shapiro state in their classic study of changing public opinion, "Collective policy preferences are generally stable; they change in understandable, predictable ways."[11]

For another look at the public's environmentalism, we look at a series of questions asked by the Gallup Poll about the trade-off between environmental protection and economic growth that offers us a second view of the public's environmental feelings over time. The question is this:

> With which one of these statements about the environment and the economy do you most agree? [rotate answers] Protection of the environment should be given priority, even at the risk of curbing economic growth. OR, Economic growth should be given priority, even if the environment suffers to some extent.[12]

Although this question is widely used by researchers, it has a weakness. It forces respondents to choose between economic growth and environmental protection. Some economists argue that such tradeoffs often do not exist.[13] Moreover, a group of Michigan State University investigators has shown that a large number of people think that we can have both economic growth and environmental protection at the same time.[14] Despite the question's flaws, we think we can gain some useful insights from it.

In figure 3.3, we see the public mostly expressing strong environmentalist views, but we also see that the number of people choosing environmental protection over economic growth changed over time. From 1984 through 2000, more than 60 percent favored environmental protection. Starting in late 2000, the public's support for environmental protection declined until it bottomed out in 2003 at 47 percent. The public's desire for environmental protection then moved up again to 55 percent in 2007, but it faltered in the recession years of 2008–10.

To get a better understanding of the change in people's environmental views over time, we estimated a simple regression model to explain the percentage of the public who said that protection of the environment should be given priority.[15] We used the unemployment rate, the consumer price index, and a dummy variable coded to measure whether the president is a Democrat or Republican. The results are shown in table 3.1.

All three variables had significant effects. The biggest effect was for which party controlled the White House. Having a Republican president was associated with a 5 percent drop in giving environmental protection priority over the economy. The effect for unemployment was small, but in the direction we would expect.

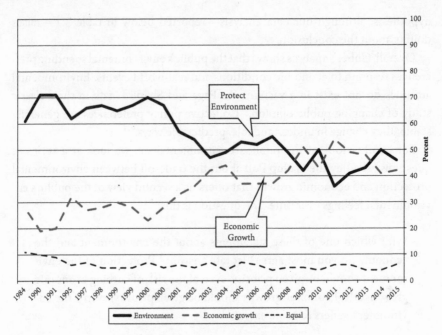

Figure 3.3 Protect Environment vs. Economic Growth.

Table 3.1 **Regression Model Explaining Support for Protecting the Environment at the Risk of Curbing Economic Growth (for the data in figure 3.3)**

Variable	Coefficients
Intercept	113.9***
	(5.8)
Unemployment rate	−2.6***
	(0.6)
Consumer Price Index	−.22***
	(0.03)
Post Sept. 11, 2001	−5.2*
	(1.9)

* p < .02
*** p < .001
n = 24
Adjusted R² = .82

Source: Data from the Gallup Poll (http://www.gallup.com/poll/1615/Environment.aspx) and U.S. Bureau of Labor Statistics (http://www.bls.gov/cpi/data.htm and http://www.bls.gov/bls/unemployment.htm)

For every 1 percent increase in the seasonally adjusted unemployment rate, support for environmental protection fell by 2.6 percent. Given that unemployment ranged from 4.0 to 9.6 percent during the years of our data, that means that unemployment accounts for about a 6 percent change over time. Finally, change in the consumer price index also had the effect that one would expect. For every 1 percent increase in the consumer price index, support for environmental protection fell about two-tenths of a percent. Although changes in inflation ranged from 0.1 to 6.1 percent over the time period, most of the time it ranged narrowly between 1.5 and 3.5 percent, so this impact was far smaller than the unemployment effect. Overall, the basic finding from both our analysis and Guber's is the same. When the economy turns sour, the public's enthusiasm for environmental protection declines.

Support for Offshore Oil Drilling and the Price of Gasoline

Just as we see environmentalism rise and fall with the nation's economic health, we might also expect to see support for energy development policies rise and fall with the state of the economy and specifically with the price of oil and gasoline. Most people can easily see the connection between the supply of oil and the price of gasoline. During energy crises, oil companies and their political allies loudly remind the public about the connection, arguing that opening up more areas for oil drilling in the United States will cut the price of gasoline. Their critics correctly point out that opening up new areas for development will not affect gasoline prices for five to ten years if at all. Nevertheless, both sides are talking about drilling and gasoline prices, which helps the public make the connection. Therefore, we can see why support for domestic oil drilling should rise when the price of gasoline rises and fall when it declines.

We have two sets of survey data on offshore oil drilling that allow us to look at the connection between oil prices and public opinion on offshore oil and gas drilling—a series of national polls conducted by Cambridge Research International and a series of polls of Californians conducted by the Field Institute. In both cases, we see the public's view of offshore drilling responding to the price of gasoline.

Figure 3.4 presents the results from Cambridge Research International surveys. Its question, first asked in 1976 when many Americans believed the country was in the midst of an energy crisis, is this:

> I'm going to read you several proposals for dealing with the energy crisis, and I'd like you to tell me whether you generally favor or oppose each one. . . . Expanding offshore drilling for oil and natural gas.[16]

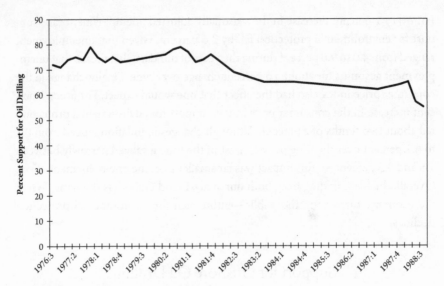

Figure 3.4 US Support for Offshore Oil Drilling.

Support for more oil and gas development was overwhelming. Throughout the 1970s, from 70 to 80 percent of Americans said they favored expanding offshore drilling. Support only began falling in the 1980s as the price of oil fell.

To explore why support for oil development varied over time, we estimated a regression model, shown in table 3.2, using the same three variables we used to explain support for environmental protection plus the percentage of people born since 1945 (one of Guber's explanatory variables). Our model of support for drilling reveals that two variables had significant impacts. As gasoline prices rose, so did support for offshore oil and gas development. In addition, as the years passed and the number of people born since 1945 grew, support for oil development slowly fell. The long-term trend of growing environmentalism, which Guber found in her analysis of environmental spending preferences, reappeared.

The California data, shown in figure 3.5, present a different picture in which public opinion tracks gasoline prices much more closely.[17] An important difference between the US and California polls is that the level of support for offshore oil and gas drilling among Californians is far lower than the level shown in the national data. Two differences may account for these results. First, the question asked of Californians does not refer to an "energy crisis." It merely asks to agree or disagree with a statement that additional drilling should be allowed: "Oil companies should be allowed to drill more oil and gas wells in state tidelands along the California seacoast."[18]

Table 3.2 **Regression Model Explaining National Support for Offshore Drilling (for the data in figure 3.4)**

	Coefficients
Intercept	93.2***
	(8.8)
Price of gasoline, inflation adjusted	0.145***
	(.05)
Unemployment rate	.035
	(1.08)
President (Rep=1, Dem=0)	−3.29
	(2.20)
Percent born since 1945	−0.92***
	(.11)

** p < .05; *** p < .01
n = 35
Adjusted R^2 = .80

Source: Data from the Cambridge Research International, quoted in William G. Mayer, *The Changing American Mind* (Ann Arbor, MI: University of Michigan Press, 1992), the U.S. Energy Information Administration, *Annual Energy Review 2010*, and the U.S. Bureau of Labor Statistics (http://www.bls. gov/bls/unemployment.htm).

The Cambridge Research International question's reference to the energy crisis may have pushed respondents to support steps to deal with the crisis. Second, Californians may feel a direct connection to the Pacific Ocean and the offshore oil and gas production along its edge, a connection that most Americans lack. A majority of Californians live in coastal counties and have easy access to the coast. In addition, the 1969 Santa Barbara Channel oil spill, which helped launch the modern environmental movement, also made the struggle over oil and gas drilling along the California coast a major political issue in the state. Consequently, the differences between the national and California data that we see in figures 3.4 and 3.5 probably result both from the differences in questions and the differences in how strongly Californians feel about their coast and the issue of offshore drilling.

Looking at figure 3.5, we see that at the end of the 1970s, support for off-shore oil drilling grew in California along with the rising price of gasoline (the dashed line in figure 3.5), peaking at 57 percent in 1980. The price hike was driven by the OPEC oil embargo and the energy crisis of 1979–80.

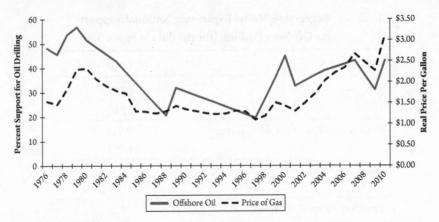

Figure 3.5   California Opinion on Offshore Oil Development and the Price of Gas, 1976–2011.

After 1980, however, public support for offshore oil development along the California coast declined substantially along with the price of gasoline. The decline in support for oil development from 1980 to 1998 was not smooth. Figure 3.5 shows a sharp drop in support for oil development between 1984 and 1989, and a bounce upward between 1989 and 1990. The overall trend of declining support in the 1980s seems to be the result of gradually declining oil prices, but the sharp drop in support in 1989 is no doubt the result of the *Exxon Valdez* oil spill in Alaska in March 1989—shortly before the 1989 survey was conducted. The Field Poll asked its 1989 question in July, when newspapers were still covering the oil spill clean-up efforts and various legal actions against Exxon. Consequently, the level of support for further coastal oil development that we see in 1989 differs from what it would have been had people not been thinking about the recent oil-related disaster. By 1990, the *Exxon Valdez* presumably no longer jumped to mind when people were asked about offshore oil drilling, so the polls registered an increase in support for drilling over 1989 as gasoline prices moved up. However, we should note that the 1990 level of support is lower than the 1984 level. From a long-term perspective, the post-1980 decline in support for oil drilling can be seen to continue in both the 1990 and 1998 observations.

The May 2001 survey shows a sharp increase in support for offshore oil and gas development. Support rose from the historic low point of 20 percent in 1998 to 45 percent in 2001. The likely cause of the increase, of course, is the rapid increase in gasoline prices that began in 2000.

A regression analysis of the data in figure 3.5 provides an estimate of the effect of gasoline prices on the public's support for offshore oil and gas development.

As table 3.3 shows, the inflation-adjusted price of gasoline increases by one dollar, support for drilling increases by 11 percent—a large increase, but one that is just statistically significant because of the small sample size.[19] The model also included a dummy variable flagging 1989, the year of the *Exxon Valdez* disaster, and change in California Unemployment. The *Exxon Valdez* spill was associated with a 19 percent drop in support for oil drilling. The unemployment variable had no effect.

We can sum up the data in the first two sections of the chapter quite simply. The central finding is that the public's environmentalism responds to changes in the economy. As the economy weakens—for example, as the unemployment rate or gasoline prices rise—people become less enthusiastic about spending tax dollars for environmental protection, more willing to sacrifice environmental values for economic benefits, more willing to trade environmental protection for job growth, and more willing to allow offshore oil and gas drilling.

From the point of view of politicians, lobbyists, and political activists, the result is that bad economic times provide fertile ground for attempts to weaken environmental protections. For those who want more oil development, the best time to strike is when the economy is suffering and people are more willing to sacrifice the environment for economic security. The efforts may not succeed, but a poor economy offers them their best chance. In contrast, good economic times help environmental causes. The public feels better able to afford environmental advances. The economy and the price of gasoline open and close windows of opportunity.

Table 3.3 **Regression Model of California Support for Offshore Oil Development, 1977–2010**

	b	*s.e.*
Intercept 1	35.2***	10.2
Real Price of Gas	11.2*	5.6
California Unemployment	−2.0	1.5
Exxon Valdez	−19.1*	10.2
Adjusted R²	0.29	
Sample n	15	

p < .10; ***p < .01

When an Energy Crisis Strikes,
Who Changes their Opinions?

Now that we have seen that the public's environmentalism and attitudes toward energy development respond to changes in the economy, we can turn to the question, whose opinions change when an energy crisis strikes? Do all groups shift their views equally, or do some groups respond to changes in the economy while others hold steady?

Questions about which groups change and which do not are important because politicians do not just care about public opinion as a whole—they care about particular groups. Many politicians care greatly about their core supporters, care less about other groups, and feel indifferent about the opinions of their opponents' core supporters.[20] So which groups change their opinions and which do not can be an important consideration in the political calculations of decision makers.

To learn more about how various groups change their opinions when an energy crisis strikes, we will look at public reaction to the sharp increases in oil prices between 1998 and 2001. We have a pair of surveys of Californians with matching questions that allow us to look at patterns of opinion before and after prices shot up from less than a dollar per gallon to $1.73 per gallon—an 81 percent increase.[21] During that period, public support for offshore oil drilling along the California coast increased from 20 percent to 45 percent—a 25 percent point leap.[22] Our 2001 survey did not go back to the same people interviewed in 1998 and re-interview them, so we cannot track individual change in opinion over that time period. Nevertheless, we can examine how the patterns of support and opposition to oil development changed. The changes in those patterns will reveal what sorts of people changed most, and tell us something about the process of opinion change.

We need to start by saying a few words about what caused opinions to change over that three-year period. Certainly the rising gasoline prices caused people to rethink their views on offshore oil drilling, but it was far more than that. As we will show later in this book, when prices started rising during past energy crises, consumer advocates began denouncing oil companies for price gouging. Oil companies and their allies began calling for opening up the Arctic National Wildlife Refuge, the nation's coastlines, and other protected areas to oil and gas development. Politicians wade into the fray on both sides.

In the 1998–2001 price surge, the 2000 presidential campaign played a critical role. Automobile owners were reminded of the steep price hikes every time they filled their cars' gas tanks. The presidential candidates responded to the voters' concerns. Texas Governor George W. Bush argued that the best way to lower prices would be to produce more domestic oil and, in particular, to allow oil development in Alaska's Arctic National Wildlife Refuge. Vice President Al Gore responded that the way to cut gasoline prices would be to conserve energy and to put pressure on major oil-exporting countries such as Saudi Arabia to produce more oil for the world market. He fiercely opposed relaxing environmental standards to make it easier to drill for oil in the United States, and he insisted that the Arctic National Wildlife Refuge remain untouched.[23] Newspaper columnists and television pundits weighed in on both sides of the debate. As a result of both the high prices and the media attention, the price of gasoline drew more attention than any other issue throughout the election year according to surveys by the Pew Research Center.[24]

Our point is that when we see gasoline prices and public support for offshore oil drilling rising at the same time, we should not leap to the conclusion that it is a simple matter of gasoline prices driving public opinion. As we discussed in chapter 2, the problem is much more complicated than that. Advocates, media pundits, and politicians all play roles in changing public opinion. In our case, the 2000 presidential election played a role as well. People change their minds not just because they reevaluate their opinions based on the price of gasoline; they also consider the arguments put forth by various parties in the conflict.

To examine how people's opinions on offshore oil development changed over time, we use individual level data. We combine the data from two surveys conducted in 1998, when oil prices had hit a historic low, and 2001, when they had surged upward so quickly and to such a height that gasoline prices became a critical issue in the 2000 presidential election. We should note that the 2001 survey was conducted in May, well before the September 11 terrorist attacks. The 1998–2001 comparison allows us to see how the public reacts to a sudden shift in prices.

Using our merged data set, we estimated a logistic regression model explaining support for offshore oil drilling. (Readers who are uncomfortable with methods like ours need not fear. We will explain what we learned from them when we discuss our conclusions.)

Broadly speaking, we can suggest four reasons why public opinion shifted over time. (1) People may have responded to the rising oil prices based on their economic self-interests. That is, the people who were hurt worst may have moved most strongly in favor of more oil drilling. (2) People may have responded based on their ideological views. That is, people who were ideologically inclined toward oil drilling may have changed more than others. (3) People who were inclined for or against environmental causes may have changed at different rates, with those who did not agree with environmental appeals moving most strongly toward more oil drilling. (4) All groups could have moved at the same pace regardless of their economic circumstances, ideologies, or environmental views. We will discuss each of these hypotheses in turn.

The Self-Interest Hypothesis

Our first possible explanation of the shift in opinion toward greater support for offshore oil development is that people who were affected by higher gas prices might have reasoned that increased oil production in the United States would prevent gas prices from rising. That was the argument that Governor George W. Bush and his allies made during the 2000 presidential campaign, and an argument echoed by Senator John McCain during the 2008 presidential campaign. Increasing the domestic oil supply would bring down gas prices. People who accepted this argument and changed their minds from opposition to support for more oil drilling would be acting out of self-interest.

Previous research has shown that self-interest is not as simple as it might seem. A series of studies has found that self-interest generally does not influence attitudes, contrary to what one might expect.[25] The studies found instead that people with vested interests are more likely to take action on their interests. As a result, it would seem to the casual observer that self-interest influences opinions because we see people acting on their interests. However, the studies found no direct effect of self-interest on attitudes.

To test the self-interest hypothesis, we need to identify groups that were especially hard hit by rising gasoline prices. The most obvious candidates are people who felt that their financial situations were weak. They might find any increase in prices threatening. The 1998 and 2001 surveys have similar (but unfortunately not identical) questions about respondent's financial situations. In 1998 respondents were asked, "During the last few years, has your financial situation been getting better, getting worse, or has it stayed the same?" In 2001, they were asked, "Would you say that you and your family are financially better off or worse off today than you were a year ago?" For our logistic regression model, we combined the two questions into a single financial situation measure. The hypothesis is that people whose financial situations were worsening would feel economically threatened and favor more oil drilling.

A second group of people hurt by the rising gasoline prices was the poor. People with low incomes have less discretionary income, and so are likely to be harmed more by rising gas prices than those who are financially better off. We tested this hypothesis with family income as an independent variable.

The Environmentalism Hypothesis

A second possible explanation of the changing support for offshore oil is that environmentalists reacted differently from non-environmentalists to the rising gasoline prices. Environmentalists may have continued to heed the call of environmental leaders who insisted that offshore oil drilling posed a serious environmental threat, while non-environmentalists may have accepted the idea of increasing the oil supply as a way to moderate gasoline prices.

We do not have direct measures of environmentalism in our surveys, but we can measure environmentalism indirectly by using demographic variables. Previous studies have shown that age, education, and gender consistently predict environmental attitudes. In general, more educated people, younger people, and women take more pro-environment stands than the less educated, the old, and men.[26] We therefore include these demographics as independent variables in our model to see if they changed over time, which would imply (but not conclusively show) that environmentalists and non-environmentalists reacted differently to rising gasoline prices.

The Political Orientations Hypothesis

A third possible explanation of the growing support for offshore oil development is that people are responding to political leadership. The argument about political orientations is that when they come into play depends on whether political issues receive media attention and on whether the issues are controversial. When the news media ignore issues, and when politicians from opposite parties agree, partisan and ideological differences in the public tend to be small. In contrast, when the news media focus on issues and politicians from opposing parties jump in on opposite sides, partisan and ideological differences in the public tend to be large.[27]

In our case, offshore oil development did not receive much media attention and was not controversial in 1998. Gasoline prices (adjusted for inflation) hit a historic low point in 1998, with an average price of only $1.03 per gallon (in 2000 dollars) in the United States. Energy crises seemed to be events of the distant past. Neither Washington political leaders nor major oil companies were pushing to increase oil drilling off the coast of California. Democratic and Republican leaders in California joined one another in opposing offshore oil drilling. Under these circumstances, political orientations should not make much difference. In 2001, however, the situation had changed dramatically. Gasoline prices had shot up. Public opinion polls showed that the high price of gasoline was the most important issue to most Americans throughout the campaign year 2000, and politicians began to disagree sharply along partisan lines about oil development.[28] Most prominently, during the 2000 presidential campaign, Governor Bush called for opening up the Arctic National Wildlife Refuge to oil drilling, while Vice President Gore denounced that proposal.[29] As a result of these events, we should expect to see much sharper partisan and ideological differences in 2001 than in 1998. Two measures of political orientations are available in our 1998 and 2001 surveys—party identification and ideological self-identification. We include both as independent variables.

The Period-Effect Hypothesis

We take the term "period effects" from studies of change in public opinion over time.[30] Those studies divide the causes of opinion change into life cycle effects (opinion change caused by people growing older), generational effects (opinion change in the population caused by younger generations of people replacing older generations as they die off), and period effects, which are causes of public opinion that affect all groups at the same time and produce a general shift of public opinion in some direction. Of course, over the brief three years between our surveys there could not have been sufficient time for life cycle or generation effects to have caused significant change. For our purposes, the period-effect hypothesis is, in effect, a null hypothesis. If all groups moved in the same direction at the same time, then the self-interest, political orientations, and environmentalism hypotheses are all wrong.

Data Analysis

Our first three hypotheses say that support for offshore oil development increased more strongly from 1998 to 2001 among some groups of people than among others. For example, our self-interest hypothesis is that support for offshore oil grew more among people who felt financially insecure or who had low incomes than among people who felt that their financial situations were good or who had high incomes. To test these hypotheses, we need a set of interaction terms that show how relationships between the independent variables and support for oil development changed over time.

To construct the interaction terms, we multiplied respondents' scores on the key independent variables (e.g., financial status or income) by a dummy variable for year. The year dummy is scored "0" for 1998 respondents and "1" for 2001 respondents. Consider, for example, the way income is coded. The essential elements are:

Support for oil drilling = b_1 (Income) + b_2 (Year) + b_3 (Income x Year)

The first term represents the influence of income on support for offshore oil. The second term reflects the overall change in support from 1998 to 2001. The third term indicates how the influence of income on support has changed from 1998 to 2001. We can see how the equation works by focusing on the sample year. For 1998 respondents Year = 0, so the second and third terms do not come into play. We see the influence of income on oil drilling support. For 2001 respondents Year = 1, so all three terms play a role. The first coefficient, b_1, represents the influence of income. The second coefficient, b_2, is in effect a change in the intercept that affects all 2001 respondents. The third coefficient, b_3, shows the change in the influence of income from 1998 to 2001. The marginal effect of income on support for oil drilling is $b_1 + b_3$. That is, we can only see the full effect of income if we take both variables into account.[31]

Table 3.4 presents the results of our analysis. We will look at each hypothesis in turn. The self-interest hypothesis gets no support from the data at all. Neither income nor financial status nor their interaction terms measuring change over time had any effect. Whether people were rich or poor, or better or worse off was unrelated to their opinions on offshore oil development. We tested several variations on the self-interest measures, and found no effects of any kind. We have to reject self-interest as an explanation.[32]

The environmentalism hypothesis fared no better. The hypothesis is that environmentalists would resist calls for offshore drilling, while others would accept them. The variables we used to identify likely environmentalists—education,

Table 3.4 **Logistic Regression Model of Support for Offshore Oil Development, 1998 and 2001 California data**

	b	*s.e.*
Intercept 1	−1.28***	0.40
Intercept 2	−0.95**	0.40
Income	−0.10	0.07
Financial status	0.01	0.10
Education	−0.16**	0.08
Age	0.009*	0.005
Female	−0.66***	0.18
Party Identification	0.15***	0.04
Year	1.49**	0.63
Income in 2001	−0.06	0.11
Finances in 2001	0.09	0.06
Education in 2001	−0.13	0.13
Age in 2001	0.06	0.11
Party Identification in 2001	0.15**	0.07

Sample n = 674
McFadden's Pseudo R^2 = 0.11
Somer's d = 0.45
* p < .10; ** p < .05; *** p < .001

age, and gender—all worked as expected. The well-educated and women were less likely to favor offshore oil drilling than were poorly educated people and men. Older people were more likely to favor it than the young. That is what we expected to see based on previous studies of environmentalism. However, the hypothesis was that as gas prices rose from 1998 to 2001, environmentalists would remain unmoved, but support for drilling would grow among others. That hypothesis is measured by the interaction terms, none of which was statistically significant.

We should remind readers that because we had no direct measure of environmental values, we had to use demographic variables to predict environmentalist views. That makes our test weak. Perhaps better data would yield a different answer. Nevertheless, the answer we have here is that the hypothesis is not supported

Finally, we have the political orientations hypothesis, which we test by including only party identification in the model (which we will explain below). Here we meet with success. Both the party identification variable and its 2001 interaction term are significant. That means that Republicans were more pro-drilling than Democrats in 1998 and that the gap between Democrats and Republicans grew larger by 2001. We can see this in figure 3.6, which shows the growing partisan gap between Democrats and Republicans. The lower, dashed line shows the various levels of support for more oil drilling across the political spectrum in 1998. A partisan difference clearly existed, but it was not very large. Whereas 13 percent of the strong Democrats supported more oil and gas drilling in 1998,

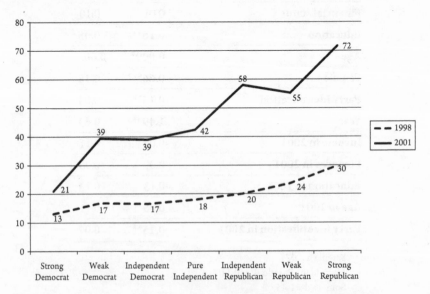

Figure 3.6 Support for Oil Drilling by Party Identification, 1998 and 2001.

30 percent of the strong Republicans supported it—a 17 percent gap. In 2001, however, the differences were far sharper. Among strong Democrats, support for more oil drilling had grown to 21 percent, but among strong Republicans, it had grown to 72 percent—a 42 percent increase.

A similar picture appears when we use ideology. Our model in table 3.4 only included party identification because party and ideology are so strongly correlated that the equation cannot disentangle them.[33] When we include one variable at a time—that is, either party identification or ideology—we get essentially the same results.

To sum up, what we see is a situation in which political orientations play a key role in opinion change. The people most likely to switch their views were the Republicans and conservatives whose political leaders told them that increased offshore oil development was the solution to high gas prices. All groups moved toward more support for drilling, which is a period effect, but the greatest movement was among those whose leaders led the charge. In contrast, what we do not see is any influence from economic self-interest. People felt harmed by the surge in gas prices, as the next section also shows, but it took more than self-interest to sway their opinions; it took political leadership.

At this point, it is useful to recall the distinction between obtrusive and unobtrusive issues, which we discussed in chapter 2.[34] When people have direct experience with an issue, it is obtrusive; when they do not, it is unobtrusive. For example, gasoline prices obtrude in people's lives because they pay for gasoline regularly, but the national debt is invisible to all but a handful of experts unless the news media explain it. The interesting point about these issues is that people can decide on the basis of their personal experience whether an obtrusive issue is important to them, but that they need guidance from the news media to assess unobtrusive issues. Yet the data we have just seen show that there is more that can be said about obtrusive and unobtrusive issues.

People can decide whether an obtrusive issue is important without relying on the news media, but they may need the media and political leaders to decide what to do about it. In the case of the rapidly rising oil prices from 1998 to 2001, people did not need anyone to tell them that it was important, but they did need guidance about what an appropriate policy response would be. The Republicans were told by their leaders to increase offshore oil drilling, and they responded positively to the idea. The Democrats were told not to allow more oil drilling and, for the most part, they held their ground in opposition to the proposal.

This leads to another point about the change in opinion in response to the energy crisis. People do not always respond so strongly to what politicians say. Many political appeals are met with indifference. Yet in this case, the opinions of Republicans shifted 42 percent—a huge change. The messages clearly fell on fertile ground. To put it in more general terms, the combination of an obtrusive issue that people found important and clear political leadership on a related issue caused opinion change.

To make this claim, we need to show that high gasoline prices directly affect people's everyday lives. Two surveys from June and July 2008, when gas prices were most recently soaring, provide the evidence.

The first question at the top of figure 3.7 captures the problem. An ABC News/Washington Post poll asked, "Have recent price increases in gasoline caused any financial hardship for you or others in your household?"[35] Three-quarters of the public said yes. In addition, 71 percent said that they had seriously considered getting a more fuel-efficient car, 66 percent said that they had cut back significantly on their driving, and 55 percent said that they had cut back significantly on their household spending because of higher gas prices. That is evidence that gasoline prices hit Americans hard.

A similar set of survey results comes from a Field Poll conducted among Californians at about the same time.[36] Figure 3.8 shows these data. More than three-quarters of the respondents said that they drove less around town or shortened weekend trips and vacations as a result of the high gas prices. Two-thirds said that they bought a cheaper grade of gas, and 59 percent said that they used their more fuel-efficient car more frequently. Other steps that people took to save money on gas, such as carpooling and using public transit, were only taken by minorities. Still, significant numbers of people adopted these other ways of saving gas.

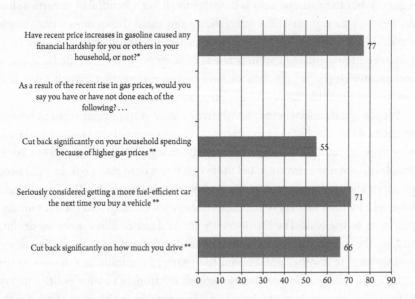

Figure 3.7 Impact of High Gas Prices in June 2008.

* ABC News/*Washington Post* Poll. June 12–15, 2008; ** CNN/Opinion Research Corporation Poll. June 4–5, 2008

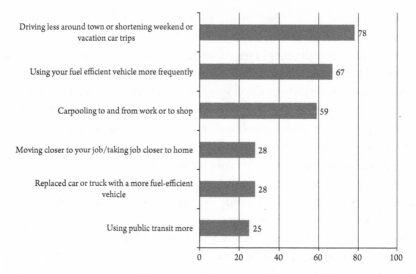

Figure 3.8 Impact of High Gas Prices among Californians, July 2008.
Field Poll, registered California Voters, July 2008

In short, people changed their driving habits and behavior. Almost everyone tried to cut spending on gasoline in some fashion. The high gas prices affected everyone, and for many, the impact was inconvenient and frustrating. The combination of an issue that had a substantial impact on people's lives and clear political leadership produced sharp movements in public opinion on what to do about the energy crisis.

Who Gets the Blame?

Blame plays a critical role in energy crises. When energy prices spike, people react angrily. Rapidly changing prices are not the norm, so people look for an explanation. They look for someone to blame.

Blame is important because it identifies potential targets for political solutions. The old adage, "There ought to be a law," comes into play. People who blame oil company profiteering demand laws regulating and punishing oil companies. People who blame environmentalists for blocking oil development in Alaska, along our coasts, and other places demand laws opening up those areas for drilling.

In principle, people might find many targets for blame during an energy crisis. The most obvious target is probably OPEC because the members act as a cartel to increase or decrease oil production in order to control the world price of oil. Of course, that is not the only way that Middle Eastern nations have affected oil prices. Two of the energy crises were sparked by Middle Eastern wars and OPEC oil boycotts. Another was the result of Iraq's invasion of Kuwait. In still other cases, oil prices have been affected by news about potential hostilities in the Middle East, such as the series of political confrontations over Iran's efforts to develop nuclear weapons and the veiled threats from the United States and Israel that they might bomb Iran's weapons labs. In short, people might blame political and military turmoil in the Middle East for high oil prices.

Looking toward home, people might blame either the president or Congress for mishandling problems with our foreign-oil suppliers or for failing to establish energy policies that provided a steady flow of cheap domestic oil. Alternatively, people could see the high price of gasoline as the result of market forces. In that case, they might blame the drivers of gas-guzzling SUVs and other consumers who were wasting energy. Or they might reason that environmentalists were to blame because they pushed Congress into restricting US oil and gas development, and thus cut domestic oil supplies. And last, perhaps people might blame oil companies for manipulating the market and driving up both prices for consumers and profits for oil companies.

On this last point, it is worth noting that the news media routinely report on oil company profits during energy crises because the profits are eye catching and newsworthy. Energy crises are bad for consumers, but as figure 3.9 shows, they are very good for oil companies. As the price of gasoline rises, so do oil company

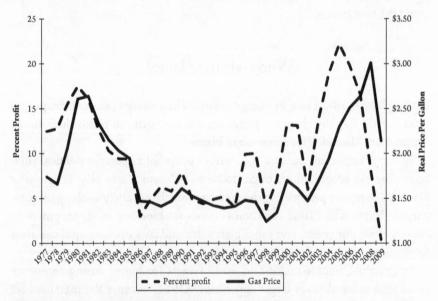

Figure 3.9 The Price of Gasoline and the Oil Company Profits.
US Department of Energy, Energy Information Administration

profits. In 1998, for example, a gallon of unleaded gas cost $1.24 and oil companies made a 3.8 percent return on their investments. By 2000, gas was selling at over $1.70 a gallon and oil company profits had jumped to almost 13.2 percent.[37] As prices continued to rise, profits hit 24 percent in 2005. With profits like that and newspaper headlines such as "Big Oil Firms Profit on Slim Output" and "Oil Industry Hums as Higher Prices Bolster Quarterly Profits at Exxon and Shell," it is easy to see why oil companies draw attention.[38]

Public opinion polls offer us a view of public thinking during energy crises. Since the first energy crisis of 1973–74, national public opinion polls have been asking people who they blame. The people's answer is clear: oil companies.

Starting in 1974, a series of Roper polls presented respondents with a list of groups and asked them to "tell me whether you think they deserve major blame for the energy crisis, some blame, or no blame at all?"[39] Figure 3.10 shows the percentage of people who assigned "major blame" to the groups. The oil companies stand out as deserving the most. "Arab countries," which came in second in most polls, were generally about 20 percent behind oil companies in the blame game, despite the fact that Arab-Israeli wars and OPEC boycotts caused the first two energy crises in 1973–74 and 1979–80. Only in the case of Iraq in 1990 did any other group come close to receiving the blame directed at oil companies. That question, of course, was asked a month after Iraq's invasion of Kuwait, and long before the United States launched its attack in the Persian Gulf War.

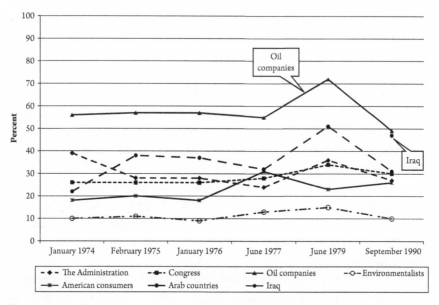

Figure 3.10 Who Deserves Major Blame for the Energy Crisis?

At the other end of the spectrum, environmentalists received the least blame from the public. This is worth noting because oil-industry supporters have argued that environmentalists are preventing the US oil industry from increasing domestic production and reducing our reliance on foreign imports. At least according to these data, that argument did not work in the past.

The relatively small number of people blaming American consumers in figure 3.10 deserves particular comment. In the ideal world of free-market economics, when shortages of a commodity are real, prices rise until demand falls enough so that supply and demand are in balance. Energy crises are a bit different in that they can seriously harm the nation's economy. So political leaders step in, calling on the public to conserve energy. Automobile owners are asked to avoid unnecessary trips and to slow down on the freeway for the good of the nation. That is, people receive both market signals (higher prices) and political signals (pleas to conserve for the nation's good). If people believe that the oil shortages were faked, however, then they might reason to themselves that the calls for sacrifice should be ignored. If the oil shortage is faked by crooked oil companies, should not the government be going after the bad guys instead of asking people to conserve oil?

To address this question directly during the first energy crisis, the Roper Organization asked,

> Some people say there is a real shortage of gasoline and fuel oil because demand has outrun the supply. Others say there really isn't a shortage of gasoline and fuel oil and the big companies are holding it back for their own advantage. What do you think—that there is or is not a real shortage?[40]

The results from their survey, along with the results from CBS and Associated Press polls with similar questions conducted during the second energy crisis in 1979 and again in 2002, are shown in figure 3.11. The public overwhelmingly believed that the oil companies were faking the oil shortages in order to make more money. Nearly three quarters of the public believed the shortages were not real, while only 18 percent thought they were. Between the two crises, in 1977 and 1978, the public's skepticism declined. But again in the second energy crisis, the conspiracy theory that the oil shortages were faked appeared again with belief ranging from 71 percent in June 1979 to 65 percent in August of that year. By more than a two-to-one margin, people said that they thought the energy crisis was faked.

The data we have presented so far are from earlier energy crises. A Pew Research Center survey from 2006 shows that who gets the most blame for high oil prices has not changed since those times.[41] Figure 3.12 shows that 31 percent of the

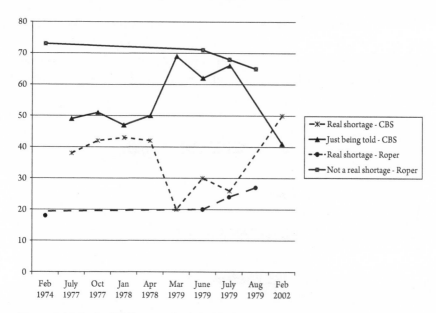

Figure 3.11 Is the Oil Shortage Real or Faked?

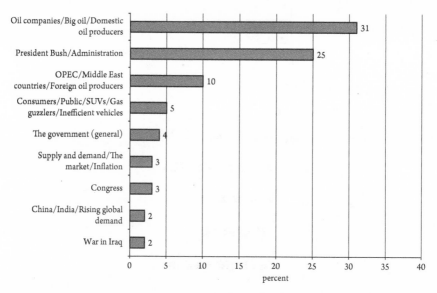

Figure 3.12 Who is Most to Blame for Rising Gasoline Prices? (Pew Research Center open-ended).
Pew Research Center, May 2–14, 2006

public blamed the oil companies, the Bush Administration came in second, and OPEC, foreign oil suppliers, and the laws of supply and demand trailed far behind. In these polls—and in every other survey we have seen—the public blames oil and gas companies above all others for high gasoline oil and gasoline prices.

There is more to the story than just blaming oil companies. The blame is widespread and has partisan aspects. Figure 3.13 and 3.14 present survey data collected during the Republican Bush Administration and the Democratic Obama Administration. In both years, oil companies and oil speculators topped

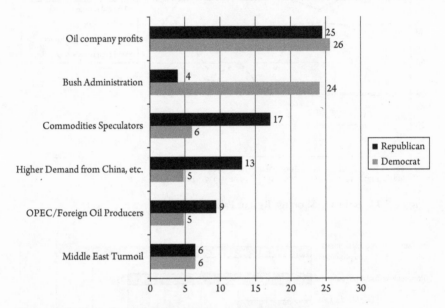

Figure 3.13 Blame for High Prices, 2008.

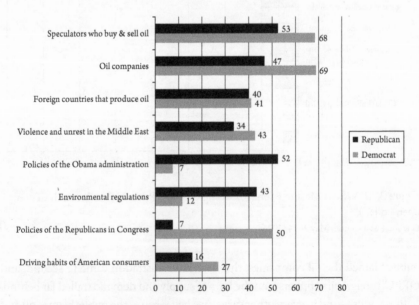

Figure 3.14 Blame for High Prices, 2011.

the blame list, although Democrats were more likely than Republicans to blame them in 2011. The partisan element stands out more sharply in assigning blame to presidents. When a Republican was in the White House, the Democrats blamed him and the Republicans looked elsewhere. When a Democrat held the presidency, the situation was reversed.

We can summarize our findings easily. The public blames the oil companies over everyone else for energy crises. With the sole exception of Iraq in 1990, even Arab countries that start wars and oil boycotts are regarded more positively. In contrast, American consumers are off the hook. Few people blame the public's wasteful driving habits for our energy problems. Environmentalists and environmental regulations are similarly regarded benignly by most people. The only twist is a partisan one. Democrats blame Republican administrations and vice versa, which is only to be expected.

Conclusions

The data presented in this chapter allow us to see the creation of windows of opportunity for change in energy policy. When energy prices rise, not only do they get more attention from the public, but people's policy preferences change as well. That sets the stage for policy change. Four conclusions stand out clearly.

First, the public responds rationally—or at least reasonably—to events in the world. The public's views on offshore oil development are not fixed. They change in response to changes in relevant conditions. Support for offshore drilling rises and falls with the price of gasoline.

Environmentalists may complain that this does not rise to a level that we should characterize as rational. People respond to the price of oil as if it depended on supply and demand in the US domestic market. If that were true, an increase in domestic oil production from offshore wells would drive down the price of gas at the pump. In the real world, however, that would not happen because the price of oil at local gas stations depends on the price of oil on the world market, not the domestic market. When OPEC decides to cut production and increase prices, the price of gasoline in America goes up no matter how much oil we produce. That explains why the price of gasoline in Canada—an oil-exporting nation that produces far more oil than it consumes—rises and falls in tandem with the US price of gasoline. In short, people are mistaken if they believe that an increase in domestic drilling will have much of an effect on prices.

Nevertheless, the public does respond to the price of oil in a manner that indicates that they think in terms of supply and demand. That is fairly sophisticated thinking, the sort of thinking that Page and Shapiro described as rational.[42] The key point is that we can predict people's opinions on oil drilling and other policies based on the price of oil. When the price of oil rises, people favor the oil development policies that the oil companies want.

Second, self-interest is not a cause of the public's attitudes toward oil and gas development. Pundits and politicians talk a lot about how high gasoline prices are hurting people, and our survey data support that claim. Yet people whose financial situations are deteriorating and people who are most easily hurt because of their low incomes are no more likely to call for more offshore drilling than those who are wealthy and prospering. Economic self-interest does not seem to be causing people to change their opinions.

Third, political orientations seem to be the most important cause of the public's attitudes toward oil and gas development. Republicans and conservatives increased their support for oil and gas far more than did Democrats and liberals. Previous research suggests that this happened because of two reasons. Republican and conservative leaders called for more oil development, while Democratic and liberal leaders opposed it. And people with Republican and conservative values are more predisposed to pro-development, free-market arguments than people with Democratic or liberal values. That is a combination of leaders sending messages and followers receiving them with their partisan and ideological biases. In addition, partisanship also plays a role in people's decisions about whom to blame for higher prices. Democrats blamed the administration when the president was a Republican far more than when he was a Democrat, and Republicans did the opposite.

Fourth, the public blames oil companies over all others. Moreover, environmental groups are regarded positively during energy crises. These facts put oil companies at a political disadvantage during energy crises. However, public opinion on domestic oil production moves in a direction that favors oil company interests—toward more support for drilling offshore and in the Arctic National Wildlife Refuge. That is, changes in public opinion favor both sides in different ways during energy crises.

Perhaps most important of all, when energy crises strike, the public is unhappy and wants something done to cut prices. Those demands open the door for policy change. They also limit what elected officials can do in response to the public demands. The public reaction to the gasoline price hikes is not a mere matter of calling attention to an important problem and then sitting back and seeing how Washington responds. People are feeling hurt, and they are watching Congress and the White House to see what the responses are. That gives the elected officials in Washington good cause to move carefully and to pay attention to what the public wants as they craft their responses.

4

The Question of Trust

When energy prices spike, people demand explanations and solutions. They want to know why prices went up and what can be done to lower them to reasonable levels. Their demands are met with a flurry of conflicting answers from energy companies, environmentalists, government spokespeople, politicians, university scientists, policy analysts, media pundits, and a host of others. Oil producers and their allies inevitably call for steps to increase production. They argue for opening up Alaska's Arctic National Wildlife Refuge, ending the moratorium on offshore oil drilling along the Pacific coast, and taking other measures designed to increase domestic energy supplies—all of which, they claim, are environmentally friendly and safe. For their part, environmentalists resist the calls for ramping up production too quickly, claiming that some proposals for more domestic oil production would damage the environment and pose unacceptable risks for people. Each side inevitably disputes the claims made by the other side. How do people choose which answers to believe? It is a question of trust.

Trust is important in energy crises because the oil industry, environmentalists, and other groups make conflicting claims about scientific facts. Is the energy crisis real or faked? Will opening up new areas for oil drilling lower gasoline prices? The set of claims people choose to believe is closely linked to the demands they place on politicians. People who believe the oil companies send one message to Congress; people who believe the environmentalists send another. Indeed, this pattern holds true in every policy area when a crisis strikes and groups disagree about the right solution.

Scientific disputes are central to many of today's major public policy issues. Is climate change real and human-caused? Are nuclear power plants and offshore oil drilling safe? Does the mercury used as a preservative in childhood vaccines cause autism? In these disputes and many others, scientific claims and counter-claims are made in efforts to sway public opinion. This fact leads to questions about trust in science and scientists. How much do people trust scientists and the scientific claims they make? When scientific claims are disputed, how do people decide which side is right?

In this chapter, we will look at the role of the public's trust in sources of information about energy issues. We will begin by taking a step away from energy crises and looking at previous psychological research on trust and persuasion. We will then return to energy issues to examine how the public responds to different kinds of experts on oil and energy policy.

Whom to Trust?

Trust plays a role in this battle for the hearts and minds of the people. There are benefits to being believable. Whether the public believes oil companies, environmental groups, or government scientists can make a difference in public policy.

Political activists of all stripes recognize that trust is a key variable in policy disputes that are fought out before the court of public opinion. As part of their strategies, policy advocates often work to build the public's trust in both themselves and the scientists whose research supports their political stands.[1] This is particularly true in environmental policy battles because these fights often turn on scientific evidence. If people trust the claims of policy advocates and scientists, then those trusted voices will carry more weight in policy debates.

These fights are most easily seen in the struggle over climate change. The editors of *Science*, the world's most widely read scientific journal, have called on scientists to do whatever they can to build the public's trust in scientists so that they can be more influential in the climate change debate.[2] On the other side, a small, well-funded industry has developed to cast doubt on climate scientists and their claims.[3] The expression "junk science" has become a well-known catch phrase of climate skeptics.

The strategy of building trust stems both from common sense and from research on persuasion. Social scientists have been studying trust for more than half a century. Psychologists had established that it was a key variable in persuasion by the 1950s. In their classic study of persuasion, Carl Hovland and his colleagues wrote, "An important factor influencing the effectiveness of a communication is the person or group perceived as originating the communication—and the cues provided as to the trustworthiness, intentions, and affiliations of this source."[4] Although there have been many advances in our understanding of communication and persuasion over the years, trust in the source of the message has continued to be recognized as an important variable. The leading contemporary theories of persuasion, the elaboration likelihood model and the heuristic-systematic model, both identify trust in the communicator as a key variable.[5]

An important aspect of the prevailing theories of persuasion is that they treat trust as the independent variable. That is, the more one trusts the source of a message, the more one is likely to believe the message. Typical psychological experiments on trust manipulate some characteristic of the person who is the source of a persuasive message so that subjects increase or decrease their trust in that person in order to measure the influence of the characteristic on message acceptance.[6] Researchers who study persuasion on environmental issues such as climate change, nuclear power plants, peak oil, or offshore oil drilling make the same assumption.[7] If we trust the scientist who is telling us about climate change or another risk, then we will believe her message.

Researchers in the closely related area of risk perception typically take a similar approach toward trust. Loss of trust in institutions and the experts associated with them is one of the most commonly proposed explanations for the failure of people to believe expert risk assessments and accept new technologies.[8] The argument is that if people do not trust the government, big business, university scientists, or other sources of expertise, then they will reject the experts' assurances that risks are minimal and that they have no reason to worry. Some scholars further claim that trust in experts has declined in the last forty years and that the United States is becoming a less trusting society.[9] The lack of trust, according to this reasoning, explains why many Americans remain afraid of nuclear power plants, offshore oil drilling, high-power electric transmission lines, genetically engineered foods, pesticides, and a host of other potential risks.

Message content was also identified in the 1950s as an important variable affecting whether people believe persuasive messages. A variety of message characteristics have actually been studied.[10] Here we are referring specifically to whether the content of the message agrees with the recipients' previously held opinions.

Psychologists working on social judgment theory found that the likelihood of people accepting persuasive messages depended on the discrepancy between their beliefs and the positions advocated in the messages.[11] This argument can best be explained in spatial terms. Messages that advocate views that are close to the listener's views tend to be accepted. Messages that advocate views that are somewhat more distant fall into a non-commitment range. Messages that advocate views that are quite distant from the listener's views are rejected. In short, the greater the discrepancy between the message and the recipient's opinion, the less likely the message will be believed.[12]

Message content, like trust in the communicator, has continued to be recognized as an influence on persuasion, but it has not received as much attention as trust from those who study politics. Psychologists studying persuasion continue to investigate the influence of prior beliefs, and they find that prior beliefs have a substantial influence on message acceptance.[13] In related work, researchers who study schemas (the ways in which people organize their knowledge about the world) and their resistance to change have found that people tend to accept scientific studies that are consistent with their schemas and reject studies that contradict them.[14] More recently, researchers have shown that people have a "defensive motivation" to maintain beliefs that are consistent with "self-definitional attitudes" such as basic values.[15] As Albarracín puts it, "A persuasive message does not impact a *tabula rasa*."[16]

To sum up, we have two sets of findings from psychology. First, trust in the source of a message causes people to accept it. The more one trusts the messenger, the more one is likely to believe the message. Second, agreement with the content of a message causes people to accept it. One is likely to agree with messages that support one's opinions and disagree with messages that contradict those opinions.

These findings raise an intriguing possibility. If people tend to reject messages that contradict their opinions, then perhaps they also tend to become less trusting of the messengers. That is, perhaps trust in the messenger is caused by agreement with the message, rather than the other way around.

The prevailing view is that trust causes message acceptance, but a few researchers dissent from the prevailing view. Howard Margolis was the first to raise doubts about the role of trust and distrust in risk assessments, which is related to persuasion.[17] He suggested that the causal path may actually be in the opposite direction. In the case of risk perception, once a person has decided that something is dangerous, he or she may tend to distrust any so-called expert who says otherwise. That is, distrust may be caused by exaggerated fears, rather than being a cause of them. Margolis produced no experimental or survey evidence to support his claim; nevertheless, his argument is certainly plausible. Moreover, a few studies have indirectly supported his hypothesis. Although most researchers assume that trust causes attitudes and risk perceptions, a few studies have treated trust as a dependent variable caused by attitudes and risk perceptions.[18]

Outside the academic world of surveys and laboratory experiments, there is also doubt about causal direction. The fact that Republican conservatives overwhelmingly rely on climate change skeptics, whereas Democratic liberals rely on climate change scientists who warn us about the threat of global warming, is well known.[19] Did all those people decide whom they would trust without regard to the scientific claims they were making? Of course not. Some people decided which scientists to trust based on other factors, such as the claims the scientists made about climate change. More broadly, we can see that in political disputes, some people choose which experts to trust and believe based on whether the experts agree with them on the facts.

This is not to say that the psychologists studying persuasion have it wrong. Experiments are, after all, a powerful method for showing causal direction.

There is really no doubt that trust in the person who is the source of a message causes people to be more likely to believe the message. Instead, we suggest that in the real world outside of psychologists' labs, causation flows in both directions. When people trust a scientist, they are more likely to believe her, but people's opinions on scientific facts can also guide them in their choices of whom to trust.

For readers who are not familiar with the idea of two variables simultaneously causing one another, we need to offer an explanation. With survey data such as ours, one way of understanding the idea is simple. In one group in the survey sample, people's thinking may be dominated by trust. They place their trust in scientists and believe what the scientists tell them. In another group, people's thinking may be dominated by their belief that climate change is a hoax. When they hear some scientists claim that it is real, they conclude that the scientists do not know what they are talking about. The result is that in the sample, causation runs in both directions. Trust causes belief and belief causes trust, but for different people.

There is more to it than that. In a single person, trust in scientists and belief in scientific facts can be forces in opposite directions. When someone whom we trust tells us something we are inclined not to believe, what do we do? Both trust in sources and belief in facts can work against one another. The result can favor one side or the other, or in some cases, the result can be uncertainty.

To summarize: we suggest that in political disputes in which scientists make factual claims about the world, trust is both a cause of and caused by the content of the claims. That is, the trust people have in scientists causes them to believe the scientists, but at the same time, people's beliefs about scientific facts cause them to choose which scientists to trust.

A Look at Some Data

To learn more about the role trust plays in energy crises, we have data from two surveys of Californians that allow us to see how the public reacted to three of the most important groups that sound off during energy crises—oil companies, environmentalists, and the government. There are two important limitations on our data and argument.

First, we are using only two surveys to examine a single issue, offshore oil development. That is not much on which to base our sweeping claim about trust in scientists and acceptance of scientific knowledge. We recognize that more tests covering more issues will be needed before we can be confident about our argument. Moreover, we think that these ideas should be tested with experiments as well as surveys. Still, we think our data go a long way toward supporting what we think is a very plausible claim—that in some cases, people choose which scientists to trust based on the claims the scientists are making.

Second, surveys of Californian are not as desirable as national surveys. For our purposes, however, we think they are almost as good. California is a large, diverse state with many similarities to the entire US population. Indeed, more than one in ten Americans lives in California. One researcher claims that California is a "microcosm" of the United States.[20] It is sufficiently close so that any broad patterns found among Californians should be found elsewhere in the United States.

Our two surveys were conducted in 1998, when the price of oil was near an all-time low, and four years later in 2002, when the price of oil had doubled and people were complaining about gasoline prices. In both cases, we find evidence that trust in scientists is both a cause of people believing the factual claims made by the scientists, and that prior belief in certain facts causes people to choose which scientists to trust.

We begin with our 1998 survey.[21] The survey asked questions about respondents' opinions about offshore oil drilling and their trust in scientists. The first question about offshore oil drilling was, "Do you generally favor or oppose increasing oil and gas drilling along the California coast?" The second asked respondents how strongly they agreed or disagreed with the statement: "Oil companies should be allowed to drill more oil and gas wells in state tidelands along the California seacoast." We should note that the first question was also the first question about energy policy in the survey, whereas the second was in a series of nine questions about energy policy that were rotated, so respondents had time to think about different aspects of energy policy before answering. This explains why the two questions are strongly related (Pearson's $r = 0.58$), but not identical. Oil drilling was not very popular at the time. As figures 4.1 and 4.2 show, just over 20 percent of the sample favored it.

To measure trust in scientists, respondents were asked, "How much confidence do you have in statements made by [government/oil industry/environmental group] scientists about potential health risks associated with living near an oil drilling site? Do you have a great deal of confidence, a moderate amount of confidence, only some confidence, or almost no confidence at all?" The order of the three versions of the question was randomly rotated. As figure 4.3 shows, people regarded environmental group scientists as the most trustworthy, followed by government scientists, followed by oil industry scientists.

To sort out the influence of trust in scientists and opinions about offshore oil drilling on confidence in scientists, we estimated the structural equation model shown in figure 4.4. In this type of model, observed variables (e.g., the answers people give to the questions about offshore oil development or confidence in scientists, shown in rectangles) are used to infer the existence of unobserved

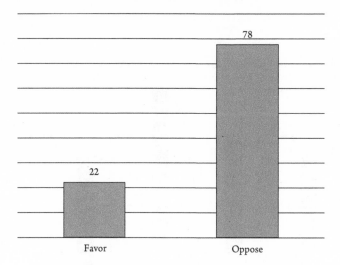

"Do you generally favor or oppose increasing oil and gas drilling along the California coast?"

Figure 4.1 Favor or Oppose Offshore Oil Drilling.

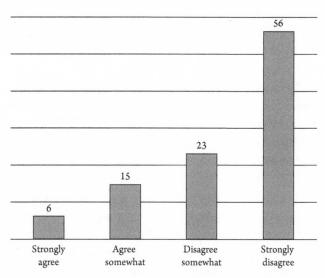

"Oil companies should be allowed to drill more oil and gas wells in state tidelands along the California seacoast."

Figure 4.2 Oil Companies Should Be Allowed to Drill.

variables (e.g., the "Support for Oil Development" and "Trusting" variables shown in circles in figure 4.4). For example, the three questions about confidence in government scientists, environmental group scientists, and oil industry scientists (shown in boxes at the bottom of the figure) and the four questions about whether people can be trusted, whether government can be trusted, whether big interests run the government, and whether smart people run the government are

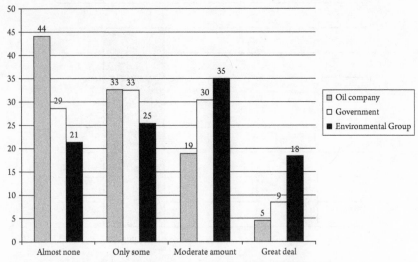

Figure 4.3 Confidence in Scientists.

used to infer respondents' underlying feelings of general trust (labeled Trusting in the circle). In other words, if a respondent expresses trust in response to a series of questions, even though we cannot directly observe that she is a person who is generally trusting, we infer that she is. In contrast, if another respondent says he has little confidence in people, government, or scientists, we infer that he is generally not a trusting person. In this way, we infer the existence of an unobserved variable, "Trusting." The statistical program we use allows us to get a precise measurement of that unobserved variable.[22]

In models like this, latent or unobserved variables are shown in circles or ellipses, and observed variables are shown in boxes. So in figure 4.4, the boxes indicate questions that were asked in our survey, and the circles indicate unobserved variables that we have estimated using our statistical program. The arrows indicate causal direction. For example, the arrows from the "Trusting" variable to the "Confidence in Scientists" variables mean that trust causes confidence in scientists.

Our model in figure 4.4 has three unobserved variables—Environmentalism, Trusting, and Support for offshore oil development. On the left hand side of the figure, environmentalism is assumed to cause four observed variables— opposition to nuclear power, and whether one favors cutting standards of living, slowing population growth, or slowing industrial growth to reduce energy consumption (see Appendix B for question wording). The variable is described as environmentalism because high scores indicate opposition to nuclear power and

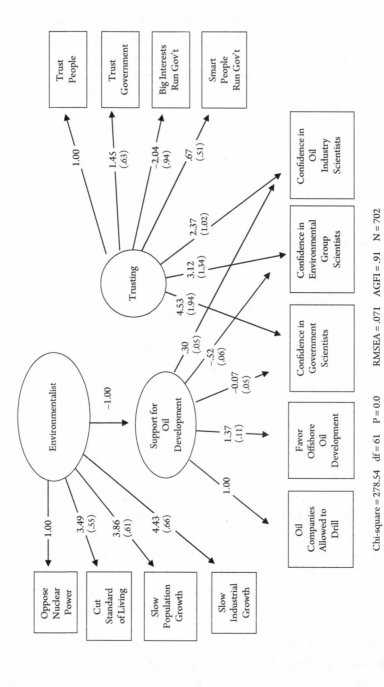

Figure 4.4 Model of Attitudes toward Oil Drilling and Trust in Experts.

Chi-square = 278.54   df = 61   P = 0.0   RMSEA = .071   AGFI = .91   N = 702

support for taking steps to reduce energy consumption. In turn, environmentalism causes people's attitudes toward oil development, a latent variable, which causes people's answers to our questions about offshore oil drilling.

On the right side of the figure, the unobserved variable "Trusting" is measured with four questions from the American National Election Studies—how much people can be trusted, how much the government can be trusted, whether the government is run by a few big interests or for the benefit of all the people, and whether the people running the government are smart. Trust also causes people's feelings of trust in government scientists, environmental group scientists, and oil industry scientists. Our central hypothesis is tested by asking whether our respondents' attitudes toward offshore oil drilling also causes these three measures of confidence in scientists.

The details of the model are presented in the appendix to this chapter, although we do want to note that all but two of the coefficients are statistically significant. Here we only want to focus on the big picture. The coefficients for the causal paths from environmentalism to the four environmental opinion variables are all reasonably large and in the expected positive directions. The coefficients for the trust indicators on the right hand side are in the expected directions, but one of them—the coefficient for believing that smart people run the government—is small and statistically insignificant. The coefficients for offshore oil attitude causing responses to the two offshore oil questions are positive and significant, as we would expect. Similarly, the coefficients for trusting scientists causing responses to our three confidence-in-scientists questions are positive and significant.

The key findings here are the coefficients for the paths from attitude toward offshore oil drilling to confidence in the scientists. The coefficient for oil attitude causing confidence in government scientists is small and statistically insignificant. In other words, whether the respondents supported or opposed oil drilling had no impact on their trust in government scientists. That suggests that people do not believe that government scientists have taken a side, which is good news for them. In contrast, the coefficients for environmental group and oil industry scientists are strong and significant. As support for offshore oil drilling increases, confidence in oil industry scientists increases and confidence in environmental group scientists decreases. In other words, one's attitude toward offshore oil drilling causes one's trust in scientists affiliated with different sides in the controversy. That finding supports our hypothesis that people choose which scientists to trust based on their beliefs.

To pursue the question of whether opinions about oil drilling influence how much confidence people have in scientists, we turn to our 2002 data.[23] An experiment was embedded in this survey.[24] It consisted of a question with six variations that were randomly asked of respondents. The question was this:

A team of [government/oil industry/environmental group] scientists recently reported the results of their research showing that because of new technology, offshore oil drilling is far [riskier/safer] than previously thought. How much confidence do you have in that claim—a great deal, a moderate amount, only some, or almost none at all?

The three possible sources of the report were government, oil industry, or environmental group scientists. The two possible messages were that offshore oil drilling was either riskier or safer than previously thought. The result is a 3×2 design that allows us to look at the effects of the source of the message and its content. If people are more likely to accept scientific claims that agree with their previously held views, this experiment should show it.

Figure 4.5 shows the basic results of our experiment. The two columns on the left show the respondents who were told that the scientific report was from environmental group scientists. The pair of columns in the middle show the respondents who were told that the report was from government scientists, and the columns on the right show the respondents who were told the report was from oil industry scientists. In each pair of columns, the left column indicates that the message was that oil drilling was riskier than previously thought, and the right column indicates that oil drilling was safer.

One finding immediately jumps out. Californians generally have more confidence in expert claims that offshore oil drilling is riskier than previously thought than they have in claims that it is safer. Fifty-eight percent of the respondents express a great deal or moderate amount of confidence in expert claims that

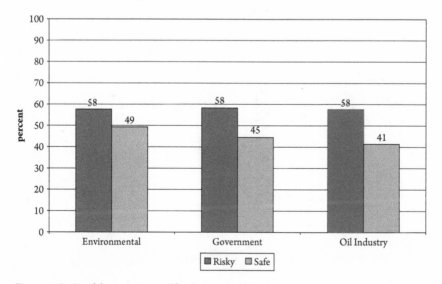

Figure 4.5 Confidence in Report by Source and Content.

offshore oil drilling is riskier than previously thought, but only about 41 to 49 percent express that same confidence when told that oil drilling is safer than previously thought, depending on the source. An ANOVA analysis confirms that the difference between riskier and safer messages is statistically significant.[25] Bad news about offshore oil drilling is well received. This finding is consistent with previous research showing that people are more likely to accept bad news about risks than good news, a point to which we will return in our discussion.[26]

The other result in figure 4.5 is that the source of the messages had no effect on acceptance of the report that offshore oil drilling is riskier than previously thought, but the interaction between the source and the content of the message did have an effect.[27] This is because when the message is that oil drilling is safer, environmental group scientists were the most trusted, followed by government scientists and oil-industry scientists.

Figure 4.6 extends our examination of the basic relationships in the experiment by controlling for self-identified ideology. This allows us to see how message sources and content interact with core values. The three pairs of columns on the left show how liberal respondents reacted to the questions; the three pairs of columns in the middle show moderates, and the three pairs of columns on the right show conservative respondents. Again, in each pair of columns, the column on the left shows the results with the "riskier" message, and the column on the right shows the results with the "safer" message. This allows us to test the message content hypotheses, which says that people are motivated to maintain beliefs that are consistent with their basic values.

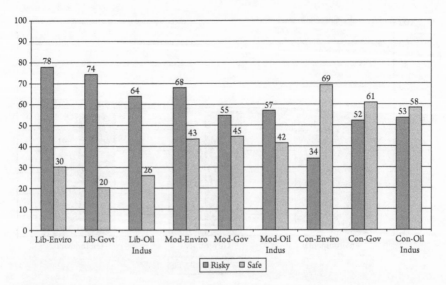

Figure 4.6 Confidence in Report by Source, Content, and Ideology.

The results in figure 4.6 strongly support our hypothesis about message content. Liberals have overwhelming confidence in the claim that offshore oil drilling is riskier than previously thought, no matter what the source of the report. Conservatives place more faith in the message that oil drilling is safer than previously thought, although the relationships are not as strong as among liberals. Given that liberals are generally pro-environment and conservatives are generally pro-development, this is exactly what the hypothesis would predict: ideology and the content of the message interact.[28]

People who describe themselves as politically "middle-of-the-road" are also quite interesting. The message content hypothesis offers no prediction here because it is not clear that moderates think of themselves as environmentalists. Nevertheless, they have far more confidence in the message that oil drilling is riskier than previously believed than they do in the message that it is safer than previously believed. This finding casts new light on the results shown in figure 4.5. Californians as a whole were more likely to believe claims that oil drilling is risky than that it is safe. Yet figure 4.6 shows that this view is held most strongly by liberals and by majorities of moderates as well, but the view is not shared by conservatives. From the perspective of practical politics, environmentalists win because two-thirds of the California public describe themselves as either liberal or middle-of-the-road.[29]

Last, we present the results for respondents who either favored or opposed offshore oil drilling.[30] This allows us to see how message sources and content interact with prior beliefs. Figure 4.7 presents our experimental results controlling for attitude toward oil drilling. The three pairs of columns on the left represent those who oppose offshore oil drilling; the three pairs on the right represent those who favor it. The results are striking. First, all groups find reports favoring their position to be far more credible than reports opposing it.[31] Respondents who opposed oil drilling, for example, were far more likely to have confidence in reports saying that it was riskier than previously believed.

The Role of Trust

Taken together, the results in this chapter show that the role of trust is more complicated than it might seem at first glance. The editors of *Science* may think that all they have to do is to persuade the American public to trust scientists, and then their problems will go away. People will accept the advice of scientists, and Congress will act on climate change, energy policy, childhood vaccines, and the wide variety of other issues on which scientific consensus exists. Sadly, that is not the case.

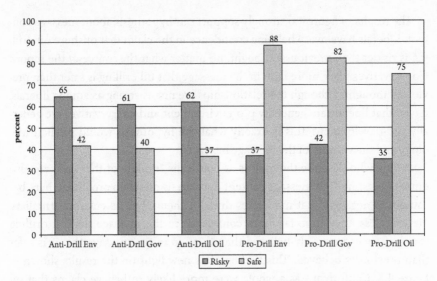

Figure 4.7 Confidence in Report by Content, Source, and Support for Drilling.

Trust does cause acceptance of claims made by scientists, but beliefs about science also cause people to choose which experts to trust. That, at least, is the conclusion to which our data point. As we noted at the beginning of the chapter, we only have two surveys looking at one narrow issue—offshore oil drilling. More data are clearly needed to support our argument. Nevertheless, we think it likely that our claims will hold up when it is tested more thoroughly.

Two conclusions follow from our work on trust. First, the strategy of building trust in scientists, which some advocate, is likely to have some impact, but not necessarily enough to be a winning strategy. A public relations campaign urging all Americans to trust scientists is not likely to win because people are increasingly seeing scientists as taking sides and not being neutral.[32]

Second, the lack of trust in science and scientists makes it difficult to achieve compromise and design effective policies. To some extent, people are not only choosing sides based on their values—liberal, conservative, or whatever; they are also picking teams. When trust in science on any number of issues is increasingly divided along ideological or partisan lines, policy decisions are even more difficult to achieve. Even more problematic are two facts. First, individuals are increasingly living in "ideological silos" in which they associate only with those who share their views. Second, selective exposure reinforces and amplies their distrust in science. Unfortunately, science denial today is more commonly found among the political right. If the proposed remedy to this is to create public relations campaigns, urging Americans to trust scientists, such public relations campaigns will likely be viewed skeptically by those on the right. This is not a conclusion that is likely to bring joy to the heart of the scientific community.

For energy crises, our results imply that the voices of scientific reason will be able to do little to calm the waters and point the public toward sound policy steps to take in response to energy price shocks. Scientists may indeed be able to identify policy changes that would either improve or worsen a crisis. For example, economists have identified regulatory steps that actually made the California electricity crisis more severe in 2000 and that should not have been taken.[33] Yet persuading the public to believe economists when they call for no price freezes in markets with rapidly rising electricity rates would be difficult to do. Based on our findings, we think that people would be likely to compare the policy recommendations to their own prior beliefs and weigh the results with their own partisan biases. In short, scientists are just one more set of policy advocates among the advocacy coalitions fighting over changes in public policy.

PART II

THE POLITICAL DYNAMICS
OF ENERGY CRISES

5

The Yom Kippur Arab-Israeli War

The Crisis of 1973–74

The preceding chapters familiarized readers with the theory of agenda setting with special attention paid to the logic of punctuated equilibrium and focusing events and the role of public opinion in relation to energy crises. The theoretical framework therefore demonstrates that policy is dynamic and also that focusing events and episodes can reorganize the political landscape so that new players and new solutions play a role in policy change. The present chapter and those that follow consider each energy crisis in greater detail. The aim herein is to provide the reader with a more comprehensive and detailed look at the politics of the energy crisis of 1973–74—the players, the politics, and the outcomes.

A Look Back

In the decades following WWII, America's industrialization, urbanization, and growing love affair with the automobile greatly increased its dependence on cheap and plentiful oil. In fact, between 1950 and 1974, oil consumption in the United States had more than doubled.[1] With just under 6 percent of the world's population,[2] the United States was consuming one-third of the world's energy.[3] However, by the late 1960s and early 1970s, America's demand for oil had begun to place significant stress on its own petroleum supply, as domestic production had leveled off and even began to fall. As a result, the United States more and more relied upon foreign imports to fill its energy gap. By 1970 the United States relied on foreign imports for 30 percent of its petroleum needs.[4] At the same time, the growing dependence on foreign oil coincided with energy shortages, the first of which occurred in September 1970 when electricity brownouts hit the Northeast after a long summer heat wave and thus made the term "energy crisis" very real for Americans. The energy situation continued to worsen with additional energy shortages in the winter of 1972–73 and again the following summer. Furthermore, the energy problems were exacerbated by government-mandated price controls that discouraged domestic oil production while encouraging rampant consumption. As a result of the rampant consumption of oil, the growing dependence on imported Middle Eastern petroleum, and short-sided policies, the United States was ever-more vulnerable to Middle Eastern politics and events and none more so than the Arab-Israeli war and subsequent oil embargo in late 1973.

In an effort to force Israel to surrender captured lands, Egypt and Syria launched a joint attack on October 6, 1973, Yom Kippur, and started what was to become known as the fourth Arab-Israeli War. Shortly thereafter, the Organization of Arab Petroleum Exporting Countries (OAPEC, consisting of the Arab members of OPEC plus Egypt and Syria) announced that they would no longer ship petroleum to nations that supported Israel. While the Unites States had initially wished to stay out of direct involvement, doing so remained difficult as the Arab forces benefited greatly from a massive Soviet resupply effort.[5] When the United States realized how massive the Soviet resupply was and how much Israel was now threatened, on October 14 the United States made efforts for a covert airlift to Israel, which turned out to be anything but covert. In the meantime, in an effort to punish the United States for its support of Israel, Arab countries agreed to an oil embargo that cut production 5 percent from the September level, and each subsequent month was met with another 5 percent cut.[6] These production cuts were seen as much more severe than merely banning petroleum exports to an individual country, because petroleum shipments could be easily redirected and therefore be cause to a mere inconvenience. Supply cuts were far more threatening because of the how much Americans had grown to depend on petroleum as a way of life.

On October 19, Nixon proposed a $2.2 billion military-aid package for Israel. Later that day, Libya initiated a full embargo on all oil shipments to the United States. In the days to come, all the other Arab states had done or were about to do the same.[7] The United States now found itself in a petroleum pickle. The end result of the embargos was quite disrupting to the United States, for it came at a time when the country had grown dependent on cheap and abundant oil. Moreover, with the decline in domestic crude oil production, greater reliance on imported oil (17 percent of the United States' total 23 percent crude imports at this time were from OPEC countries),[8] and OPEC production cutbacks, the embargo further cut into the supply of oil and elevated prices for Americans to levels previously thought impossible—oil prices jumped from about $2.90 per barrel in September 1973 to $11.65 per barrel in December.[9] Panic prices were the result of war, cutbacks in supply, embargoes, shortages, desperate consumers, the specter of further cutbacks, and the possibility that the Arabs would never restore production.[10] According to the Energy Information Administration, the 1973 Oil Embargo was the first oil-supply disruption to cause major price increases and a worldwide energy crisis.[11] Nonetheless, while the United States' energy problems were exacerbated by the Arab boycott, it was fairly evident that even without the boycott, the United States would have experienced a deepening energy crisis by the winter of 1974.

The preceding events illustrate the beginning of a sequence of events that we term the "energy crisis cycle," with the energy crisis serving as a focusing episode. The soaring demand for cheap oil by Americans, accompanied by the sudden supply shortage resulting from the aforementioned Yom Kippur war and Arab production cuts and oil embargo, led to a sharp and significant jump in the price of energy. While the energy crisis felt very real to consumers, the energy producers—the domestic oil industry—received a windfall from the increase in oil prices. As a result of the high prices and huge profits, the energy industry was targeted by politicians and interest group advocates who raised claims that the energy industry manipulated prices—or even worse, fabricated the energy crisis—in an effort to increase their own profits. Public outrage at the belief that they had been duped by the oil industry led to demands that the government take remedial steps without any additional cost to consumers. While remedial action by government officials was fairly swift, the best that it did was to subsidize the oil gluttony and forestall the end of the energy crisis. Briefly, this is the cycle of energy crisis, and the following will describe this cycle in detail as it applies to the 1973–74 energy crisis.

The Arab oil embargo hit the United States during an already tenuous set of circumstances regarding oil. As mentioned above, petroleum shortages first were noticed in the summer of 1970, the same year that domestic oil production had reached its peak at 11.3 million barrels per day and surplus capacity had dropped to about a million barrels per day.[12] The electricity brownouts in 1970 foreshadowed events to come, with spot shortages of heating fuel in the Northeast during the winter of 1972–73 and the following summer. Yet the circumstances resulting from an energy policy, long cobbled together over the years, created an environment that made energy shortages and high prices inevitable. To help understand the inevitability of the 1970s energy crisis, it is important to know something about what came before.

The history of congressional regulation of oil began early in the twentieth century, when oil producers, feeling vulnerable to new oil discoveries in Texas, welcomed government action with the National Industrial Recovery Act of 1933 (NIRA), later ruled unconstitutional by the Supreme Court and replaced with the Connally Hot Oil Act of 1935. The purpose of the Connally Hot Oil Act was to create a domestic oil cartel that would protect the industry from contraband oil,[13] help stabilize the quickly falling price of oil, and encourage the conservation of US crude-oil deposits. Such efforts were seen as the obvious solution to protect an industry—and a politically attentive one—from bankruptcy resulting from the glut of oil from new oil discoveries in Texas. If Congress had not acted, the supply of oil would have increased to the point of driving the prices low enough to bankrupt domestic producers. Members of Congress, therefore, sided with the domestic oil industry, which had vociferously lobbied Congress for remedy in the form of regulation. The oil industry benefited while the consumers lost insomuch as they suffered a missed opportunity for a significant drop in the price of oil.[14]

In 1955 Congress once again acted to protect domestic oil producers and approved a quota system, Section 7 of the Trade Agreement Extension Act, which limited the import of foreign oil. A significant consequence of the prorationing of the market to regulate demand and control prices was a distorted market. Both the prorationing and the quotas worked to the benefit of oil producers at the expense of the consumers: world oil prices were falling deeply, but the price of oil for Americans was much higher than it would have been had the market been left to operate freely or had it been imported from abroad. Moreover, another effect of both policies was that they restricted the domestic production of oil largely because it had grown cheaper to produce oil abroad and import it. The quota system stayed in place until Nixon abandoned all import quotas in 1973, when domestic reserves became tight.

Price controls on oil were imposed by President Nixon in August of 1971 as part of an economy-wide freeze on wages, prices, and rents. Nixon's comprehensive plan was the result of his focused attention on the issue of inflation, which had been a central concern of his since he first took office. The plan did nothing to curb consumption or induce the exploration of new oil reserves, as it kept petroleum prices artificially low when world oil prices were rising. In addition to stimulating consumption, the price controls stymied domestic exploration, making the situation worse. Although the mandatory freeze was temporary, lasting ninety days, when the immediate crisis had ebbed and the mandatory freeze was lifted, Nixon called for voluntary price controls that were mostly ineffective, as the price of heating oil shot up 8 to 10 percent.[15] The demand for oil continued to surge well into 1973, and gasoline shortages were imminent. When President Nixon lifted the quotas on imported oil in April 1973, the effect was frenetic buying that stirred up a panic and sent the price of oil sky-rocketing. As Smith observes, "Insofar as the nation had an energy policy, it was making the situation worse."[16]

Public Reaction: The Pinch at the Pumps

For more than one hundred years, Americans had been spoiled by the fact that their consistently increased use of energy (doubling every twenty to twenty-five years or so) had the welcome effect of lowering the price of energy.[17] It was not until the 1970s, when rampant consumption, strained domestic oil supplies, ad-hoc energy policies, and America's expanding dependence on Middle Eastern oil, eventually led to the abolition of import quotas. With the abolition of quotas, the world oil market, also suffering from scarce excess capacity, experienced a "major new demand in an already-fevered market."[18] Prices were quickly rising, doubling from 1970 to 1973. Some stations began rationing the amount of fuel available to each customer, and other stations operated under a reduced schedule, as they were unable to meet the demand for gasoline. While clues of the energy crisis had appeared prior to the spring of 1973, neither politicians nor the public was aware of how critical the problem was becoming. However, as summer approached the mounting crisis became imminent, capturing the attention of the public and politicians. It so motivated then Georgia Governor Jimmy Carter to order State Troopers to drive slower and reduce their number of highway patrols in an effort to conserve gasoline. Furthermore, with the peak travel season approaching and fuel shortages looming, panicky residents in Martha's Vineyard, Massachusetts began queuing up at gas pumps at 6 a.m.[19] By May 1973, already 562 gasoline stations across the country had closed, with another 1,376 threatened due to short supplies.[20] Additionally, predictions began to circulate of even greater shortages the following winter. Even still, it was not until the Mideast oil boycott, announced in October 1973, that the reality of the shortage so captured the attention of Americans. In fact, up until October 1973, a large portion of the public was not aware that the United States imported any oil at all.[21]

Within months, indicators of an energy crisis were ever-present. Americans faced a huge jump in the price of gas, long gas lines at the gas pumps abounded, motorists were forced to wait up to two hours for gas, and many gas stations displayed signs that read, "Sorry, No Gas Today." Some gas stations employed a gas allocation system where license plates ending in an even number received gas on even-numbered days and odd numbered plates on odd-numbered days. New car sales declined and bicycle sales increased.[22] Public reaction to the crisis at times was intense: as a *Time* magazine article reported, people began to turn to violence—an "owner of a South Miami filling station had to call police after a motorist to whom he refused to sell gas on Saturday night swung a hose at him, shouting: 'I am going to get some gas even if I have to kill somebody'. . . [and] in Hanford, California, a station owner who had closed at the President's call found that a competitor across the street was open on Sunday and doing a hopping business. So the patriot hauled out a pistol and shot up six of his rival's pumps."[23]

American motorists immediately felt the effect of the oil embargo as prices at the pump climbed quickly and significantly. Over the course of a week in early November 1973, the price of gasoline rose between 1¢ and 4¢ per gallon.[24] A November 1973 *Time* article stated that at present, motorists were paying about 40¢ per gallon for gasoline, and by winter's end the price was expected to jump to 50¢ per gallon.[25] In September, Oregon Governor Tom McCall actually banned outside commercial and display lighting and also made the Grinchish suggestion that Christmas-light displays might also be prohibited.[26] As the embargo wore on and winter settled upon the United States, consumers were harshly aware of the energy crisis as their homes and offices were chillier with thermostats turned down, schools closed for extended holiday breaks, gas lines were long with up to a two-hour wait, and motorists were now traveling the highways at 55 mph. Yet even with the embargo, which lasted until March 1974, and the continued high price of energy, the public's concern about the seriousness of the energy crisis peaked in November 1973 and then steadily declined in subsequent months. In November 1973, Americans were asked, "How serious do you think the energy shortage is in this country?" Fifty percent of respondents indicated that it was very serious, and 37 percent of respondents indicated that it was somewhat serious. In January 1974, those numbers changed: only 34 percent indicated that the energy shortage was very serious, 45 percent indicated it was somewhat serious, and 17 percent, almost double the November figure, indicated that it was not at all serious.[27]

Part of the explanation for the declining proportion of the public who considered the energy shortage a serious problem was due to the increase in the proportion of Americans who considered the energy crisis to be artificial and a ruse crafted by the American oil industries in an effort to drive up profits. With the considerable profits of energy producers, politicians and interest group advocates charged them with manipulating prices and even asserted that the crisis was fabricated. The public believed the suggestion that there was price manipulation by the industry and rejected claims that the energy crisis was real, and, as a result, they demanded that the government fix the problem. The trend in public opinion supports the notion that the public was increasingly skeptical of industry claims about the legitimacy of the oil crisis. Therefore, the events of 1973-74 energy crisis can easily be understood within the framework of the "energy crisis cycle."

Soaring Prices: Soaring Profits

At the start of January 1974, seemingly overnight, gas prices increased in many parts of the United States by two to seven cents per gallon. As a result, in the early weeks of 1974 there was growing skepticism by the public that the oil industry was unfairly profiting from the recent rise in gas prices. That is, the public was concerned that the industry was taking advantage of fuel shortages to reap large profits. Again, the increase in gas prices, reports of price gouging, and violations of price ceilings by station owners—all coinciding with reports of windfall profits—only heightened suspicion and frustration of the American public regarding the veracity of a fuel shortage.

Indeed, rumors of an orchestrated shortage and profiteering began as early as June 1973, when many independent station owners began to claim that big oil had created a "phony shortage to drive them out of business by shutting off their supplies."[28] The claims made by these independent station owners were supported by the attorneys general from six states (Massachusetts, North Carolina, Florida, New York, Connecticut, and Michigan).[29] In July 1973, during the summer gas shortage, the evidence continued to mount and skepticism grew regarding the veracity of the energy crisis as the crisis wore on. In fact, on July 17, the Federal Trade Commission officially filed a complaint claiming that the eight major oil companies had colluded to create a monopoly practice and that the high price of gas that consumers paid was the result. Regardless, until the Arab embargo hit, causing a major disruption in oil supplies and oil and gas prices to soar, the public's attention was not acutely focused on the issue. Once the embargo was underway and American citizens were busy preparing for the coming winter and cold weather, enduring long gas lines and other sacrifices such as fuel rationing, anger about the mendacity of the oil industry were reaching a fever pitch. The words of one Californian seem to sum up the nature of Americans' skepticism quite succinctly: "There was a gas-shortage scare but we haven't run out after the big scare. The oil companies are trying to make everyone believe there is a shortage so they can jack prices up, drill in the Santa Barbara Channel, and get the Alaska Pipeline. The oil companies can make the whole country sweat."[30]

In the early fall of 1973, not only was the American public growing suspicious of profiteering by the companies, but government officials were also becoming increasingly concerned. Public opinion polls demonstrate the nature of public thinking during energy crises, and since the first energy crisis of 1973–74, polls have been asking people who they blame. Clearly, the public blames oil companies. As chapter 3 detailed, the public assigned "major blame" to oil companies, followed by "Arab countries," which was actually a distant second. As a result of public concern, government officials began to act on their suspicions about the rising gas prices and mandated justifications by oil companies in order for them to raise the price of gasoline. For example, the government mandated that Atlantic-Richfield Co. (ARCO) "justify a 1¢-per-gal. increase on gasoline and a 2¢-per-gal. hike on fuel oil that the company posted Aug. 20."[31] The government's attention, however, had more to do with the negative effect that the rapidly rising gas prices was believed to have on inflation and the belief that such pricing was the result of collusion by the industry than it did with excess or "windfall" profits. Nevertheless, with the oil embargo *and* an energy crisis in full swing, an October 1973 *New York Times*[32] article finally substantiated the profiteering rumors with concrete evidence that showed the sharply rising profits for the American major oil companies. The *Times* article, dated October 25, presents data from the major domestic oil companies' third quarter's (July to September 1973) net profits and percentage gain over the third-quarter earnings from the previous year, shown in table 5.1.[33] Overall, Exxon collected the biggest windfall, with net earnings of $638 million (an 80 percent increase over its 1972 figures), and Gulf produced the largest percentage gain (91 percent) from 1972, which translated into $210 million net earnings. Nearly half of the fourteen companies listed below showed a 50 percent gain over their 1972 profits! Particularly questionable about the huge profits was that they came on the heels of a five-year period where profits were almost perfectly flat, even with a big growth in demand.[34]

Moreover, with 1974 oil stocks higher than 1973 levels, there was additional evidence to help substantiate doubts about the reality of an oil shortage. One theory put forth about the energy crisis was that "oil was plentiful but the crisis was hyped by oil companies in order to generate price increases and that the Administration was involved in an effort to help its industry friends generate a profit from the crisis."[35] This "devil theory," as a *Time* magazine article coined

Table 5.1 **Oil Company Profits: Third Quarter 1973**

Oil Company	Net Earnings (in millions)	Percent Gain over 1972
Exxon	$638	80%
Texaco	307	48%
Mobil	231	64%
Gulf	210	91%
Standard Oil (Indiana)	147	37%
Shell	82	23%
Atlantic Richfield	60	16%
Phillips	54	43%
Continental	54	38%
Getty	32	71%
Marathon	31	35%
Cities Service Co.	27	61%
Ashland	24	17%
Standard Oil (Ohio)	18	14%

it, united many Americans, including members of Congress, government officials, consumerists such as Ralph Nader, and environmentalists such as Barry
Commoner. There existed several reasons for the record profits; the most immediate jump was the result of foreign operations, where domestic industries
developed foreign reserves. Other factors that contributed to the rapid increase
in profits included the slow pace of refinery construction as well as, for example, reduced capacity of existing refineries, swelling environmentalism, governmental tax credits, and tax advantages given to the industry. Regardless of
the multitude of probable causes, according to public opinion in January and
February 1974, there was widespread public consensus (mean = 40 percent)
that the federal government and the oil and gas companies bore the responsibility for the energy crisis, while less than 5 percent of the public placed blame
for the crisis on individual consumers, Russians, Israelis, or environmentalists.[36]
Moreover, a February 1974 poll conducted by Roper demonstrated that an
overwhelming majority of Americans (73 percent) believed that there really was
no shortage but that big oil companies were holding it back for their own advantage.[37] People were so convinced of conspiracy that one law firm in Detroit filed
a $270 billion class-action lawsuit that accused the twelve major oil companies
of causing the crisis in order to generate increased profits. The lawsuit sought
$1000 in damages for "each person in the United states who had paid 'unfair
prices for fuel products.'"[38] The public wanted government to act and solve the
energy crisis, dialing back the price of oil to "the good old days" while still main-
taining an adequate supply.[39]

Government Responds: Subsidizing
Overconsumption

Congress is a significant player with respect to national problems and policymaking, and the energy crisis of the early 1970s is no exception. Yet it is difficult
to characterize Congress's handling of energy policy because of the major, and
sometimes contradictory, shifts it took with regard to energy policy. In the 1930s
Congress supported oil producers by creating a domestic oil cartel to restrict
production. In 1955, Congress again acted to the benefit of domestic producers
by enacting an import quota system, thereby limiting the amount of foreign oil
imported into the United States. The tide of Congressional support changed in
the 1970s, when consumers were favored over producers with Congress's implementation of price controls. The price controls that Congress implemented,
however, had the effect of subsidizing consumption. In most respects, at every
turn from at least the 1930s on Congress has only aggravated the energy situation as it tried to respond to competing interests.

In the early 1970s, in the wake of the growing energy shortages, congressional action was focused on alleviating the cost of gasoline to consumers, which had the unfortunate effect of encouraging energy consumption rather than conserving it. Therefore, the work that Congress did only seemed to exacerbate the problem. Additionally, as discussed previously, Nixon's initial solution of phased price controls kept energy prices artificially low and encouraged consumption by consumers. Moreover, the Emergency Petroleum Allocation Act (EPAA) in 1973, passed by Congress and signed into law by Nixon, created a two-tier pricing system on domestic oil and, as a result, yielded many distortions in the market and exacerbated the shortages it was designed to remedy. Later, in the midst of the 1973–74 energy crisis, sharply rising industry profits fueled the growing public resentment over the high cost of energy, which had shot up 33.5 percent in 1974, and the public's attention became keenly focused on energy, oil, and the economy. While both Congress and President Nixon began efforts to deal with the deepening energy crisis prior to the Arab oil embargo, once the embargo hit and energy prices soared, the energy crisis was pushed to the top of the national agenda, thereby forcing government officials to respond to the public's demands to do something.

In the spirit of the "energy crisis cycle," this section will largely deal with how government responded to public demands for action with regard to rising energy prices, oil scarcity, and the changing economy. In doing so, we will discuss how Congress and the president balanced competing demands made by advocacy groups (e.g., industry, environmental, and consumer) on different sides of the issue and used the crisis as a means to push through their own policy objectives. Additionally, we will discuss how Congress, individual members, and the president responded to the growing sea of public discontent surrounding the oil industry's reported record profits generated by the oil industry at the height of the crisis.

Up until the 1970s, when energy was still abundant and cheap, there was little need for a comprehensive energy policy or for congressional intervention with regard to energy policy. In fact, congressional intervention was minimal and only existed insofar as it established price controls, depletion allowances, tax credits, and import quotas. With the increasing energy shortfall, the Arab oil embargo, and the surge in petroleum prices in the early 1970s, public opinion, lobbying by special-interest groups, and presidential activism with regard to energy compelled governmental action. In an effort to respond to public demands, government efforts were focused on shielding the public from the high price of gasoline. In fact, President Nixon, with power given to him via the Economic Stabilization Act of 1970, implemented comprehensive price and wage controls on August 15, 1971. The price controls were set to last 90 days, and, unfortunately, once expired, caused the price of oil to shoot up 8 to 10 percent.[40] In 1973, after an abnormally cold winter, soaring energy prices, and energy brownouts, Nixon once again implemented price controls. In retrospect, the August 1971 price controls and those he implemented again in March 1973 did more harm than good, as the price controls encouraged energy consumption in a time of growing shortage. It was not until the 1980s, when oil was deregulated, that consumption actually declined due to rising prices in addition to the encouragement of conservation.[41]

Presidential Response: The Nixon Administration

In these early days of the energy shortage and rising prices, President Nixon in particular focused on protecting consumers from the high price of fuel. Early in his first term and responding to the demands of independent oil companies, Nixon considered removing a major law that protected the control that Rockefeller had over international oil—oil-import quotas. Removing the oil-import quotas would thereby allow independents more level footing with regard to expanding into the US market and potentially alleviate the high prices for consumers. Additionally, in 1971, Nixon tried to expand energy production. Some have suggested that these efforts along with the price controls were the result of his desire to win sway with the public due to the presidential election that was quickly approaching. Nevertheless, Nixon's efforts were piecemeal, and the early years of his presidency can be characterized by his failure to enact a comprehensive energy program. What Nixon's efforts, however, *can* be characterized as is mostly organizational. That is, Nixon spent the early years of the crisis reorganizing executive agencies and creating new, temporary units associated with energy, including the appointment of Charles J. DiBona as a special consultant for an office that later became the National Energy Office.[42] The real focus of his administration vis-à-vis the energy crisis was to consolidate power related to energy by creating the Federal Energy Administration (FEA) to deal with the immediate shortages created by the embargo; the Energy Research and Development Administration (ERDA) to begin R&D efforts to facilitate energy independence; and the Department of Energy and Natural Resources (DENR), which would consolidate the functions of the FEA and ERDA and manage long-term energy and natural-resources policy.[43] Historically, industry representatives had dealt directly with Congress and bureaucracy in a sub-governmental-type relationship, and no overarching energy policy existed. Moreover, many legislative proposals supported by Nixon at best contradicted others he supported—the National Environmental Policy Act was often viewed as contradictory to Nixon's goals of energy independence.

President Nixon seemed a more likely leader in dealing with the growing energy crisis than did Congress, initially. However, and again, many of his efforts fell short, as they tended to aggravate the problem or were broad and debatably empty gestures. Many also criticized his efforts as benefitting industry representatives. Nevertheless, Nixon likely would have argued that it was Congress's idleness with regard to national energy policy that had contributed to the worsening energy situation, as he had already demonstrated his focus on the issue earlier in his administration, when, in June 1971, he delivered the first-ever message to Congress on energy. However, it was not until 1973, well into the energy crisis, that Nixon sent to Congress a list of specific energy proposals that were designed to avert the oil crisis both in the short and long term. That he referred to the situation as an "energy challenge" rather than as a "crisis" underscores Nixon's attitude that the situation was not yet dire and therefore did not require "extreme measures."[44] Therefore, his second of three messages, "A Special Message to Congress on Energy Policy,"[45] delivered to Congress on April 18, 1973, was more short term in nature and more focused on increasing supply than it was on lowering consumption. In his message, Nixon outlined the general and specific legislative goals he believed would help solve the current and emergent energy dilemma. In terms of general objectives, Nixon's proposals included increasing domestic production of all forms of energy; conserving energy more effectively; meeting energy needs at the lowest cost consistent with the protection of national security and natural environment; reducing excessive regulatory and administrative impediments; acting in concert with other nations to conduct research in the energy field and to find ways to prevent serious shortages; and utilizing the nation's scientific and technological capacities so current energy resources could be used more wisely and also so that new sources and forms of energy could be developed.[46]

Also, Nixon chided Congress for its failure to pass several proposals, including deregulating natural gas, constructing the Alaskan pipeline, and the simplifying of licensing for nuclear plants, electric facilities, and deepwater ports. Moreover, Nixon's appeals stressed energy development more than protections of the environment. That is, while Nixon did value environmental protection, he began to temper it with the fact that energy development might likely be limited by adhering to some of the stricter environmental standards stipulated in the Clean Air Act of 1970:

> If we insisted upon meeting both primary and secondary clean air standards by 1975, we could prevent the use of up to 155 million tons of coal per year. This would force an increase in demand for oil of 1.6 million barrels per day. This oil would have to be imported, with an adverse effect on our balance of payments of some $1.5 billion or more a year.

Such a development would also threaten the loss of an estimated 26,000 coal mining jobs.

If, on the other hand, we carry out the provisions of the Clean Air Act in a judicious manner, carefully meeting the primary, health-related standards, but not moving in a precipitous way toward meeting the secondary standards, then we should be able to use virtually all of that coal which would otherwise go unused.[47]

Nixon's April 18 message to Congress outlined several specific executive actions he was taking to deal with the energy situation. Nixon's actions focused on improving federal organization of energy activities and included (1) directing the secretary of the interior to strengthen the department's organization via expanding the responsibilities of the new assistant secretary for energy and minerals to incorporate all departmental energy activities, develop the structure for the collection and analysis of energy data, and creating an Office of Energy Conservation; (2) granting the Department of the Treasury authority for directing the Oil Policy Committee (via Executive Order 11703); (3) enhancing the ability of the Executive Office of the President to deal with top-level energy policy matters by creating a special energy committee (via Executive Order 11712); and (4) creating a new division of Energy and Science within the Office of Management and Budget.

Finally, Nixon's April 18 message included Proclamation 4210, with three important policy changes, including (1) removing all existing tariffs and quotas on imported crude oil and refined products; (2) suspending direct control over the quantity of crude oil and refined products that could be imported; and (3) instituting a graduated schedule of licensing fees for importers of crude oil and most petroleum products. The function of such proposals was to help stimulate US domestic oil production and readjust what had by then appeared a failing of US oil-import policy.

In the third message, sent two months later on June 29, 1973, President Nixon proposed the appointment of Governor John A. Love (R-CO) to head the Energy Policy Office, which was part of a newly created office in the Executive Office of the President. Nixon also proposed a $10 billion, five-year energy R&D effort.[48] On November 7, 1973, during the Arab oil embargo, Nixon again addressed the nation, announcing his launch of Project Independence. Project Independence was Nixon's effort to secure energy independence for the nation and included some bold steps with measures that did not require the action or approval of Congress, including reducing fuel allocations for commercial aircraft, curbing the conversion to oil from coal by industry and utilities, hastening the licensing of nuclear power plants, and a 15 percent cut in the supply of heating oil for homes and offices. Also, Nixon proposed emergency energy legislation including the following short-term fixes: a return to daylight savings time, a reduction in the speed limit to 50 mph, congressional funding for R&D and production from Naval petroleum reserves, and authority to implement gas rationing and emergency conservation measures (e.g., restricting working hours for shopping centers and other commercial establishments) as well as to relax environmental regulations on a temporary, case-by-case basis. In order to combat the energy shortage over the long haul, Nixon once again urged Congress to authorize construction of the Alaska pipeline and to remove any irrelevant and unnecessary provisions in order to pass the legislation; to grant legislative authority to encourage production of the United States' vast quantities of natural gas; to provide the legal ability to set reasonable standards for the surface mining of coal; and to establish the organizational structures needed to meet and administer the nation's energy programs.

> Let us set our national goal, in the spirit of Apollo and with the determination of the Manhattan Project, that by the end of this decade, we will have developed the potential to meet our own energy needs without depending on any foreign energy sources. Let us pledge that by 1980, under Project Independence, we shall be able to meet America's energy needs from America's own energy resources.[49]

Not quite a month later, on December 4, 1973 Nixon reshuffled the energy bureaucracy and replaced the Energy Policy Office with the Federal Energy Office. William E. Simon, the deputy treasury secretary (who had no experience with the energy or oil industry), was selected to head the department when Love resigned the day previously. "The FEO. . . was to collect and analyze information on the supply and use of energy, develop the allocation plans required by emergency legislation, regulate energy prices, and formulate plans which would achieve the president's goal of energy self-sufficiency."[50] Simon, as head of the FEO, became known as the energy czar. In his efforts to combat the energy shortfall, Nixon also urged tax incentives for oil exploration, the streamlining of the siting process for additional electric power plants, reconsideration of federal mineral-leasing laws, exploratory shale-oil development, and passing a land-use bill that would provide funds to states to allow development of mining and electric-plant siting. In all it seemed as though Nixon was doing what he could, even though he confronted obstacles and disagreements regarding two issues: fuel allocation and gas rationing.

The winter of 1974 was met with a worsening energy crisis and gas shortage. The effects were widespread and included the following: declining production for US automakers, with risk of major layoffs and furloughs; a trucking strike, which rendered major supermarket chains vulnerable to panic buying, and which forced them to airlift supplies to stores in regions where supplies were needed most; and increased airfare costs. In order to address the shortage, Simon, as head of the FEO, oversaw the administration of the EPAA, which extended price controls for petroleum products but also required government to allocate the petroleum products and crude oil regionally "as equitably and efficiently as possible."[51] That is, the Act sought to move oil from regions of the country with a surplus to those regions with a shortfall. Allocations were determined by the oil industry based on usage from the corresponding month in 1972. And, for whatever reason, the FEO revised allocations on a near-weekly basis, thus continuously complicating the process. In the end, however, the allocation system proved to be nothing more than an albatross, and even Simon later admitted the allocation programs was "a disaster."[52] Nixon's attention had, at this point, been consumed mostly by Watergate. It was probably a relief to him when the embargo was lifted on March 18. One of Nixon's last acts as President was to sign the Federal Energy Administration Act of 1974 on May 7, 1974, which was also his first energy proposal to be voted out of Congress. The Act established the FEA as the successor to the White House Federal Energy Office and would oversee the tasks of gasoline allocation, emergency rationing, petroleum price regulation, data collection and analysis, energy conservation, and Project Independence.

Once the embargo was lifted, state after state dropped their gasoline rationing and distribution policies, and Americans just as quickly abandoned their efforts to conserve fuel. In late April, data showed that gas demand increased 9 percent in one week.[53] Even though fuel had become more plentiful with the lifting of the embargo, the FEO continued to issue quotas for the states.

Nixon resigned the office of the presidency on August 9, 1974 as a result of revelations of his involvement in the Watergate scandal, and his legacy with regard to energy policy was his significant expansion, consolidation, and restructuring of the federal government and agencies tasked with overseeing energy policy, including regulation and research and development. His sweeping reforms sought to expand energy resources and encourage conservation, and his proposals included the following: Project Independence; decontrolling natural gas; offshore oil exploration; increased funding and incentives for research and development, including oil exploration; expediting the permit process for nuclear power plants and electrical power plants; terminating the oil-import quota; and relaxing environmental standards that he and others believed to be stymieing the development of energy sources. Nixon is also remembered for his efforts to organize a national bureaucratic apparatus that was capable of dealing with this type of crisis, and, as a result, he organized and re-organized offices and departments many times. Unfortunately, many of Nixon's proposals were thwarted by Congress, demonstrating the embattled relationship they had. When he resigned, Nixon passed on to Ford a legacy of strong involvement with the energy sector, as Nixon had assumed control of the energy policy apparatus and held on to it for the length of his administration.

The Ford Administration

When Ford assumed the presidency, his efforts to handle the energy problems in many ways resembled Nixon's. Many of his policies were those that Nixon had proposed before his resignation. For example, Ford immediately put people to work on Project Independence, and an 800-page blueprint was produced by November 1974.[54] Another of Nixon's proposals, the Energy Reorganization Act, was also ushered in along with the policy process enacted by Congress in October 1974. However, Ford ultimately backed away from full-fledged energy independence and instead opted to support a more realistic path by supporting "reasonable self-sufficiency."[55]

In part, Ford inherited from Nixon problems that were complex and widespread. Although the lifting of the oil embargo in March 1974 by OPEC had indeed eased the nation's oil shortage, the energy problems had become so closely woven to the nation's economic problems (including simultaneous inflation and recession) that there was a need for continued focus by Ford and Congress. The complaints of Americans were no longer so focused on long gas lines, but rather on climbing prices, especially high-energy prices. In 1974, consumer prices increased 12.2 percent, but energy prices climbed 33.5 percent.[56] Moreover, the unemployment rate continued to increase, and in December 1974 it reached 8.2 percent, its highest level since the Great Depression.[57] Economic experts were befuddled and split on how exactly to remedy the multi-layered problem.

Another carryover from the Nixon to the Ford Administration was a chilly relationship between the president and Congress. Ford and the Democratic Congress went toe to toe on several issues, including Ford's proposed $3 oil tariffs, which ultimately delayed the implementation of the proposed increase until May 1975. There was also disagreement between the two branches over Ford's proposal to decontrol oil prices when the EPAA of 1973 expired on August 31, 1975. Congress laid the groundwork to block Ford's effort. The greatest tension between Ford and Congress regarding energy policy, however, was the result of Ford's controversial plan to decontrol domestic oil prices. His plan rallied the opposition of consumers and support of industry.

In late January 1975, Ford sent to Congress his energy plan, the Energy Independence Act (S. 594). The plan comprised thirteen major elements; the most controversial was Ford's proposal to deregulate natural gas, which Congress ultimately blocked. The other elements included the following: deregulation of interstate sales of natural gas; full-scale production from three naval petroleum reserve lands, including one at Elk Hills, California; development of a civilian national strategic oil reserve; easing of environmental restrictions to permit increased use of coal for generating electricity; delaying deadlines for compliance with clean air requirements to reduce the energy costs of such compliance; elimination of bans on fuel cost adjustment charges and passage of other legislation to aid public utilities; FEA control over the siting of energy facilities; authority for the president to impose tariffs or quotas if needed to prevent foreign oil producers from threatening domestic production by undercutting prices; mandatory federal standards for the heating and cooling of all new homes and commercial buildings; federal grants to states to assist the poor and elderly in winterizing their homes; mandatory labeling of appliances and motor vehicles to describe the amount of energy they consumed; and standby authority for the president to take a wide range of actions in case of an energy emergency or embargo.

Ultimately, however, it looked as if the most feasible way to combat energy problems was to implement a plan that would nurture energy conservation. However, it was not until December 1975 that a conservation bill was sent to Ford for his signature. Although Ford encountered serious opposition from industry, and concern by many supporters that it fell short of what he intended, Ford signed into law the Energy Policy and Conservation Act of 1975 on December 22. The EPCA placed previously uncontrolled new oil produced since EPAA had passed under price controls and, as a result, created a three-tier system rather than the two-tier price-control system that existed with the EPAA. Another key element of the EPCA was that it created Corporate Average Fuel Economy (CAFE) standards for automobiles and light trucks. One of the negative effects of the Act, however, was that it created and exacerbated a range of economic distortions, including increasing the incentives to import and decreasing consumer incentives to shift from oil to other energy sources or to conserve.

Ford's success with Congress with regard to energy policy was mixed. In 1975 he was successful in ushering the following through Congress: a one-billion-barrel national strategic petroleum reserve; an extension of federal authority to order power plants to burn coal over oil or natural gas, to require energy labeling of major appliances and autos, and to grant the president a variety of standby authorities to use in an energy emergency. Ford, however, fell short at convincing Congress to pass the following: approving a windfall-profits tax; allowing public utilities to make basic changes in rate structure; formulating a plan for siting new energy facilities; allowing private industry to take over from the federal government the business of uranium enrichment and development of nuclear fuel; authorizing the creation of a $100 billion Energy Independence Authority; and providing incentives for the commercial production of synthetic fuels via loan guarantees, price supports, and construction grants.[58] Early in Ford's presidency he had approximately sixteen policy proposals dealing with the energy crisis awaiting congressional action. However, by 1976 Ford had seen only eight of his bills passed while fifteen remained, on which Congress ultimately did not act.[59]

Congressional Response: Action Jackson

Initially, in the wake of the embargo Congress did little to jump into action and alleviate the burden of high gas prices and quell the fear and suspicion of Americans during the crisis. Part of the cause of legislative inaction was the result of the sparked activity by environmentalists who were increasingly concerned that the need for energy would undermine long-worked-for environmental laws. In fact, concerns of Eskimos and Alaskan natives delayed the construction of the Trans-Alaskan Pipeline. However, it was a wide coalition of environmental activists who, in the wake of the 1969 Santa Barbara oil spill, were successful in halting the development of the Trans-Alaskan Pipeline by a Federal court injunction, issued in 1970 by invoking the recently passed National Environmental Policy Act (NEPA) of 1969. NEPA was intended as a basic agreement for protecting the environment and whose main objective was to put greater environmental control in the hands of the public by diminishing the power of developers. Specifically, NEPA included two primary goals: (1) to inform federal decision makers about the environmental impact of their action *prior* to deciding to take action; and (2) to involve the public in discussions with decision makers *prior* to taking action. For nearly four years environmentalists successfully delayed the construction of the pipeline based on concerns ranging from protection of Alaska's permafrost, to caribou migration, fish spawning, oil spills, and even pollution that could result from the construction workers' camps.

Another significant roadblock to legislative solutions resulted from a serious game of blame-trading by both President Nixon and Congress. Nixon blamed Congress for not responding to his 1971 warnings of an impending energy problem, while Senate Majority Leader Mike Mansfield articulated Congress's sentiments when he responded that when it came to legislation, "[Nixon] is wanting." In addition, Congress charged that the Nixon Administration was unable to centralize energy proposals and frequently reshuffled that responsibility.[60] Overall, the shortcomings in Congress had more to do with its perennial problem of multiple committees with overlapping jurisdiction over energy policy than a lack of policy experts capable of handling the issue.

Congressional involvement at the height of the oil crisis appeared minimal, and the most active involvement came from Presidents Nixon and Ford. However, Nixon's efforts were often viewed as motivated more by his 1972 presidential election bid than the crisis itself. That is, he hoped any effort he made to deal with the energy crisis would help him win sway with the public and secure his likelihood for reelection. In late fall of 1973, there was an ever-present fear that Americans would be unable to stay warm during the coming winter due to a lack of fuel for adequate heat. One White House aide, Melvin Laird, was quoted as offering the following bit of advice, "I'd buy a sweater."[61] Yet, according to Representative John J. McFall (D-CA), the House Democratic Whip, "Energy dominated the work of Congress last year, with 28 committees in the House and Senate devoting more than 500 hours to hearings on energy related matters."[62] McFall also asserted that Nixon's efforts were "little more than restatements of actions already taken and pronouncements already made, or calls for programs already under consideration by Congress."[63] According to our own count, Congress held 515 hearings related to energy matters between 1970 and 1975 (see figure 5.1). Clearly, Congress rightly considered itself the heavy lifter when it came to the energy crisis and was taking an active role in responding to constituents' ire over the rapidly rising prices of oil and gas, the widespread shortages, and the exorbitant profits that industry had been reaping during the crisis. In comparison with President Nixon's efforts (figure 5.2), which included four energy messages to Congress and nine Executive Orders, plus several more that dealt indirectly with the energy crisis but directly with economic stabilization and price controls, this assertion seems fairly accurate. Moreover, the nine executive orders comprise a small proportion of the total 346 that Nixon issued during his presidency. One might also note that when the energy crisis was nascent, Nixon provided both written and oral statements regarding the energy crisis. And while the trend lines of both slowly increase over the course of the crisis, clearly Nixon, and later Ford (with a remarkable 140 oral statements on the topics of "energy crisis" and "petroleum"), spoke more frequently about the

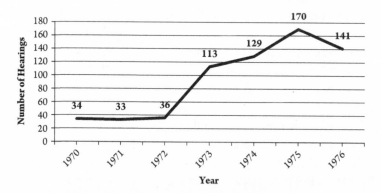

Figure 5.1 Number of Congressional Hearings Related to Energy, 1970–1976.
The Policy Agendas Project (http://policyagendas.org/page/trend-analysis)

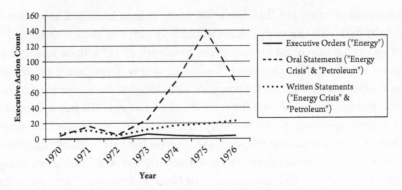

Figure 5.2 Executive Action Related to Energy, 1970–1976.
The Policy Agendas Project (http://policyagendas.org/page/trend-analysis) and the American
Presidency Project (www.presidency.ucsb.edu)

crisis and petroleum as the crisis ebbed, which indicates that while the acuteness
of the crisis was over, the politics of energy policy remained.

As evidence of its focused involvement in the crisis, the EPAA was passed by
Congress in November 1973; Nixon signed it into law on November 27, 1973
(Public Law 93-159). The purpose of the EPAA was to protect consumers from
gasoline shortages and high fuel prices by evenly distributing scarce fuel supplies, creating a two-tiered pricing system for domestic crude oil, and establishing equitable prices. Additionally, throughout 1973, Senator Henry M. "Scoop"
Jackson (D-WA), as chair of the Senate Interior and Insular Affairs Committee,
which handles a great deal of energy-related policy, "initiated hearings on developing a national energy policy, and also sponsored bills that would increase
research and development, institute a mandatory fuel allocation program and
establish a strategic 90-day stockpile of oil reserves."[64] In fact, by Congress's adjournment in December 1973, several key pieces of legislation had wended their
way through Congress, including the authorization of the Trans-Alaskan Pipeline
(PL 93-153), Emergency Fuels and Energy Allocation Act (PL 93-159),[65] year-
round daylight saving time (HR 11324—PL 93-182), and lowering the national
speed limit of 55 mph (PL 93-239 and PL 93-643). Finally, Congress also passed
several transportation-related measures that were predicted to have a positive
impact on the conservation of fuel.[66]

Most congressional efforts to handle the energy crisis came in the form of
proposed legislation on which action was not completed as Congress adjourned
at the end of 1973, including the creation of a Federal Energy Administration
(S. 2776, HR 11793) and National Emergency Energy Act of 1973 (NEEA)
(HR 11450, S. 2589), which would give the president emergency powers to deal
with the nation's fuel shortage. Although the NEEA was never actually passed, it was
introduced in the Senate by Senator Henry Jackson. NEEA restricted advertising

lighting, car speed limits, and indoor temperatures; rationed gas; curbed energy consumption; controlled fuel choices of utilities; and regulated refinery operations. The measure also gave Congress veto power of the president's implementation of the bill's measures. The bill stalled in conference largely as a result of the administration's objections to the congressional veto power, the windfall-profits tax, and federal aide to workers who lost their jobs due to the energy shortages.[67]

Several other legislative proposals sponsored by Senator Jackson were also not completed when Congress adjourned in December 1973. Jackson's proposals included the National Coal Conversion Act of 1973 (S. 2652), which would help preserve "the national security and protection of the public health, safety, and welfare by conserving scarce petroleum and natural gas resources; and substituting domestic coal for these fuels in electric power generating plants and other industrial facilities."[68] Essentially, S. 2652 would encourage the maximum use of coal resources to meet energy needs of industrial users but doing so in a manner that commits to environmental protection. Additionally other proposals were still incomplete at the end of 1973 including one to reorganize and consolidate particular and related functions of the executive branch in a new Department of Energy and Natural Resources (S. 2135, HR 9090), and a bill to create an Energy Research and Development Administration (S. 1283), which would coordinate federal research programs (this eventually was passed by both houses of Congress and signed into law (P.L. 93-577) on December 31, 1974).

Some of Senator Jackson's proposals, however, made greater progress in 1973 including a bill (S. 2176) that would provide for a national fuels and energy conservation policy and establish an Office of Energy Conservation in the Department of the Interior. In addition, other members of Congress introduced more minor proposals in an effort to deal with the crisis. For example, one resolution (HR 716) sponsored by Representative Silvio Conte (R-MA) to conserve energy, would reduce the number of operational days and hours in federal buildings and offices. Other bills introduced during the 93rd Congress ranged from a proposal expressing the support of the House for the formation of an Organization of Petroleum Consuming Nations (HR 801) introduced by Representative Robert Steele (R-CT) to one that would temporarily suspend certain air-pollution requirements (HR 1082) sponsored by Representative Richard Bolling (D-MO), and a bill (HR 1137) that would give full consideration to solar energy in the construction of federal buildings, introduced by Representative Dick Shoup (R-MT). While the above legislative action was in an effort to deal with the immediacy of the energy crisis, none of the proposals did anything to quiet the skepticism of the public, which was overwhelmingly focused on oil-industry profits and suspicious that the oil crisis was really and truly orchestrated by the major companies in an effort to reap such record profits.

In early 1974, the press out-and-out accused the oil industry of collusion in an effort to increase the price of oil and increase their profits.[69] As the energy crisis cycle predicts, increased profits of energy producers caused politicians and others, namely interest group activists, to charge them with manipulating prices, and to claim that the crisis was fabricated. The public believed the industry critics and did not accept claims that the energy crisis was real, so they demanded that the government fix the problem. So, in line with the theory, in January of 1974, members of Congress who were just returning to Washington from visits to their districts communicated the concerns of their constituents about the energy crisis in general and whether it indeed was real. In fact, for some members their constituents seemed far more concerned with the energy crises than whether Nixon should be impeached. As Alan Cranston, a Democratic Senator from California, remarked, "'There is a very widespread suspicion that the crisis is a conspiracy by the oil companies to create a situation to make more money'....Cranston quickly voiced 'great support' for a windfall-profits tax on oil companies."[70] Representatives Richard W. Mallary (R-VT) and Neal Smith (D-IA) also expressed similar thoughts about their constituents' suspicions that the energy crisis was the result of some conspiracy or even the fault of government. Representative Ralph S. Regula (R-OH) summed up the sentiment of not only his constituents but many Americans at the time: "People are willing to sacrifice so long as they are satisfied that this is a real, genuine, honest-to-God crisis."[71] By all appearances, members of Congress were forced by the growing public skepticism to respond to rumors of oil-industry profiteering, and many returned to Washington after their winter recess with a focus on doing just that.

Very few Americans believed the assertions made by the oil industry—it was impossible to overlook the facts. In January 1974, as oil companies began to announce an additional increase in the price of oil, a Gallup poll (released on January 9, 1974) showed that the public blamed both oil companies and the administration for the current energy crisis.[72] In a February 1974 Roper poll, 74 percent of Americans believed that there was no real shortage of oil.[73] It is no mystery as to why Americans were so skeptical about the energy shortage, since the survey came on the heels of the release of the oil companies' fourth-quarter profit statements. And once again, the profit statements showed that while Americans were busy making sacrifices in the name of energy conservation, the oil companies were busy making money hand over fist. Union Oil Co. of California reported on January 23 that fourth-quarter earnings were up 55 percent (or $51 million) and annual net income was up 47 percent (or $58.3 million). That same day, Exxon released its fourth-quarter and annual net income, both of which were up 59 percent from 1972. The following day, January 24, Texaco released its fourth-quarter earnings, which were up a record 72 percent from the previous year (or $453 million). Texaco's annual earnings also reached record levels of $1.29 billion (or a 45 percent increase from 1972).[74] Over the course of the next few days, the other oil companies released their earnings statements, and the story was all too similar. The data showed the public that American oil companies had not only profited from the energy crisis but that their profits were huge. Again, Americans who had spent the previous year conserving energy and emptying their pockets in order to fill their gas tanks found such exorbitant profits insulting.

In what appears as a direct response to public doubt and frustration about the nature of the energy crisis and windfall profits, in early January 1974 four Congressional subcommittees announced that they would initiate hearings to determine the veracity of the energy problems. The hearings, incidentally, came at the same time that Ralph Nader added volume to the choir of those concerned about the truth behind the energy shortage: "To this very hour . . . the industry refuses to disclose its reserves to the government. If there was a real energy shortage, that is the first thing they would want to show. Basically, this country is groaning in a sea of oil and gas."[75]

Congress made its most notable mark on the issue when the Senate Permanent Subcommittee on Investigations, chaired by Senator Jackson, who was planning a run for the presidency, held its own hearing wherein executives of the seven major oil companies were questioned about their business operations and record profits. After months of speculation and suspicion that the oil crisis had been contrived in order for domestic oil companies to score a windfall, Jackson declared, "The American people want to know if this so-called energy crisis is only a pretext; a cover to eliminate the major source of price competition—the independents, to raise prices, to repeal environmental laws, and to force adoption of new tax subsidies. . . . Gentlemen, I am hopeful that we will receive the answer to these and other questions before we leave here today."[76] Over the course of three days, Jackson revealed that industry profits increased by 46 percent during the first nine months of the 1973, while sales only rose by 6 percent over the same period. Moreover, the subcommittee members focused on reports that, at the time, were recently released by some oil companies and indicated their inventories were higher than they were a year previous. However, in an effort to defend themselves against accusations implied or otherwise, the industry's response was that the previous year's (1972) figures were abnormally low.

Part of the problem was the lack of adequate data provided by the oil companies on the status of their oil reserves. Such data are fundamental, as the government relied on the data for government projection on fuel production. Energy-producing companies were withholding too much information or classifying it as proprietary. For example, Jackson requested oil companies respond to questionnaires, but only two, Mobil and Gulf, fully complied. Exxon had apparently stamped "proprietary" when answering each question—many seemingly innocuous questions such as "how many stations they own and operate, how many stations are independent customers and how many have closed over the past year."[77] Moreover, what information they did supply to government often lacked independent verification. With inaccurate or incomplete data, the government was unable to make accurate projections.[78] According to testimony before a House Select Committee on Small Business' subcommittee, "Four energy policy experts said the oil industry had been able to reap advantages from the fuel shortage by keeping the government 'in the dark' about their supply and price information."[79] Union leaders from the United Mine Workers urged Congress to act against energy conglomerates due to, as Arnold Mill, the union's president charged, big oil's "possible anti-trust action to separate oil and coal interests" and that "[the energy crisis is a] crisis of secrecy, greed and manipulation, but not a crisis of supply."[80]

As a response to the growing public discontent, congressional hearings were underway and probing into big oil's profits, and other Washington insiders were busy drafting legislation likely perceived as anti-oil, including measures that would require the oil industry to reveal its fuel holdings and place both a tax and a limit on excess profits. Because 1974 oil stocks were higher than 1973 levels, there was further doubt about the reality of an oil shortage:

> Many people are taking a line that goes roughly like this: the companies have plenty of oil to sell, but they have been talking up a crisis so that they can get big price increases. The Administration has helped companies in this campaign . . . because the White House wants to help its business friends create a crisis.[81]

In January, 1974, Representative Les Aspin (D-WI) asserted that

> Four hundred and thirteen directors, senior officials and stockholders of 178 oil and gas companies had contributed $4.98 million to President Nixon's re-election campaign . . . [approximately 10% of his total receipts] . . . [and therefore Nixon's hands are tied [and] . . . there is little he can do to control them.[82]

Other efforts by Congress to deal with the public's ire toward windfall profits included its reconsideration of S. 2589, the National Emergency Petroleum Act. Upon returning for its second session in January 1974, S. 2589 was once again sent to a conference committee wherein debate centered on whether to substitute an oil-price ceiling for the windfall-profits tax and weakening the clean-air standards. Despite widespread public support for a windfall-profits tax, it was replaced with a rollback, which set the maximum price of oil to $5.25 per barrel for all domestically produced oil.[83] The provisions of S. 2589 also included auto-pollution limits and a relaxation of industrial emissions. Withstanding the extraordinary lobbying efforts by the administration and Congressional members from oil-producing states, including an extended December filibuster by Senator Russell B. Long (D-LA), who opposed the excess profit tax, a conference report was passed by both the House and Senate in February 1974 only to be vetoed by Nixon on March 6, 1974 based on his opposition to three of its provisions: the price ceilings, congressional veto, and unemployment compensation.[84] The Senate was unable to override Nixon's veto. The final attempts, S. 3267 and HR 13834, were introduced on March 6, 1974 in the Senate and House, respectively, and included many of the same provisions as the vetoed bill. After Nixon issued his veto, William Simon, head of the Federal Energy Office, relayed to Congress that due to the embargo being lifted, an omnibus emergency energy bill was no longer needed. Rather, Simon urged Congress to tackle those energy proposals that the president's administration supported.[85] So while Congress tried to do right by the public and create legislation that would ease the problems associated with the energy crisis, Nixon's actions relating to national emergency energy legislation demonstrated his longstanding and often-criticized relationship with the oil industry.

Then, in April of 1974, oil companies began to release first-quarter 1974 profits and the tune was all too familiar—the profit reports showed sharp increases over the same period the previous year. Texaco's first-quarter profit statement showed a 123 percent increase from the previous year (from $264 million to $589.4 million), and Occidental Petroleum Corp, the eleventh largest, reported a 718 percent profit increase over the previous year's profit.[86] Moreover, the media's focus began to turn to the record profits of oil companies and, as a result, Americans' doubt regarding the authenticity of the energy crisis continued. The American public continued to vocalize its discontent and demand that government work to fix the problem.

Senator Jackson's hearings, although part political theater, could be interpreted as a direct effort to respond to public ire and skepticism about the energy crisis. Even without hard and convincing evidence that the crisis was the result of industry manipulation, the hearings did little to salvage the industry's already tarnished reputation. Senator Jackson and his Democratic colleagues scrutinized and rebuked the assertions made by oil-industry executives, who defended themselves against the unrelenting attacks and argued that the shortage was indeed real and that the increased earnings were needed to finance exploration for new sources of oil. This reasoning was hard to believe, especially when a number of oil companies had increased their dividends and offered salary upgrades and bonuses to their executives. With the hearings televised, public condemnation toward the oil industry and its executives was heightened. In the end, "between 1973 and 1975, fifteen of the thirty-nine permanent committees of the U.S. Congress conducted investigations into the energy crisis,"[87] yet the ability to identify the oil industry as a chief conspirator was elusive.

With Ford in the White House and Democrats still in control of Congress, it was evident that Congress was no more willing to work with Ford than with his predecessor. Ford's proposed energy plan fell short in the eyes of Congressional Democrats, and thus they were forced to put forth their own plan. In April 1975, Congress passed its own energy bill. While Ford's bill dealt more with deregulation, Representative Al Ullman, Chair of the Ways and Means Committee, introduced a conservation policy that imposed oil import quotas, an incremental gasoline surtax, a tax for gas guzzlers, an energy trust to help with the development of new energy technologies, and so on. The Senate also worked on similarly spirited bills (S. 3424) that would provide federal assistance for state and federal governments to implement conservation programs, require thermal standards for buildings (S. 2191), and stipulate regulations for lighting and car use (S. 1149).[88] Due to public concern about the environment and the increased focus on conservation efforts, Congress seemed to work toward that end—it was a politically safe pursuit, as by pursuing conservation Congress was acting responsively to public preferences.

Ultimately, Senator Jackson's energy bill, the EPCA, and discussed above, was signed into law (PL 94-163) in December, 1975 and was intended to impose "Draconian Federal intervention in the marketplace."[89] Ford was also likely swayed by the force of public opinion to sign the legislation, although it is well documented how much he regretted doing so. "If I could [have acted] unilaterally, on my own, I probably would have decontrolled period, immediately. There would have been a little turmoil for a short period of time. But we would have opened the markets and the markets would have corrected things rather quickly. But that was not the real world. The real world was that I had to deal with Congress."[90]

Interest Group Activity

Aside from the oil embargo, the energy crisis, and Watergate, the 1970s can be characterized by the immense proliferation of interest groups in the political process, especially those that are described as citizen-oriented (e.g., environmental and consumer) groups or public-interest groups.[91] According to *Washington Representatives*, a reference book, in 1977 there were estimated to be approximately 1,300 Washington-based associations.[92] Additionally, of the groups active in 1980, 40 percent had been formed since 1960.[93] Much of this explosion of interest groups is the result of groups responding to each other—once a group forms on one side of an issue, a group on the other side of the issue forms as a counterbalance.

In terms of interest group politics, crisis offers interest groups an opportunity to mobilize. "[Political space] expands as new policy problems appear, as governmental policy changes, and as political expectations are raised. It contracts as activist concerns are satisfied or as public attention shifts away from a sector's concerns."[94] This perspective aligns with our theory of the energy crisis cycle. According the energy crisis cycle, spokespeople for a wide range of business interests join the political debate regarding how best to deal with the energy crisis and offer a chorus of requests to relax environmental regulations in order to produce more energy. To them, the energy crisis is an opportunity to beat back environmental advances. On the other hand, environmental groups resist business demands and propose their own green solutions to the energy crisis.

Indeed, our theory conforms with much of reality. Specifically, consumers were vociferous about the quickly rising cost of gas, utilities, and goods in general—the high prices being the result of simultaneous energy shortage and an economic downturn. Although the modern environmental movement was in its infancy, environmental groups were particularly active and quite successful at thwarting what they perceived as unfettered economic and energy development that was detrimental to the health and welfare of people, wildlife, and the environment. For a long time, however, the oil industry put the blame of the worsening energy crisis on environmentalists: "Watching the energy panic roil the nation, energy lobbyists joked confidently that the country would keep warm that winter of 1973–74 by burning environmental protection laws."[95] As is often the case, government policy is often the result of "the most dominant or organized group,"[96] and this is true with regard to energy policy in the 1970s. Indeed, during the energy crisis, interest groups took aim at each other in order to pursue their favored objectives.

Again, environmental activists found the energy crisis an opportunity to push forward their interests, including clean-air standards, energy conservation, developing renewable energy sources, and protecting the environment from unfettered energy development, especially in Alaska. Environmental concerns were not unfounded. In fact, environmental concerns were increased when Congress enacted its emergency legislation to deal with the energy crisis. Such emergency legislation was considered by environmentalists as an assault on many of the standards for which they had fought in the preceding years. Air standards were delayed or relaxed; land-use concerns surfaced over efforts to step up strip-mining activity (Ford even pocket-vetoed a bill, S. 425, which would have imposed strict controls over surface mining coal); risks of nuclear safety seemed to be increasingly glossed over in an effort to meet the growing energy gap; and exemptions from federal and state water standards were issued.

One of the major issues on which environmental groups were exceptionally vocal was the Trans-Alaskan Pipeline. Environmentalists halted the construction of the Trans-Alaskan Pipeline via court injunction. Their primary concern was that companies were "trying to move too fast, without sufficient study, understanding, skills, or care and that the proposed pipeline was poorly planned."[97] Furthermore, environmentalists believed that before construction on the pipeline commenced, the United States should implement an energy conservation program. The Sierra Club was particularly opposed to the pipeline; its president, Phillip Berry, believed that if Americans only conserved energy, the development of new energy would be unnecessary. Moreover, Berry doubted that the North Slope would actually meet America's energy demands.[98] Stewart L. Udall, former secretary of the interior, believed the problem was not the Arab embargo but America's "unsatiable appetite for energy and resources and its wasteful use of them."[99] Finally, with regard to the heightened discussions about the switch from oil to coal, environmentalists were exceedingly worried because coal was considered ecologically disastrous due not only to the effects of mining but also due to the pollution and health risks it created when burned.

While the oil industry blamed environmentalists, by all appearances, public opinion was on the side of environmentalists more than that of the energy industry. Americans' conservation efforts appeared to be successful, and the American public still targeted its anger toward the oil industry for the windfall profits and the utilities for their increases in customer utility rates. Moreover, environmentalists, including David Brower's Friends of the Earth, Barry Commoner, and Ralph Nader worked to lift the veil and expose the cozy relationship that the oil industry had had with government.[100] Commoner was among one of the early skeptics who demanded Congress investigate the oil industry in order to uncover the reality of nation's oil supplies.[101]

In reality, the energy crisis could be considered a good thing for environmentalists insofar as the crisis gave environmentalists an engaged public and an opportunity to work to shape legislation, politics, and nurture a culture of conservation and environmental values. For example, environmentalists not only worked to attach far-reaching provisions to industry-sponsored legislation, they also promoted policies of conservation and the development of alternative energy sources such as solar and geothermal. Moreover, environmentalists were extraordinarily successful in thwarting the development of nuclear-energy facilities.

One of the most well-known environmental lobbies, the Sierra Club, firmly placed itself in the middle of the environmental activism of the 1970s. Operating under the motto, "Not blind opposition to progress, but opposition to blind progress,"[102] the Sierra Club's involvement in energy policy stems from the overlap that exists between energy and the environment. During the energy crisis, the Sierra Club opposed nuclear power,[103] strip mining, and the development of the Wyoming-Montana coalfields, offshore oil development, and shale-oil development. On the other hand, the Sierra Club supported conservation and research and development of alternative energy sources. The group took no position on deregulation of gas and oil or the reorganization of the oil industry.

Another source of concern for environmentalists was the move toward off-shore oil drilling. While many considered offshore oil to be the best source of domestic oil and a way to reduce the need on foreign petroleum, environmentalists were rallied by the memory of the1969 blowout of an oil well in the Santa Barbara Channel and the resulting environmental catastrophe. In fact, the Santa Barbara accident was a key motivating factor in passage of the National Environmental Policy Act of 1969. However, the debate about offshore oil drilling was not necessarily about if it should happen but the pace at which it was being pushed. A lobbyist for the Sierra Club, Richard Lahn noted, "I'm not opposed to Outer Continental Shelf development, but I am opposed to the way the administration is going about it. They want to proceed as rapidly as possible regardless of what effects it might have on the environment or the onshore effects."[104]

After President Nixon's energy message, delivered on November 7, 1973, where he called for a speed-up in the licensing and construction of nuclear power plants, exemptions from federal and state air- and water-quality laws and the National Environmental Policy Act, the conversion of plants from oil to coal, and "reasonable" standards for strip-mining in an effort to help fill the energy gap,[105] environmentalists were most acutely concerned that land would be devastated by strip-mining and that safety would be compromised in a rush to build nuclear power plants. Nixon's Project Independence, therefore, was a rallying cry for environmentalists who believed that conservation was far more important than self-sufficiency. To environmentalists, self-sufficiency meant "a new raid on resources at huge environmental costs."[106] In the wake of the oil embargo, and as a result of concern over pricing, energy security, and the intense lobbying efforts and public relations campaign by the oil industry, construction of the Trans-Alaskan Pipeline was fast-tracked. As the first major energy bill enacted in 1973, S. 1081 passed both houses with large margins (77–20 in the Senate and 356–60 in the House). PL 93-153, which authorized the construction of Trans-Alaskan Pipeline and prohibited any court review on environmental grounds, was signed by President Nixon on November 16, 1973.

The oil industry and other energy developers considered environmental laws, such as the Clean Air Act of 1970, to be a major source of the energy crisis and were diligent in trying to delay and/or weaken hard-fought-for environmental legislation. The concern of energy developers was that the recent strides in environmental protection hampered development. For example, while energy producers urged the development of the national energy resources, including offshore oil drilling, shale, and strip mining, environmentalists were intensely concerned about the environmental costs that accompanied the mining and burning of coal (problems with re-vegetation after strip-mining, pollution of air and ground water, water requirements for coal conversion). The American Petroleum Institute's (API's) president, Frank N. Ikard, claimed that "factors producing the energy shortage—all beyond the industry's control—included delays in building the Alaskan pipeline and holding offshore lease sales, gas-gobbling cars . . . and federal price controls on natural gas and crude oil."[107] As a result of Nixon and Ford's commitment to Project Independence, the energy industry was in a real predicament. Additionally, with the economic condition so bound to the energy situation, energy producers' hands were tied—they had no option but to push for the development of a variety of energy sources and for an easing of environmental laws.

The decontrolling of natural gas involved energy interests, including the API, the American Petroleum Association of America, and the Natural Gas Supply Company, which were very supportive of the administration's proposal to de-regulate. However, this issue was not without controversy. On the one hand there was significant support for deregulation. In particular, deregulation was supported by Presidents Nixon and Ford, William E. Simon, John C. Sawhill, as well as Senator John G. Tower, (R-TX) who offered his own bill, S. 371. However, there was active opposition that the industry was up against, and the most ardent opposition came from the Consumer Federation of America, the American Public Gas Association, as well as many members of Congress, in-cluding Representative Torbert H. Macdonald (D-MA), Representative Harley O. Staggers (D-W.VA), and Senator Warren G. Magnuson (D-WA). The logic with deregulation was that due to the Federal Power Commission's set rates, the price of natural gas was too low and therefore contributed to a shortage. By lift-ing these controls, it was believed that prices would adjust and demand would fall. Critics argued that by removing price controls, the energy industry would reap windfall profits. Moreover, consumer groups and their allies in Congress argued that deregulation would leave consumers at the mercy of major oil companies.[108]

Major gas and oil trade associations were quite present and vibrant in Washington prior to and during the energy crisis. These included the Indepen-dent Petroleum Association of America, Interstate Natural Gas Assocation of America, National Oil Jobbers Council, National Petroleum Refiners Association, American Gas Association, American Public Gas Association, and the Association of Oil Pipe Lines. These associations and their Washington rep-resentatives were active in a variety of legislative efforts, including the deregu-lation of gas and oil and further exploration. The API, however, was the most significant player in terms of representing the energy industry in energy policy. In 1975 its membership included 350 oil and gas companies and 7,000 indi-vidual members, and it represented all aspects of the industry, from refiners to producers, distributors, transporters, and more.[109] During the 1970s, API's representation in Washington doubled and its influence grew.

The legislative interests of API during this time were determined by how cohesive the group was. That is, API did not take a position on controversial issues that divided its membership, such as the quota system.[110] One of the issues that rallied the support of its members across the board was the development of the Trans-Alaskan pipeline. Additionally, while the American public and Congress were devoted to limiting industry profits during the energy crisis, API was successful in thwarting such efforts. For example, initially API supported emergency energy legislation, S. 2589; when the conference version included the House-approved restrictions on windfall profits, API pressed for its defeat. Other issues supported by API concerned government-sponsored R&D, authorization of deepwater ports, depletion allowances, easing of clean air standards, and the construction of new refineries and nuclear facilities.

Independent gas station owners (aka "independents") urged Congress to pass the mandatory allocation rather than the voluntary measure that was currently in place.[111] These small, independent stations argued that the large oil companies were making it impossible for them to survive the fuel crunch and were slowly driving them out of business. Independents essentially had relied on the large oil companies for fuel, which they then turned around and sold for a discount at small, independent gas retailers (e.g., convenience stores).

When the energy crisis ebbed, the energy industry was a bit fractured as the different players fell on different sides of the proposals and issues before them. For example, some major integrated firms wanted immediate decontrol of petroleum, whereas others accepted the need for gradual phase-out.[112] The large independent refineries (Independent Refiners Association of America) wanted controls continued temporarily (what they really wanted was an allocation system and entitlements), but smaller ones wanted indefinite extensions. Retail marketers such as the National Congress of Petroleum Retailers, representing forty-seven associations of 70,000 gas station operators, also favored extension of controls, as did the New England Fuel Institute and the Society of Independent Gasoline Marketers of America. Terminal operators and wholesale jobbers all feared a margin squeeze and demanded protection. With regard to the windfall-profits tax, independents opposed any windfall-profits tax; however, some of the larger firms actually thought it was a reasonable proposal.[113]

The automobile industry used the energy crisis to push for delays and modifications to newly enacted (although fairly controversial) laws and rules, including those associated with the Clean Air Act. In fact, between 1973 and 1977, the auto industry was successful in four separate delays or modifications to national clean air standards, including those associated with emissions regulation. In June 1974, President Nixon signed the Energy Supply and Environmental Coordination

Act, which enacted a series of amendments that eased regulations and deadlines set by the Clean Air Act. As a result, the auto industry was provided a three-year reprieve (until 1978) for the full implementation of auto-emission standards. The auto industry was also successful a year later with another delay that would extend existing hydrocarbon and carbon monoxide standards for another year, and again in 1977 with their success in weakening emissions standards associated with the Clean Air Act Amendments through supporting a Senate filibuster that ultimately strong-armed Congress into caving on the emissions standards in favor of industry preferences. It has been said that one of the key strategies in the industry's success at winning such governmental favor was its claim that pollution regulation and energy shortages had negatively impacted sales and therefore negatively impacted jobs.[114] However, there seemed to be little evidence of that. Rather, the success seemed more to be the result of their change in tactics regarding lobbying, putting significant energy toward their lobbying efforts. Part of this success is attributed to the industry's ability to galvanize the support of various industry stakeholders, including parts suppliers, dealers, and the 1.5 million-member United Auto Workers Union.[115] "The auto companies' success in 1977 was due to one key factor: they employ so many God-damned people."[116]

Consumer-oriented advocates and groups including the Consumer Federation of America (CFA), Consumers Union (CU), and Ralph Nader were actively involved in issues directly related to the energy crisis. CFA's ties to energy stemmed from its member affiliations to consumer groups and federations of public power companies and rural electric co-ops. As a result, CFA's interests focused on energy development and production versus environmentalism. During the energy crisis, the CFA was vocal on issues related to corporate energy policies, and, as a result, it supported a federal oil and gas corporation; CFA was also opposed to the deregulation of oil and gas and the appointment of oil executives to federal policy-making positions.[117]

CU is known for its publication *Consumer Reports*. CU's energy activities consisted mostly of lawsuits on behalf of consumers with regard to pricing of oil and gas and interpretation of the EPAA. For example, CU's lawyer, Peter Schuck, won a lawsuit that challenged the FEA's policy that allowed unleaded gas to be priced the same as premium gasoline even though the former costs the same as regular to be produced.[118]

Ralph Nader has long been a significant fixture in policy debates, taking the liberal side and using his notoriety to advocate on behalf of consumers, including championing the Consumer Protection Agency, motor vehicle safety, safe drinking water, and the Environmental Protection Agency. Savvy as Nader is, he too was able to use the energy crisis to push his public-interest-oriented agenda. For example, in 1973 Nader joined Friends of the Earth in a suit to shut down twenty nuclear power plants due to concerns over safety and fear of a nuclear meltdown.[119] Nader is also known for eschewing largess and, as a result, maintains many smaller organizations (rather than one mega-organization) that oversee all the various aspects of his advocacy work, such as lobbying, fundraising, and so on. With regard to energy in the 1970s, Nader had five organizations dedicated in some capacity to the issue: Public Citizen, Inc., Congress Watch, Critical Mass, Tax Reform Research Group, and Public Interest Research Group.[120]

One of Nader's fundamental roles during this period was to serve as a leader of the antinuclear movement organizing a variety of other organizations also opposed to nuclear energy; another of his roles was to coordinate the dissemination of information to the public on the issue of nuclear-energy development. During the energy crisis, Nader was also busy fighting the good fight on behalf of consumers, siding with the notion that the crisis was a ruse set forth my major oil companies. His motivation was based on the belief that the government's energy policies were managed by major oil companies. "There are 52 former oil executives now employed by the Federal Energy Office under William Simon and they will be going right back to those oil companies."[121] As a result, Nader was among those vocal against proposals to deregulate oil and natural gas. Nader's organizations supported the Fisher amendment proposing a tax on new cars with high gas consumption, the Udall proposals to control strip mining, and also measures that supported the development of alternative energy sources (such as solar) and energy conservation.[122]

According to Andrew S. Mcfarland, Common Cause is an organization that was founded in 1970 and focuses on issues related to government reform, including campaign finance, regulation of lobbying, but also engaged in the anti-war movement, lobbying in opposition to the Vietnam War.[123] In 1975, Common Cause began to participate in lobbying regarding energy. The overriding concern of Common Cause during the energy crisis was on structure and process of government and political action and influence. For example, Common Cause "emphasized reforms of the structure and process of government at the national and state levels, such as regulating campaign finances, regulating the activities of lobbyists, requiring disclosure of financial holdings of top officials, requiring that meetings of decision-making bodies be open, reforming congressional seniority system, and so forth."[124] Due to the group's focus on procedure, substantive issues such as energy were secondary. Therefore, the group was not exceptionally influential in terms of energy policy. Yet the group combined its primary goal and its concern for energy in an effort to reform the "decision-making process of some of the energy agencies in the federal executive branch."[125] One way it achieved this was by persuading presidential appointees to publicly commit to particular reforms in the process of confirmation, which was done in the confirmation hearings of both FEA administrator nominees John Sawhill and Frank G. Zarb, as well as Stanley Hathaway's confirmation hearings as the interior secretary-designate.[126]

With regard to its position on energy matters, Common Cause believed in conservation but was realistic enough to also believe that the development of additional energy sources was inevitable. As such, they urged that effective environmental standards guide such energy development, including that of coal conversion and offshore oil leasing. Common Cause, however, opposed the issuance of construction permits for nuclear energy until there was convincing proof of its safety. While the group did support R&D funds for renewable energy and nuclear energy, it did not support the level proposed by the Ford administration. Specifically, Common Cause supported a conservation-oriented oil-import quota, backed an amendment to Representative Al Ullman's conservation bill that would tax gas-guzzlers and provide a tax incentive for automakers to produce cars with higher gas efficiency. However, due to pressure from oil-state Democrats, compromises were made in order to get the bill, by then watered down, voted out of committee despite Republican opposition. Also, as part of a lobbying coalition, Common Cause was successful in getting oil depletion allowances repealed in the spring of 1975.[127]

Conclusion

The 1973–74 energy crisis was a focusing episode and thereby created a flurry of activity with regard to national energy policy. During the crisis, Americans' attention was sharply focused on the issue due to the inconveniences they faced at the pump, and heating their homes with the rapidly climbing cost of energy. Public opinion polls of the time demonstrated how concerned Americans were, and, as a result, politicians were forced to respond. The events of the 1973–74 energy crisis illustrate the convergence of Kingdon's[128] three streams—that is, a problem was widely recognized, there existed appropriate policy solutions, and the political situation was ripe for change, with strong advocacy coalitions prepared to act. As a result, the focusing event or episode drew attention to the problem, and a sequence that led to change was initiated. Crucial to this sequence was the role of public opinion and how the public could compel politicians to respond to them when they wanted something. Underlying focusing events and episodes were public desires and demands, but once energy prices fell, public attention faded.

While the Middle Eastern oil embargo was lifted on March 18, 1974, the problems Americans would face with regard to energy crises, oil prices, and industry profits would ebb and flow as time marched on. Once the dust began to settle after the embargo was lifted, the casualties of the crises could be counted. All told, the "nation's economic output declined by $10–$20 billion during the first quarter of 1974"; the civilian labor force shrank by about

500,000 people (approximately 80 percent of industrial layoffs were traced to the decline in demand for autos or recreational vehicles, and another 150,000–200,000 jobs, mostly in gasoline stations or airlines, were lost as a direct result of employers' inability to acquire sufficient petroleum); the shortage of petroleum also caused a loss in state and federal gasoline taxes, which for seventeen states in February 1974 amounted to a nearly $700 million loss in revenue; the high fuel prices caused a rise in the Consumer Price Index; and finally, nearly 20,000 gas stations, mostly independent, closed during the 12-month period ending June 30, 1974.[129]

The events of the early 1970s were part of a cautionary tale, and many experts warned that additional shortages should be expected. In hindsight, we understand that such warnings were warranted. In fact, as we demonstrate in the next three chapters, the United States experienced additional energy crises, all of which can also be understood via the same theoretical lens. Furthermore, blame for the protracted 1973–74 crisis could be placed on many different actors: Congress, long a victim to problems of collective action, did little early on to create a national energy policy, whereas President Nixon and the executive branch could have done more to urge congressional action. Consumers demanded energy at a clip that far outpaced supply, and the federal government maintained incomplete information on the supply of US reserve but this was ameliorated after the crises by the formation of the Strategic Petroleum Reserve and the Energy Information Administration (EIA).[130] Industry, especially big oil, also shared part of the responsibility, and could have been keener to ensure alternatives when demand surpassed supply.

At the height of the energy crisis, public attention was more sharply focused on the issue. As a result, widespread public concern forced the hand of public officials, especially those in Congress. Senator Henry M. Jackson in particular turned a steely gaze upon the major oil companies for what many Americans and members of Congress believed to be an artificial crisis created for the purpose of self-benefit and windfall profits. With the high prices and energy shortages, the public and a variety of interest groups pushed their policy preferences, and the government was forced to respond and attempt to balance competing demands. Yet once the embargo was lifted and the intensity of the energy crisis ebbed, public attention followed. Consequently, policies meant to deal with some of the major issues associated with the energy crisis—which, many feared, would rear their heads again—were hindered. With hindsight we know that government's receding attention to energy issues, helped ensure subsequent crises. Nevertheless, we demonstrate how these events show that the cycle of energy crises correspond to the theory of agenda setting and punctuated equilibrium, with the energy-price spikes serving as focusing episodes.

While the 1970s energy crisis is the first case we use to illustrate these theories, in the remaining chapters we apply the framework to the subsequent national energy crises—in 1979–80, 1990–91, and the 1999–2000 and 2007–8. In every case, we will demonstrate how soaring oil prices spark concern in the public and renders the government groping for answers on how best to handle the issue. As with any policy domain, solutions are usually watered-down versions of the original, as politics is the result of compromise, especially with interest groups competing against each other for their political preferences. Ultimately, one of the major lessons to come from the 1970s energy crisis was how problematic it was for a nation so dependent on energy to be without a national energy policy. Even in the midst of the crisis, when the need for such a policy seemed dire, the US government still failed to come up with a national energy policy. What resulted was an ad-hoc and short-term approach built on compromises between conflicting factions, pitting consumers against producers, major gas companies against independent stations, northeastern states against southeastern states, domestic against imported, and so on. Unfortunately, and as we shall see, the subsequent energy crises were also unable to foment commitment toward a comprehensive policy.

The Iranian Oil Crisis: 1979–80

The 1976 presidential campaign presented the public with two contrasting approaches to address the energy vulnerability brought to light by the 1973–74 oil embargo. The Democratic Party platform offered specific proposals to solve the energy crisis through conservation and research on alternative fuels. In contrast, the Republican Party platform highlighted energy self-sufficiency through the expansion of energy supply and increased exploration into traditional energy sources as well as solar and wind. In terms of policy solutions to the energy problem, the choice was distinct for the public: either conserve or increase supply. The Carter/Mondale ticket ultimately prevailed over the Ford/Dole ticket by fifty-seven electoral college votes, and Jimmy Carter was inaugurated as the thirty-ninth president of the United States in January 1977.

Upon his inauguration, President Carter inherited an energy situation that had continually worsened since 1973, despite the regulatory and legislative efforts of Congress and his predecessors. Energy consumption had grown, even in the face of higher prices, and domestic production had stabilized, thereby increasing America's dependence on imported oil. More so than his predecessors, Carter was far more willing to target the problem of energy shortages through conservation efforts among the public rather than relaxing environmental regulations to free up supply.[1] And while plans that call for conservation and price increases might sound good to the public in the abstract during a campaign, these policies can be difficult sell to the public and lawmakers in reality. Carter openly recognized the political trouble that such an approach might cause, noting himself that these proposals would mean "some very difficult decisions will have to be made by Congress. . . . I'm going to take as much of the disapproval and disappointment of the American people on myself as President to make it easier for Congress to move forward."[2] A poll published in late April conducted by Gallup found that 45 percent of the respondents felt that the energy situation was "very serious" but also ranked "high cost of living" and "unemployment" above "energy problems."[3] It seemed clear that while the majority of Americans recognized energy as an important issue for the new president to address, it would have to be done in a way that was sensitive to American pocketbooks during an unsteady and inflationary economy.

Prior to his inauguration, Carter reportedly told a visitor that he was determined to reform the nation's energy habits "even if it costs me another term."[4] Entering office with what he believed to be a mandate for energy reform, President Carter and the newly appointed secretary of energy, James R. Schlesinger, quickly set forth to create a comprehensive energy plan that would address national energy production and consumption. To rally public and congressional support for this undertaking, on April 18, 1977, President Carter delivered a televised speech announcing his energy proposal and declaring that energy policy reform was the "moral equivalent of war— except that we will be uniting our efforts to build not destroy."[5] In this speech, Carter outlined ten "fundamental principles" of the energy plan, including protecting the environment and reducing energy demand. Overall, the address was motivational and designed to set the stage for the forthcoming energy plan, though it was largely void of specific policies and details.

However, eleven days later, on April 29, 1977, Carter publicly issued the objectives of his National Energy Plan, a program that is often referred to as "NEP I." There were four prominent goals included in this initiative: to reduce the annual domestic growth rate of national energy demand to 3 percent; to reduce national gasoline consumption by 10 percent; to lower foreign oil imports from twelve to six million barrels per day; and to establish a one billion barrel strategic oil reserve.[6] In order to achieve these ambitious objectives, the Carter Administration proposed five measures. The first was a new gasoline tax that would increase by $.05 per year until the established conservation goals were met. The second was the elimination of price controls on gasoline. The third measure was to establish tax credits and grants to encourage private conservation. The fourth was to decontrol the price of new oil and natural gas as well as a wellhead tax on oil. Finally, the proposal included the conversion of industries and utilities to coal and support for the development of solar and geothermal energy sources.[7]

The focus of NEP I was on changing habits, conserving energy, and increasing fuel efficiency rather than simply making more energy. The enforcing mechanism behind NEP I was based largely on tax policies that would allow the federal government to reach its goals by encouraging conservation though higher prices and the punishment of excessive energy use. Carter's plan, in simple, was to raise the cost of energy in order to encourage public conservation. As was somewhat expected, there was general public support for the energy plan and its objectives, except for the added tax on gas and all aspects that would raise the costs for consumers.

Fundamentally altering American consumption patterns was only one part of the equation, however; on the other side was creating a governmental infrastructure to facilitate energy reform. Due in part to existing "iron triangles," or long-established relationships among interest groups, congressional committees, and executive agencies, the energy policy infrastructure in place following the previous energy crisis was characterized as fragmented, inefficient, and conflicting. Carter and Schlesinger believed that the best way to enact energy reform was to centralize all of the energy-related agencies into a new consolidated agency termed the Department of Energy (DOE). The proposed DOE would absorb the Federal Energy Administration (FEA), the Energy Research and Development Administration (ERDA) and the Federal Power Commission (FPC). The new department would assume the regulation of oil, natural gas, and electric power and share the management of resources on federal lands with the Interior Department. Carter stated that the purpose of this reorganization was to "give us one governmental body with sufficient scope and authority to do the massive job that remains to be done."[8] The legislation to create the DOE was passed through Congress and signed by President Carter on August 4, 1977.

The public and Congress backed the reorganization of executive agencies and the creation of a centralized Department of Energy. However, the public did not agree with Carter's assessment of the severity and scope of the current energy crisis. Public opinion polls at the time showed that the public was concerned about energy but that they were skeptical of the presence of a true energy "crisis." The success of NEP I relied in large part on the public's willingness to change their behavior and make sacrifices in order to stem the energy crisis. Carter's appeal to the public succeeded in convincing only one-third of Americans that the energy situation was as bad as he suggested, and even that support quickly waned. Carter was calling for the public to change long-established patterns of consumption—a formidable task that required a shift in public mentality, not just slightly higher prices at the pump. Ultimately, and consistent with the predictable patters of the energy crisis cycle, the impetus for change came from an external shock that followed the fall of the Shah in Iran and significant cuts in foreign oil supply.

Not only was the public skeptical of the urgency of the energy crisis as Carter had framed it, but they showed little trust in the companies and industries that control energy nationwide. Only a few years had passed since the first energy crisis, where reports confirmed speculation about soaring profits for the oil companies during the crisis. As a result, oil companies were generally viewed as narrow-minded money-grabbers who benefitted during times of public distress. The public believed that oil companies profited far more than they actually did, estimating they earned $.62 per dollar taken in, when they actually earned $.06.[9] An Associated Press/National Broadcasting Company poll found that

54 percent of the 1,600 adult respondents surveyed believed that the energy shortages were a hoax designed to increase oil-company profits.[10] Many in the American public felt that oil companies did a poor job of balancing public interest with making a profit, and when asked to name industries where power rests in the hands of too few companies, oil was mentioned more often than any other business.[11]

Distrust in the oil industry and historical accounts of artificial perpetuation of energy crises for oil-company profits threatened to stagnate Carter's energy plan. In an effort to harness the public's distrust for oil and use it toward his advantage, Carter put pressure on Congress to approve his bill by stating that the nation "will risk the biggest rip-off in history" unless Congress approved his plan, including controls that would limit oil-industry profits.[12] Without an imminent threat to spur them into action, the public was reluctant to proactively conserve energy or bear the additional costs at the pump that Carter's plan proposed. As Carter's approval ratings steadily declined from 75 percent in January to 46 percent in December 1977, his persuasive power with the public waned, and Carter stood little chance of winning over Congress's support.

Congress was reluctant to back the NEP I plan since its initial proposal. Though members of Congress were able to recognize that there was a need for some action, they were equally concerned about the economic ramifications of such a program. Under serious doubt that Carter's proposal would be effective in meeting any energy crisis, the House Ways and Means Committee eliminated the proposed standby tax on gasoline and eliminated rebates to car buyers who invested in smaller, more efficient vehicles.[13] Amid partisan deadlock over the bill, Congress left the plan on the table as they went home for the holidays in December. Frustrated by his fading proposal and rancorous debate in Congress, Carter called the decision to ignore America's energy troubles until the New Year "regrettable."[14]

Despite escalating concern in parts of the Middle East that would eventually cement the second major oil crisis, a *New York Times*/CBS poll reported that only 33 percent of those polled felt that the energy crisis was "as bad as the president said."[15] To be fair, there was a reported glut of oil at the time due to increased supplies that would begin to come from the North Slope and the North Sea.[16] Reports speculated that the world could anticipate a glut of oil lasting into 1981, perhaps even "too much" oil for the infrastructure to handle.[17] Not only were such reports not helping President Carter convince the public that the energy crisis was genuine and imminent, but these forecasts were counterproductive and harmful to his energy agenda. A Washington official from a major oil company commented, "That's going to be Carter's biggest problem, convincing people to conserve when we're awash in crude oil."[18] Increasing oil production and reports of a global surplus undermined Carter's program and his credibility. Additionally, such reports further increased cynicism among the public regarding the energy crisis while causing them to lose sight of the need for a long-term energy plan.

Waning public support doomed Carter's energy program. Polling showed that the administration's attempt to galvanize public opinion behind energy-policy reform had failed. Though Carter tried to maintain an image of openness and dialogue with the public and interest groups on his energy proposal, the truth of the matter was that it was drafted quickly and by non-political technicians. In fact, one of the many factors that led to the weakening of the bill was that Carter did not include interest groups in the drafting, and this made it particularly difficult to pass through a Congress that relied on interest groups for services and campaign contributions. Additionally, the bill lacked a concerned constituency to advocate for its passage. Coupled with active lobbying against the bill by a broad range of special interests, the bill had little chance. Over the following year, the energy bill was debated and minimized to a point of non-recognition.

When the battered legislation was finally placed on Carter's desk for a signature in October 1978, it hardly resembled the initial proposal the administration had put forward. Carter's proposal to save 4.5 million barrels of oil per day by 1985 through taxation, incentives, and regulatory authority had been deflected by Congress. The proposed standby tax on gas, if consumption goals were not met, was rejected. The final bill was vastly weakened, but it did maintain some significant elements, including a phased deregulation of natural gas by the late 1980s. This portion of the bill called for newly developed industrial plants and utilities to use fuel other than oil in their operation and also called for the eventual conversion of all utilities off gasoline and oil by 1990. Additionally, state regulatory agencies were encouraged to consider conservation procedures, and significant effort was put toward the insulation of facilities such as homes, hospitals, and schools for better efficiency. While the final legislation still held onto some portions of the initial proposal, it was severely weakened and a reflection of the low public support for energy conservation programs.

Though Carter was elected to office on campaign promises of energy reform and a program centering on conservation rather than increased production, when push came to shove the public lacked the motivation needed to support these policies. NEP I was introduced as a significant package of changes that held promise to reform energy consumption patterns in America. However, without public willingness to bear the costs of the program, Congress was unwilling to inflict price increases on their constituents. While the National Energy Act (NEA) was ultimately passed through Congress, it was a shell of the original proposal. Carter had tried to rally the public by comparing the energy situation to the "moral equivalent of war"; James Flung, head of the Energy Action interest group, said that Carter signing the NEA was the "functional equivalent of surrender in the moral equivalent of war."[19]

NEP I is a good example of the failure of a policy window to open. The energy crisis cycle suggests that policy windows open as the result of a specific sequence of events: energy prices spike; the public places upward pressure on government, which opens policy windows; and then change occurs. This cycle does not work as effectively from the top down, however. Without an imminent energy shortage, there was little discussion of energy-company profiteering, scant anger focused at the oil companies, and little public demand for action. The ordering of events in the energy crisis cycle is paramount for windows to open and policy change to take place. Just a couple of years later, in the presence of a global oil shortage and significant increase in prices resulting from political events in Iran, Carter took another stab at major energy reform and was far more successful.

Iranian Revolution: The Second Energy Crisis

Escalating politics in the Middle East once again began to cause concern for the United States and the global community. The 1977–78 negotiations at Camp David between Egypt and Israel, resulting in the Camp David Accord, led to peace between those countries and the withdrawal of Egypt from the anti-Israeli struggle. However, this policy result, among other issues, angered and worried much of the Middle East, breeding anti-American sentiment in the region.[20] Because of his favoritism toward the West and pro-American policies, dissatisfaction with the Shah of Iran, Mohammad Reza Pahlavi, grew among the Iranian population. Exiled Shia cleric Ayatollah Ruhollah Khomeini was perpetuating domestic opposition to the Shah by disseminating propaganda through cassette tapes made in Iraq. These actions revived a very old battle between the royal house of Iran and the dominant Shia Islamic fundamentalists that would ultimately spell the end of the Shah's reign over Iran and serve as the focusing episode of the second energy crisis.

In addition to general displeasure about the Shah's friendliness with the United States, domestic pressures mounted against the Shah as the urban Iranian infrastructure was unable to absorb the increasing revenue from oil. Under the Shah, the public sector exhibited poor urban planning, bottlenecks in development, over-congested ports, soaring housing costs, and a flawed monetary policy that lead to rising inflation. Overall, the state was not prepared to handle the demands placed upon it, and public discontent grew as a result. Eventually, violence and protest erupted among the population in Iran calling for the removal, and worse, of the Shah. After Iranian soldiers killed ten students during a protest where protesters were throwing rocks and chanting insults, martial law was imposed in Iran in September of 1978.[21] Later in October, strikes in the oil sector, calling for the release of political prisoners and the arrest of corrupt officials, led to a 40 percent drop in oil production, ushering in the second major oil crisis.[22]

Behind Saudi Arabia, Iran was the second largest exporter of oil to the United States and a major supplier to Western Europe and Israel.[23] Iran shipped around 900,000 barrels of oil per day to the United States, or roughly 8 percent of US daily imports.[24] In total, of the 5.5 million barrels of oil Iran produced each day, 4.5 million were exported while the rest was consumed domestically.[25] By November 1978, overall production declined to less than a million barrels per day—barely enough to satisfy domestic needs—just as the winter demand for oil began to surge.[26] The ramifications of the Iranian oil crisis were quickly felt abroad. Shell Oil was the first to start rationing to dealers in December, and price of gas in the United States was reportedly already up 8 percent from the previous year.[27]

Due to the enduring strikes among oil workers and sustained political struggle in Iran, oil production fell even further to 500,000 bpd. On January 16, 1979 the Shah, suffering from cancer and wildly unpopular, fled Iran, leaving it in the hands of a ruling coalition. On February 1, 1979 Ayatollah Ruhollah Khomeini, previously exiled for his denunciation of the Shah's regime, was allowed to return to Iran whereupon he seized control of the Iranian government, replacing the Shah's monarchy with an Islamic Republic. Oil production picked up slightly after the fall of the Shah; however, oil production and exports from Iran remained very low until the late 1980s and to this day remain far below production levels reached during the mid-1970s.

The focusing episode that spurred the larger energy crisis occurred between November of 1978 and the fall of 1979. Shortages of premium-unleaded gas in the United States began in November 1978, and by February of the following year President Carter was calling for voluntary gas conservation efforts from the American public to offset the dip in Iranian production. The response was not limited to the United States; in fact, the United States and nineteen other countries in the International Energy Agency all agreed to cut their collective oil demand by 5 percent.[28] Cuts in demand among these countries could take the form of using national oil reserves, increasing domestic output, or cutting consumption to meet the 5 percent mark, the equivalent of two million barrels of oil per day. Together these countries initiated an effort to head off a global shortage and price escalation; without this cooperative effort, the crisis would have surely been much worse.

Despite the global efforts to minimize the impact of short supply from Iran, overall oil supply to the United States fell by 8 percent and oil prices rose by 150 percent. The discrepancy between the small oil shortage and the massive price increase suggests that perhaps there was another mechanism other than simple market forces at work driving prices up. To compound this suspicion,

Saudi Arabia agreed to increase their level of production to compensate for the loss of Iranian oil. Saudi Arabia, unlike other members of OPEC, feared the long-term implications of increasing oil costs haphazardly: they feared that oil would price itself out of competition on the energy market. As a result, there should have been little change in the price of oil because of Saudi's assistance and global conservation efforts. So, what happened to cause this "crisis"?

Daniel Yergin suggests in *The Prize* (1991) that the answer to this question lies in panic—panic triggered by five circumstances: First, the public believed that consumption was growing. Second, there was disruption of contractual agreements within the oil industry, which led to further speculation. Third, there were contradictory and conflicting policies of consumer governments that added stress and tension to the issue. Fourth, this was an opportunity for oil exporters to capture additional high rents, and they manipulated supplies to affect the market. Lastly, emotion played a large role; stress, fear, anxiety, and confusion all led to increased panic.[29] Others agree that the "second shock happened when the interruption of production in Iran brought on a speculative panic. The short fall of Iranian production would not have had such a dramatic effect if it were not for the general belief that prices were set to go higher."[30]

The energy shortage was real to an extent, but it was socially constructed panic that made it a crisis. It was largely the buyers, not the suppliers, who made the situation worse by buying up extra oil to stock reserves in fear of a repetition of the 1973 crisis. Companies bought excess oil when they thought prices were going to go up so that they could afford to buy less of the expensive oil in the future. "Companies bought well in excess of anticipated consumption, not only because of price, but also because they were not sure they would be able to get any oil later on. And that extra buying beyond the real requirements of consumption, combined with hoarding, dizzily drove up the price, which was exactly what companies and customers were struggling to avoid in the first place. In short, the panic of 1978–1979 was self-fulfilling."[31] The increased demand by oil companies, combined with worry-driven demand among utility companies and the public, led to an excess increase in demand over consumption by three million barrels per day. Panic buying, coupled with opportunistic OPEC exporters, not a major shortage of oil, drove the price of oil from $13 per barrel to $34 per barrel by 1981.

Dynamic domestic and international forces coupled to initiate the second major energy crisis cycle. Domestically, the United Statees had just elected a new president who prioritized energy policies that would help to lower consumption and preserve the environment. Additionally, the public was primed to consider energy as a national priority, although the slow economy made them resistant to policies that drove prices up. Learning from previous energy crisis cycles, interest groups and oil companies knew they had to be very active in order to protect their interests amid a second crisis. Congressional representatives recognized the need to plan long term for a sustainable energy policy, but were reluctant to do so in a way that raised prices on the public and jeopardized their reelection chances. At the international level, oil supply was unpredictable due to rising tension in the Middle East and specifically in Iran. While Saudi Arabia increased production to offset lower exports from Iran, the market was paranoid and prices skyrocketed. Carter soon realized that the second energy crisis might provide the immediacy necessary to corral public support and finally pass long-term, sweeping energy reform.

Public Reaction

The severity of the growing world oil shortage triggered by the fall of the Shah in Iran was not felt immediately in the United States because Iran only supplied 8 percent of American oil. However, the cascading effects eventually found their way to US shores. Beginning as early as November 1978, shortages of premium gasoline started to appear at American gas stations, and the price of gas started to climb. In December, the Automobile Association of American (AAA) reported that gas prices were up 8 percent from the previous year. Shell began rationing gas sales to dealers, and Exxon announced a policy to sell crude only to Exxon affiliates. By February 1979, President Carter called on Americans to voluntarily conserve gas as a way to offset the shortages.

In preparation for the uncertain future, Carter proposed a standby gasoline-rationing program to Congress that would go into effect in the event of a serious restriction on energy supply. The program proposed to use vehicle registrations to distribute coupons for gas that could be used to purchase limited quantities of fuel. Alternatively, the coupons could be bought and traded on a "white market." Carter's gas-rationing program passed the Senate with a convincing vote of 58–39, but was ultimately killed in the House. There are several explanations for the bill's failure. After passing the Senate, the administration altered the bill several times and left representatives confused as to how this program might affect their constituents. Many representatives also felt that the coupon program the bill proposed would unfairly hurt the poor by allowing those with means to buy up all the coupons. Ultimately, the standby nature of the program lacked the imminent threat that the public would require to tolerate gas rations, and the rumored energy crisis still seemed distant to most Americans.

In California, however, gas shortages had arrived, and the state began rationing gas sales in certain counties on May 9, 1979. California required that cars with odd and even license plates purchase gasoline on alternating days.[32] The gas shortage caused many to turn to desperate measures in order to fill their tanks.

Long lines grew in front of gas stations where motorists would wait, often over-night, for the opportunity to purchase gas in the morning before the station ran out. There were many reports of gas theft by syphoning gas from other cars. The price spike, panic, and annoyance of the gas shortage and energy crisis caused anger and concern within the public.

California was by far the worst off of all the states. The national formula for gas allocation established under the Nixon Administration had left California in a lurch, and the lines and rationing were making national headlines. Other areas of the country were still supplied amply with gasoline, but panic began to set in as consumers anticipated California-style lines to reach their pumps next. Lawrence Martin, a reporter for the Canadian newspaper *Globe and Mail* wrote, "In Washington, there weren't serious shortages. The people manufac-tured a crisis. They let their insecurities flourish. They heard the gloomy reports from California, they heard the pessimistic forecasts from the energy depart-ment and went running to the pumps."[33] The energy crisis that seemed imagined and distant just a year before quickly became a very real part of daily life, and the growing sense of frustration among the public fell largely upon the oil industry.

As discontent grew, the public demanded accountability—but from whom? As the energy crisis cycle predicts, when oil becomes scarce and energy prices rise, public trust and confidence in energy institutions such as the government, utility companies, and fuel suppliers plummet.[34] Demanding accountability, however, required identifying the source of the problem, and the public was quick to place blame on energy institutions, especially the oil industry. Targeting the oil industry as the source of the problem was based on recent memory of the 1973 energy crisis and lingering suspicion about its practices. In fact, there are a host of other contributing factors, such as consumption patterns that deserve more blame than they traditionally receive. Farhar et al. write, "Attribution of the primary responsibility for the energy problem, then, is to institutions in the society rather than to individuals taken en masse."[35] Interestingly, a poll taken in 1979 revealed that whether or not a person believed the energy crisis was "real" affected where they cast blame for the energy crisis. Those who believed the en-ergy crisis was real were more likely to attribute its cause to wasteful consump-tion patterns, whereas those who did not blamed the oil companies.[36]

Two things are seemingly clear from this: First, the majority of the public doubted that the energy crisis was real and therefore attributed blame, deserved or underserved, to the oil companies. Second, information about the energy crisis, reported oil glut, profiteering, the Iranian revolution, and energy planning was abundant, albeit challenging for the average citizen to synthesize. Part of the reason that the public may have been so unclear on what was happening and who was to blame may have been that the public was generally uninterested in en-ergy information, making it difficult to assimilate fast-changing and occasionally contradictory data related to energy. In 1979, 15 percent of the American public surveyed said that they were "familiar" with President Carter's proposals to address the energy problem, 41 percent said they knew "something" about it, and 44 percent were entirely uninformed.[37] Regardless of who was actually responsible for the energy crisis, it was clear that the public generally lacked information on energy policy and could be reactionary during times of energy crisis, often placing the most blame on the oil industry.

The public's lack of trust in the oil industry was not entirely unwarranted. The first energy crisis taught the public that oil companies are often the largest profiteers during times such as these. A majority of the public (54 percent) believed that the gas shortages were a hoax perpetuated by the oil companies for profit.[38] A nationally representative CBS/*New York Times* poll conducted in March of 1979 asked respondents, "Do you think the shortage of oil we hear about is real, or are we just being told there are shortages?"—to which 20 percent responded that it was real and 69 percent responded that they believed that the public was being lied to.[39] Over 60 percent of the public believed that the oil industry was not regulated enough and demanded more oversight to protect the public interest. The international media supported the contention that Western oil conglomerates were perpetuating the crisis for profit by lowering production to drive up prices. As the energy crisis cycle predicts, we again see that upon an increase in profits among energy producers, either real or perceived, politicians and interest group advocates will charge them with manipulating prices and even suggest that the crisis was fabricated. As a result, the public believes these claims of manipulation and demands that the government step in to help solve the problem.

As lines started to grow around the country in response to gas shortages, Sen. Howard Baker (R-TN) became openly critical of oil companies retaining their profits or returning them to stockholders rather than reinvesting in production to increase supply. Baker reportedly told an oil industry representative, "If you don't get those profits plowed back into production and less of it into dividends, this country will turn on you and devour you."[40] Hinting at nationalizing American oil companies, Baker said, "If the public gets the idea that the oil companies are gouging, they might be headed for something far worse than controls."[41]

Gasoline was rapidly becoming scarcer and prices were rising. Public concern about energy generally began to rise in response to increasing prices and long lines. As figure 6.1 shows, by the second quarter of 1979, over 25 percent of Americans sampled indicated that energy was one of the "most important problems" in America today. The distant energy crisis that the American public had trouble imagining or prioritizing had finally arrived. It seemed to the public that America was suffering while the oil companies profited. And yet, despite the rising prices and growing lines, many in the public were still skeptical of

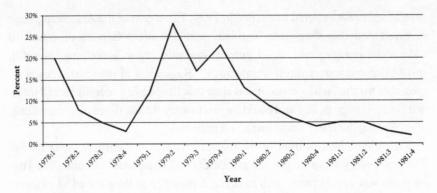

Figure 6.1 Quarterly Proportion of Respondents Who Identify "Energy" as "Most Important Problem," 1978-1981.

The data used here were originally collected by Frank R. Baumgartner and Bryan D. Jones, with the support of National Science Foundation grant numbers SBR 9320922 and 0111611, and were distributed through the Department of Government at the University of Texas at Austin. Neither NSF nor the original collectors of the data bear any responsibility for the analysis reported here.

a "real" energy crisis. As Lester Sobel writes, in *Energy Crisis* "There were still many people however, who argued that the shortages were largely artificial, that they were created deliberately for the profit of the energy industry of the oil-producing countries."[42] In 1979, the oil industry reached record-setting profits with Exxon leading the pack. It was increasingly obvious that big oil was making big gains, and this evoked sharp criticism from consumer advocates, the Carter Administration, and the public to which the government had to respond.

Government Responds to Public Upset

The public demanded the Carter Administration, Congress, and representative interest groups to respond to the growing crisis. The nation wanted truth, accountability, and a solution. Carter's appeal for increased conservation efforts among the public would continue to suffer without clarity among the public about the source of the energy problems they were faced with. Carter, however, still saw the evident crisis as an opportunity to pass a second national energy plan. During this time, Congress sought to appease their constituents without surrendering unnecessary power to the executive branch. Interest groups from all areas of the energy sector were mobilized to have a part in crafting a solution to the crisis and to represent their interests in long-term planning. Unlike 1978, when Carter proposed NEP I, the public was now more concerned about energy issues and expecting significant action from government. Furthermore, the press was very attentive to the crisis, related public panic, and proposed energy

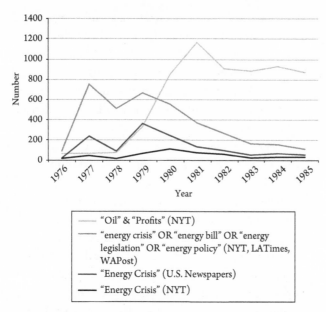

Figure 6.2 Articles Related to Energy Crisis in *New York Times* Index and US Newspapers, 1976-1985.

changes in the halls of government. A count of news stories related to energy in major newspapers shows the story count increased significantly at the onset of the crisis (see Figure 6.2). Heightened public concern and media attention helped Carter move his proposal forward.

Presidential Response: The Carter Administration

In response to growing concern about oil-company profiteering, Carter ordered the Department of Energy to look into the claim that the oil industry was intentionally withholding oil from the market to drive up prices. In May of 1979 Carter directed the Department of Energy and the Federal Trade Commission to investigate the matter. These two high-level investigations concluded, "Fluctuating government policies had contributed more to the shortfall in gasoline supplies than an alleged conspiracy by the nation's oil companies. The companies had decided to restrict gasoline output in favor of more lucrative petroleum products like jet fuel and petrochemicals."[43] These reports effectively cleared the oil companies of accusations about hoarding; nonetheless, the rumors of price gouging lingered.

US oil companies were accused many times of charging illegally high prices. The *Wall Street Journal* reported that the DOE drive against overpricing had resulted in civil charges against over a dozen major oil companies. In 1979 the Department of Justice brought criminal charges against Conoco for deliberately evading petroleum price controls in 1973 and 1974.[44] Many oil companies witnessed 100–200 percent change in profits between 1978 and 1979.[45] The sharp growth in profits brought on blunt criticism by consumer advocates, the White House, and other sources. In August of 1979, the AFL-CIO called for the nationalization of oil unless the oil industry showed stronger inclination to act in the public interest. Most of the allegations involved cost inflation by bypassing provisions of federal regulations governing the price of crude oil and its byproducts.

Carter responded to public demand for accountability from the oil companies because doing so allowed him to advance his energy-reform agenda. If Carter could demonstrate at a minimum that the oil companies were not responsible for some large hoax against the American public, then perhaps the public would come to see that big oil was not as culpable for the present circumstances as they had originally presumed. By pursuing the oil companies and vetting their involvement in price gouging and oil hoarding, the administration was able to clear the companies of some of their accusations, leaving the public with fewer factions to blame other than their own consumption patterns. As prices rose on oil across the nation and world, the public became increasingly aware that the energy crisis Carter had warned them about was real and had arrived. Additionally, the investigations had cleared the oil companies of the allegations that they had manufactured a crisis to make money. The combination of these events created a unique window of opportunity for the Carter Administration to appeal to the public for conservation efforts to affect demand, lower prices, and shift energy needs away from crude oil. With their pocketbooks pinched, and less ability to blame the oil companies for this mess, public support began to shift in favor of Carter's policies.

The window of opportunity for policy change expanded with the partial nuclear meltdown at the Three Mile Island nuclear reactor in March 1979. Prior to this incident, the National Academy of Sciences issued a statement supporting the further development of nuclear power plants and coal burning as the way to meet the energy demands of the country in the future. Prior to the incident at Three Mile Island, public opinion was divided on nuclear power in the United States. While many protested nuclear power with demonstrations at nuclear plants in Washington, California, and Oregon, many others also believed in nuclear power as a solution to our dependence on fossil fuels. After the accident at Three Mile Island, protests against nuclear power increased and nuclear energy was mothballed as a solution to our energy dependency. A poll conducted in April 1979 showed that the percentage of Americans who favored a cutback in nuclear plant operations until stricter safety regulations could be put in place increased 16 percentage points from a similar poll taken three years earlier. Taking nuclear power off the list of possible solutions to American energy demands placed even more focus on consumer conservation as a viable solution.

Carter opportunistically decided to use this period of heightened public attention to energy prices and consumption to initiate a second national energy program, "NEP II," which contained three major initiatives. NEP II proposed to establish a new Energy Mobilization Board to fast-track the development of new energy projects; it prioritized synthetic fuels through a multibillion-dollar development effort; and it proposed a massive windfall profits tax to recuperate profits that would result from Carter's decision to deregulate oil prices. These were the largest initiatives of the plan; however Carter also proposed to immediately levy import quotas on oil and required utility companies to increasingly burn coal instead of oil over the coming decade.

As Carter marched ahead with a second round of conservation initiatives driven by higher prices, he continued to explain the program to the public as a "restoration of American values" and common purpose.[46] By deregulating oil, raising prices to world levels to discourage consumption, and recapturing profits to the oil industry through windfall taxes, Carter hoped to shift American values toward energy conservation as a long-term solution. Although Carter was not afraid to champion this cause unilaterally and increasingly used executive orders to advance his cause as shown in Figure 6.3, in order to advance his energy agenda in significant ways, he required the cooperation of Congress.

The first, and most controversial, of the initiatives was to create an Energy Mobilization Board (EMB) to facilitate the fast-tracking of energy development projects by navigating red tape that slowed development. The establishment of the EMB was hotly debated because many viewed it as a power grab by the executive branch. The EMB as originally proposed would be able to take over state and local facilities, impose timelines, and waive environmental regulations to speed energy projects through. The EMB would also guarantee citizens access to

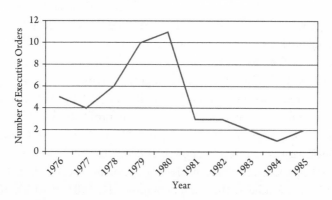

Figure 6.3 Executive Orders Related to Energy, 1976–1985.

information regarding projects that would enable a more valid role for the public in the planning process.[47] James E. Katz writes, "Their concern was based on EMB's power to impose time limits for regulatory decisions on projects classified 'critical energy facilities,' take over the state and local agencies' decision-making powers if time tables were not met, and waive environmental regulations."[48] This was a major proposal from the Carter Administration, and it was met with equal resistance in Congress and from state and local interest groups.

The second branch of Carter's NEP II was to establish an Energy Security Corporation (ESC) that would serve to fund the research and development of a synthetic fuels (or "synfuels") industry in the United States. Synfuels would help ameliorate US dependency on volatile foreign suppliers by taking advantage of ample domestic supplies of coal, oil shale, and alcohol derived from crops.[49] According to Carter's proposal, liquids and gases from coal, biomass and peat, oil, shale, and unconventional natural gas would provide a major alternative to imported oil. If the estimated thirty to sixty new plants were operating, it was estimated that the United States could rely on synfuels to make up the equivalent of 2.5 million barrels of oil by 1990. Carter's initiative behind the development of synthetic fuels was designed to produce more energy domestically, but also to send a message to OPEC to discourage them from raising prices with impunity.

The initiative to invest in the development of synfuels was not uncontested. The development of synthetic fuel is an old idea, but one that never received continuing attention and improvement. As a result, there were many valid questions among government officials, environmental interests, and corporations about the scientific viability of the synfuels proposal and the environmental implications. Walter Rosenbaum writes, "Existing data, some of it theoretical, strongly warn of potentially grave liabilities. Yet control technologies or newer processes may emerge to reduce the risks to acceptability."[50] Push-back against the synfuels proposal also came from the Department of Energy, where concern was expressed about the amount of water needed, potential violation of clean-air laws, production of tons of solid waste, pollution from coal and shale mining, and the endangerment of workers.[51] By proposing the synfuels bill, Carter was placing a big bet on science to develop to a point that would allow for safe and clean alternative fuels to replace oil.

The third part of NEP II was Carter's highly contentious proposal to deregulate oil and put in place a new Windfall Profits Tax (WPT) to recuperate excess and undue profits to oil companies and use the profits to fund the new ESC. The Energy Policy and Conservation Act of 1975 made it so that Carter did not have to seek permission from Congress to deregulate oil. Under the authority granted to the president, price controls were optional and at the discretion of the president between June 1, 1979 and September 31, 1981, at which point they would expire.[52] With this power, Carter proposed a two-year plan to decontrol all oil prices. The benefits that Carter sought from price deregulation were varied. Carter hoped that decontrol would raise oil prices for consumers and reduce demand. It was estimated that decontrol would reduce demand by 900,000 barrels per day in 1990, which in conjunction with increased domestic supply, would decrease oil imports by 2.1 million barrels per day by 1990.[53]

In conjunction with the deregulation of oil prices, Carter proposed a WPT that was similar to the plan previously proposed by the Nixon Administration. The WPT was effectively an excise tax on the first sale of each barrel of oil.

> Thus for each type of oil a base price (generally an approximation of the controlled price plus an adjustment for future inflation) was defined. The actual selling price, minus this price was the tax base, or the "windfall profit." Under the President's proposal, a 50 percent rate would be applied to this amount to determine the amount of the tax. Thus the tax as proposed was not a true income of profits tax because it did not take into account the costs of producing the oil. Although there were provisions in the later bill that limited the tax base to 90 percent of the net income from the oil, there were many complaints that calling the tax a profits tax was a misnomer.[54]

The combination of deregulating prices to stem demand and reduce US foreign dependence for oil, while syphoning excessive profits away from oil companies to put toward the development of synfuels to be fast-tracked by the EMB, was a massive overhaul to American energy policy.

The window of opportunity for new energy policy, which Carter saw in April of 1979, grew wider in November during the consideration of NEP II when an armed group of young Iranians occupied the US Embassy in Tehran and took the staff hostage. At the time, the Shah of Iran was seeking medical treatment in New York. The militants, under the direction of the leader of the Islamic Revolution, Ayatollah Ruhollah Khomeini, demanded that the Unites States return the Shah to Iran to stand trial in exchange for the release of the American hostages. The United States refused to return the Shah to Iran, and while many non-Americans, women, and blacks were subsequently released, 50 hostages remained in the embassy.[55] President Carter ordered that the United States stop purchasing oil from Iran on November 12; not to be outdone, Iran canceled all contracts with US oil companies that also supplied non-US markets three days later. The Iranian oil embargo reduced American oil imports by 750,000 barrels per day and took off the market an additional 700,000 barrels that American companies would export to other countries. The inherent risk involved with foreign oil dependence had never been more obvious to elected officials, industry, interest groups, and the general public, and it helped to usher in most of Carter's NEP II.

Congressional Response

NEP II contained many aspects that concerned members of Congress, not only because it called for higher prices on their constituents, but also because several aspects threatened the balance of power in the federal government. The Energy Mobilization Board (EMB) in particular raised many red flags because the original version of the bill proposed to significantly empower the executive branch and potentially violate environmental protections currently established. Concern was concentrated around the EMB's ability to impose time limits for regulatory decisions on critical-energy facilities, take over local- and state-level decision-making abilities if timelines were not met, and waive environmental regulations to speed approval.[56]

During the mark-up session for the EMB bill on September 19, 1979, the Senate Energy Committee empowered the EMB to override substantive state and federal law to facilitate the development of new energy programs. The exception was if the project would "unduly endanger public health or safety."[57] Unsatisfied with the bill that emerged from committee, Senators Abraham Ribicoff (D-CT) and Edmund S. Muskie (D-ME) proposed a substitute bill that imposed significant restrictions on the ability of the EMB to waive state and local laws, but the bill was defeated 58–39. Recognizing the legitimate concern for environmental protections, Sen. J. Bennett Johnson (D-LA) agreed to a compromise on the floor by allowing the secretary of the Interior or the Environmental Protection Agency to veto any wavier of law that the EMB proposed. On October 25, 1979, the Senate passed the Energy Mobilization Bill largely intact, 68–25.

The passage of the EMB bill by the Senate was indicative of a different climate of opinion when compared to the NEP I proposal. Katz writes, "While the Senate's approval did not guarantee passage of Carter's whole program, it indicated that Congress viewed the energy situation as critical and conceded that governmental obstacles to certain kinds of industrial construction have become so insurmountable that specific mechanisms were necessary to overcome them."[58]

The EMB success in the Senate was due in part to the simplicity of its legislative path to the floor. In the House, however, two widely varying bills emerged from the House Interior Committee and the House Commerce Committee. Sen. Morris Udall (D-AZ), chairman of the House Interior and Insular Affairs Committee, introduced a compromise bill that more closely resembled the administration's initial proposal; however, Udall's bill was defeated 191–215. Finally, on November 1, 1979, the House approved creation of the Energy Mobilization Board, 299–107. The House's version differed significantly from the Senate's. The House version of the bill included an additional power endowed to the board that allowed it to override substantive federal laws, such as environmental guarantees with the consent of the president.

Significantly more liberal than the Senate version of the bill, the two met in conference committee where the collective opposition of members concerned about states' rights, environmental interest groups, and state and county officials ultimately stopped it. The nail in the coffin came from Sen. Udall, who had previously been an advocate for the administration's version. While in conference committee, the Carter Administration had indicated that they would accept any version of the EMB bill that the committee could agree upon, which Udall took as an affront to his support for greater power for the EMB, and in turn he rallied opposition against a compromised version of the bill. With fervent opposition born out of compromise and waning Republican support as the general election drew near, the House effectively killed the EMB bill by sending it back to committee.

The proposal to create the Energy Mobilization Board was the first portion of Carter's NEP II proposal to be considered by Congress. While the EMB proposal did not fare well, Congress was far more excited about the prospects of synthetic fuel development in the United States, and Rep. William Moorhead (D-PA) introduced HR 3930, the Defense Production Act Amendments of 1979 on May 3, 1979. This bill would help to facilitate the development of the synfuels infrastructure and industry by guaranteeing demand from the federal government to the tune of 500,000 barrels of synfuels per day (bpd) by 1985 and 2 million bpd by 1990 to be used for defense needs. Additionally, the bill authorized $3 billion worth of synfuels price supports.[59] The bill was overwhelmingly supported by the House and passed by a vigorous voice vote on June 26, 1979.

In the Senate, the synfuels initiative received equal support. In April 1979, Sen. Proxmire William (D-WI) introduced the synfuels bill to the Senate, where it was referred to the Senate Energy Committee and the Senate Banking Committee. The Energy Committee proposed a large program establishing a synthetic fuels corporation that would own or operate plants funded by $20 billion initially, then $65 billion after three years if Congress approved. The Banking Committee produced a more moderate version of the program that limited expenditures to $3.9 billion in loan guarantees and price supports rather than direct federal outlays.[60] The Senate adopted the Energy Committee's version of the bill on November 8, 1979, and the bill went to conference committee with the House, where it emerged as the Energy Security Act (PL 96-294) and was signed by Carter on June 6, 1980.

The synfuels bill passed through Congress fairly easily, but it was not without challenge from outside forces. Oil companies, interest groups, liberals, and conservatives alike found themselves asking valid questions about the ability of the oil companies to produce the fuel needed with methods untested. Many industry experts criticized the initiative as technologically premature and felt that the timeline that was passed was unrealistic. A consultant for the Senate Budget Committee stated at a meeting that the established production goals would take "wartime effort and significant diversion from the rest of the economy."[61] Additionally, several traditionally oil-friendly members of Congress broke ranks with their oil alliances and voted in favor of the synfuels program. Sen. J. Bennett Johnson stated, "This country has had enough. People are tired of hearing 'wait a couple more years' from a few huge international oil companies with enormous financial interests in conventional oil reserves located overseas."[62] It was clear that although there were still lingering questions about the feasibility of the synfuels program, there was an urgent need to take proactive measures to free America from foreign-oil dependence.

The final aspect of Carter's energy proposal left to be addressed by Congress was the deregulation of oil prices and the proposed Windfall Profits Tax. Because Carter had the unilateral authority to decontrol oil prices under the EPCA of 1975, the only option that pro-control forces had was to pass legislation that would prohibit this power. While there were significant forces that opposed the deregulation of oil, it was clear that the votes were not there to support such legislation. After all, there were many benefits that could be derived from the deregulation of oil, including reduced risk associated with oil imports, improved international relations, and the elimination of direct regulatory costs and long-term efficiency losses.[63] Furthermore, it had the simple benefit of raising prices and lowering demand, which fit perfectly with Carter's quest for conservation.

Despite the benefits that could be derived from the decontrol of oil prices, there was no question that it would raise consumer costs, and this was not without effect. Steitz writes that the costs of decontrol were two-fold: "Decontrol would result in severe short-term macroeconomic losses, and it would result in massive transfers of income that appeared inequitable."[64] Price decontrol threatened to lead to increased inflation and unemployment resulting from slowed market growth as a function of increased costs. Furthermore, without a WPT in place, the massive transfer of profits to the oil companies, estimated at $600 billion in new pretax revenue, seem wholly "inequitable" and unfair. Pro-control advocates also expressed concern about the average public consumer. Sen. Edward Kennedy (D-MA), a consumer advocate, ardently opposed the deregulation program, calling it "a sham that will set poor against rich and worsen inflation."

Overall, the opponents of Carter's oil deregulation plan could not find the votes needed to revoke his power to decontrol prices. In light of this, attention turned toward the Windfall Profits Tax, which was squarely in Congress' court. On May 3, 1979, Rep. Al Ullman (D-OR) introduced HR 3919 to the House of Representatives, where it was referred to the House Ways and Means Committee of which Ullman was the chair. The fight in the Ways and Means Committee was split along party lines; liberal Democrats wanted a higher taxation rate, and conservative Republicans wanted either no tax at all or a "plowback provision" that required oil companies to reinvest their marginal profits in energy production or exploration. The bill emerged from committee with a higher tax rate and no concessions for the Republicans. On the House floor, the bill was amended to lower the taxation rate on oil and, counter to Carter's original proposal, to allow for the eventual phase-out of the WPT. Strong oil-loyalists Rep. Jim Jones (D-OK) and Henson Moore (R-LA) spearheaded these compromises. The House of Representatives passed the bill on June 18, 1979.

The Senate bill was referred to the Finance Committee chaired by a well-known friend of the oil industry, Sen. Russell Long (D-LA). Long ran a notoriously tight ship on the Finance Committee and maintained a level of control that far surpassed most other committee chairmen. Despite broad support for Carter's proposal among other committee members, the bill that emerged from committee was far weaker than Carter's proposal or the bill that passed the House. Long had orchestrated the inclusion of many exemptions to the tax and reduced the overall revenue by half. When the bill was reported out of committee, a bipartisan group of eleven members of the Finance Committee wrote a statement opposing the diluted version of the bill. They concurred that many aspects of the bill were acceptable, but "several special exemptions are allowed which are unjustified because they do not enhance production and because they significantly reduce badly needed revenue."[65]

Under the pressure of Majority Leader Robert Byrd (D-WV), and despite a filibuster from Sen. Long, the bill was amended to include an additional tax on newly discovered oil and finally approved by a vote of 74–24 on December 17, 1979. The House and Senate versions of the bill were reconciled in conference committee, and President Carter signed the Crude Oil Windfall Profit Tax Act of 1980 into law on April 2, 1980 (PL 96-223).

Interest Group Activity

Interest groups play a vital role in the energy crisis cycle and steering public opinion. However, with the development of NEP I, the Carter Administration opted for less interest group involvement in order to push legislation through faster. Carter promised during his campaign that he would propose a national energy plan within ninety days of his inauguration. Carter delegated this quick but massive task to energy advisor James Schlesinger. Schlesinger quickly assembled a small team of advisors including S. David Freeman, former director the Ford Foundation's Energy Policy Project, and Robert Nordhaus, chief aide to

John Dingell, the chairman of the House Subcommittee on Energy and Power. Notably, the advisory committee was not inclusive of the established energy institutions such as the Energy Research and Development Administration (ERDA) or the Nuclear Regulatory Commission (NRC), or outside interest groups. National energy planning obviously involves many and varied interests, including the oil sector, labor interests, environmental interests, and manufacturing, to name a few. The decision to use an insular committee to draft NEP I exchanged the complexity of building a supportive coalition invested in the plan for swiftness, a decision that had a clear effect on the final, weakened version of Carter's NEP I when it eventually cleared Congress.

Interest group involvement and investment in the drafting of new and major policy is important to the development of a solid base of supporters and advocates. The Carter Administration chose, however, to opt for narrower involvement, presumably in order to meet the ninety-day promise that Carter had made during the campaign. Regarding the value of interest group involvement, John Chubb writes,

> Interest groups are bound to play important parts in the planning process. The DOE cannot expect its long-term goals and policy proposals to be accepted by Congress or implemented successfully unless it builds a supportive coalition during the planning process. If it does not mediate the interest conflicts that attend so many energy policy initiatives, the conflicts may subsequently be resolved in a manner inconsistent with the department's plans.[66]

Undeniably, the decision to omit the standing energy institutions and many interest groups from the planning of the NEP I made for a weaker plan ultimately. NEP I neglected to consider important aspects such as nuclear-licensing reform, supply-side stimuli, and important existing policy in need of revision. The failure to consider energy in a broad and comprehensive way made it easy for Congress to find objections to the proposed plan and ultimately contributed to its deterioration as NEP I moved through Congress.

The efforts that the Carter Administration did make to reach out to the energy-related interest groups were superficial and ineffective at getting buy-in from the community. The administration invited extracommittee involvement through the solicitation of written comments, ten regional "town meetings," and several White House "mini conferences" where representatives from over 400 interest groups were in attendance. While nearly 28,000 responses were received and over 800 individuals commented during the town meetings, very few changes were made to NEP I. It became clear that the forums allowing for public comment were more for political theater than for true planning and consensus building. Failing to significantly involve environmental and conservation interest groups in the drafting of NEP I—which relied heavily on public conservation efforts—frustrated the groups, and they ultimately became reluctant to work for the bill.

The Carter Administration and DOE realized that greater involvement from the interest groups in the planning of NEP II would be necessary to ensure a better outcome. When crafting NEP II, the DOE actively reached out to environmental and electric-power groups as well as labor unions and commercial interests for help with planning, strategy, and public relations. Additionally, the DOE looked to conservation and renewable-energy groups and consumer public-interest groups for significant help with congressional strategy and public relations. Despite far better efforts to include interest groups in the policy formulation process of NEP II, many groups were still opposed to aspects of the plan.

As was the case in Congress, the most controversial portion of NEP II was the EMB proposal. Although Carter's public dialogue promised to maintain his commitment to the environment, the proposal to streamline development at the potential cost of environmental protections alienated Carter's environmental friends. Environmentalists were particularly concerned with the EMB proposal because it allowed for the waiver of air- and water-quality regulations. Friends of the Earth called the EMB proposal "simplistic and dangerous. They threaten to unravel the very principles of our government; government by law; equal justice . . . checks and balances, and the delegation of authority between the states and the federal government."[67]

Additionally, state- and local-government advocates such as the League of Cities and the National Governors Association opposed the EMB legislation.[68] Concern from local constituencies came because the EMB would allow the federal government to override local laws in the event that projects exceeded established timelines. Fearing the threat of a federal power grab, state and local advocates were strongly opposed to this portion of NEP II. Opposition mounted by state and local groups along with environmental interests is credited with the failure of the EMB to survive conference committee, even though the bill passed both houses of Congress in varying forms.

The synthetic fuels portion of NEP II was also unpopular among most interest groups. The success of the synfuels bill in Congress might suggest that there was significant interest group support behind it; however this was not the case. Oil companies and environmentalists alike were opposed to the bill for a list of reasons. Industry-interest groups opposed the bill on the grounds that the technology behind synfuels was premature and because they feared competition from government-owned plants. In response to industry concerns, and unwilling to let this bill die, Congress offered tax advantages to private industry to allow them to be more competitive on the open market. Environmentalists were concerned about the synfuels bill because it seemed rushed and because the health effects of a booming synfuels industry were still unknown. In spite of interest group opposition, external pressures such as the events in Iran motivated Congress to continue to pursue less dependence on foreign supply, and synthetic fuel development was the most promising alternative. Rep. Millicent Fenwick (R-NJ) said, "Voters want action on energy; they don't really care how much it costs."[69]

Finally, and intuitively, the oil industry was supportive of the deregulation of oil prices; however, they were opposed to the subsequent windfall tax designed to recover additional profits. The large producers among the oil industry argued that they needed to keep all profits resulting from the decontrol of pricing in order to compensate for profits lost under price regulation in the past and to continue to search for additional sources of crude oil.[70] Despite the opposition of the oil companies, it was clear to Congress and the American public that price decontrol would bring unprecedented profits to the oil sector. The unpopularity of the oil industry and distrust among the public made it easy for Congress to move forward with the passage of the Windfall Profits Tax.

Interest groups were more influential in the crafting of NEP II compared to NEP I. However, the climate of public opinion and external pressures from the Middle East gave Congress justification to prioritize the public over particularized interest in the passage of NEP II. The failure of the EMB bill was a success for environmental and local interest groups. Conversely, interests were less powerful than the will of the public and Congress when it came to the synfuels bill and the WPT. Overall, the greater involvement of interest groups in the planning of NEP II and the shift in events and public opinion allowed the second energy plan to be passed more easily than the first, and more closely to the original intention of the Carter Administration.

Conclusion

In late September 1980, after a long history of border disputes, and fueled by concern of regional ramifications stemming from the Iranian revolution, Iraq attacked Iran, beginning the Iran-Iraq war. In its early stages, the war removed nearly four million daily barrels of oil from the world market. This reduction in supply led Arab light oil to reach the highest price yet at $42 per barrel. These global events certainly did not help to abate the American energy crisis but rather threatened to create a third oil shock that was worse than any to date. However, two factors helped prevent a third oil shock from creating further calamity.

Consumption patterns in the United States had changed. Americans demanded less oil now than they did before the 1979 crisis, and companies had extra barrels on hand to boot. During the 1979 crisis, companies stockpiled crude oil out of fear that prices would continue to climb and that they would soon be priced-out. If the 1979 crisis was good for anything, it taught governmental agencies, the public, and industry a lesson about panic buying. The International Energy Agency called on public and private sectors to draw on their stored supplies rather than buy excessively in a fit of panic, thereby worsening the effects of reduced supply. The combination of decreased consumption and reserve oil on hand definitely helped to mitigate additional crisis and further price escalation.

The second factor that helped to stem fallout from the Iran-Iraq war was increased oil production from other countries to make up the deficit. Saudi Arabia, ever the hero when global oil supplies drop, agreed once again to ramp up its production to offset the loss of supply from Iran. Within a few days of the start of the war, the Saudis had increased production by nine hundred thousand barrels per day, roughly the equivalent of a quarter of the loss from Iran and Iraq.[71] Oil production from Norway, Mexico, Britain, and the United States had increased to a point that, when coupled with decreased demand for oil, there was really no reasonable threat. Companies were increasingly willing to dip into their stored barrels when they observed that oil and gas prices were holding steady. The third oil shock from the Iran-Iraq war failed to develop into a more serious crisis.

In an effort to stave off another energy crisis, President Carter proposed several pieces of legislation that met with mixed success. Carter's first proposal for a National Energy Plan suffered from three key factors. Carter had failed to sufficiently convince the public that the energy crisis he described was imminent. Without a real cause for concern, the public was resistant to any plans that raised prices or called for sacrifice. Additionally, the American public was suspicious of the oil industry. When talk of an oil shortage became more real, the public was quick to blame the industry for propagating a fake crisis for the sake of profit. While the public was busy blaming the oil companies for the price hike, they were not taking responsibility for their own actions or making significant changes to their consumption patterns.

Finally, Carter did not include interest groups in the drafting of NEP I, and without their support his plan was effectively doomed from the start. Interest groups would have been strong allies in helping to inform the public on the true nature of the crisis and in generating support. However, without the support of interest groups or the American public, Congress took no interest in passing the bulk of NEP I.

Carter and his administration learned from this lesson, however. When the Iranian revolution caused a dip in oil production on the global market, which manifested as an energy crisis in the United States, Carter seized the opportunity to try again. This time, the problem stream and the political stream came together to open a window through which Carter could push his comprehensive energy policy. Carter had successfully dismissed many of the charges against the oil companies for price gouging and fostering a fake energy crisis. In the cases where the oil companies were guilty, the administration took legal action, and this initiative won favor with the public. The public was tired of long lines for gas and rising prices and placed upward pressure on government to respond. Additionally, Carter did a far better job of involving the interest groups with NEP II, and many worked to move NEP II through Congress.

By the end of his term, Carter had successfully implemented significant energy reforms, facilitated in large part by the energy crisis. Among the most significant of his accomplishments was the deregulation of oil and passage of the Windfall Profits Tax that would be used to develop alternative energy sources and limit dependence on foreign-oil suppliers. The deregulation of oil helped bring prices up to global levels and to secure an incentive for continued public conservation efforts. Demonstrated by the fact that a major crisis failed to emerge after the start of the Iran-Iraq war, it was clear that American consumption patterns and national energy policy had shifted. Without the presence of a national energy crisis and significant focusing episode, windows for change remain closed and energy policy holds at the status quo. In this case study, we see again how the energy crisis cycle helped open policy windows and allowed for policy change. The crisis in Iran helped to initiate a cost increase that set off the energy crisis cycle. As expected, public opinion soured toward the oil companies, which, coupled with interest group involvement in the drafting of NEP II, facilitated sufficient momentum to implement changes. This case study also demonstrates that the success of NEP II compared to NEP I was contingent on the perceived presence of a crisis and the involvement of interest groups in drafting legislation and spreading public information. Without all of the elements of the energy crisis cycle present, policy windows are generally difficult to open, which was demonstrated here by the relative failure of NEP I.

7

The Persian Gulf War: 1990–1991

On August 2, 1990, under the leadership of Saddam Hussein, the Iraqi army invaded its neighboring state of Kuwait. This hostile activity resulted in UN sanctions against Iraq, demands for withdrawal, and an embargo against Iraqi oil, which removed about four million barrels from the international market. Although political instability in the Middle East is not historically uncommon, this event caught the immediate attention of the American public and policy-makers and prompted concern about domestic oil security. Due in large part to the previous energy crises, the United States was better prepared to withstand oil-supply disruption than ever before. In fact, because of the Strategic Petroleum Reserve (SPR) and a prompt response by Saudi Arabia to increase production and offset any loss from Iraq and Kuwait, the invasion of Kuwait should not have initiated another energy crisis in 1990 at all—but it did.

The 1990–91 energy crisis is a quintessential example of the socially constructed nature of focusing episodes. Unlike previous energy crises, the crisis of 1990–1991 occurred under a well-stocked SPR. Additionally, oil consumption in the United States had declined slightly as individual behaviors changed and alternative fuels became more common. As a result, there really should not have been a "crisis" on a comparable level following the Iraqi invasion of Kuwait in August 1990 because the United States had plenty of oil available to protect domestic markets. The Bush administration estimated that the SPR could offset imports from both Iraq and Kuwait, in their entirety, for eight hundred days before a real shortage would occur; and this fails to consider the likely reality that Saudi Arabia and other nations would increase production to offset any loss from the Persian Gulf. In nearly every way, the United States was well prepared for another energy shortage, and yet the same energy crisis cycle ensued, sparked by socially constructed concern and panic-buying resulting from tumultuous events in the Middle East.

At the time of the Persian Gulf War in August 1990, the United States consumed about seventeen million barrels of oil per day, the equivalent to over seven hundred thousand gallons. Petroleum products provided the United

States at the time with 43 percent of its energy needs, with most of the oil going toward the nation's 148 million automobiles.[1] Consistent with previous crises, imported oil accounted for almost half of our total oil consumption, and therefore the public was always at least mildly attentive to issues of foreign supply and pricing. In the month preceding the Iraqi invasion of Kuwait in August 1990, inflation-adjusted oil prices were the lowest they had been in forty years. Though energy concerns remained high on the national agenda, due especially to the *Exxon-Valdez* Alaskan oil spill in the spring of 1989, American consumers were largely content because gasoline prices continued to remain low.

The Start of the Third Energy Crisis: Iraq Invades Kuwait

A key background condition that contributed to low oil prices during the 1980s was that some member states regularly disregarded the established OPEC oil quota system and exceeded their specified production.[2] In July 1990 Iraqi President Saddam Hussein threatened an attack against OPEC nations if oil overproduction did not cease.[3] This threat was made credible when Hussein moved more than one hundred thousand troops to the border of Kuwait that same month. Hussein's self-imposed role as the rule enforcer was taken seriously among the OPEC nations, and they reached an accord in Geneva to raise oil prices by $3 to $21 per barrel.[4] In response to Iraq's move toward Kuwait, Kuwaiti Emir, Jaber Al-Ahmed Al-Jaber Al-Sabah, replaced the Kuwaiti Oil Minister, who was the central focus of Hussein's criticisms. Additionally, Kuwait decreased oil production and observed OPEC pricing standards. By mid-July, the only OPEC nation that was cheating was Iraq itself.[5]

Despite Kuwait's acts of compliance, Hussein ordered Iraqi forces to invade Kuwait on August 2, claiming that Kuwait was illegally slant-drilling petroleum out of Iraq from across the border. Within hours of the invasion, Kuwaiti and US delegations requested a meeting of the UN Security Council. The council passed Resolution 660, condemning the invasion and demanding a withdrawal of Iraqi troops. Additionally, the United States ordered the 82nd Airborne Division and several fighter squadrons to Saudi Arabia to protect the region from strategically placed Iraqi troops near lightly guarded Saudi oil fields. The movement of troops into Saudi Arabia on August 7, 1990 marked the beginning of US "Operation Desert Shield." Subsequently, the US House and Senate passed similar resolutions in early October supporting US military deployment in the Gulf; however, neither chamber authorized future use of force.[6] In the weeks following, a long series of UN Security Council and Arab League resolutions were passed regarding the conflict. One of the most important among these resolutions was

Resolution 678 passed on November 29, which gave Iraq a withdrawal deadline of January 15, 1991 and authorized the use of force to expel Iraq through all necessary means to uphold and implement Resolution 660. Additionally, the UN established economic sanctions against Iraq backed heavily by the United States.

Iraq's tactics were initially seen as an intimidation strategy to ensure higher global oil prices. However, it became apparent that Hussein had much larger plans. Hussein not only meant to intimidate but wished to invade and annex Kuwait as well. Iraqi control over Kuwait would translate to greater oil-resource power and make Iraq the regional hegemon in the Middle East. While the world may have initially miscalculated Hussein's end game, Hussein seriously miscalculated the shift in world political order and the coalition that would rise in opposition to his actions. While the debate over the motivation of the United States' and other Western nations' intervention was widespread, there is no denying "oil was a fundamental role in the crisis—not just in cost control—but as a critical element in the world balance of power."[7] Even Iraq's ally, the Soviet Union, which was on its final descent and developing friendlier diplomatic relations with the United States and the West, called for a halt to international arms exports to Iraq the day after the Iraqi invasion of Kuwait.[8]

Between August and October 1990, the price of crude oil rose 118 percent on world markets.[9] In the days and months following the Iraqi invasion, oil prices immediately soared upward from $16 per barrel to $40 per barrel, costing consumers up to an extra 14¢ per gallon for gasoline. Immediately, cries of outrage were heard from citizens, the media, and Congress against the both the government's lack of a comprehensive energy policy and the oil company's price hikes. Energy policy was once again in the news and at the top of the congressional agenda.

Unlike previous oil crises, the American public did not experience any brownouts or long lines at the gas stations. In fact, the government had pumped six hundred million barrels of oil into its Strategic Petroleum Reserve, and most other major oil-consuming nations had built up their own emergency stockpiles as well.[10] Additionally, other OPEC nations, such as Venezuela and Saudi Arabia, increased their production in the wake of the crisis to help offset any production shortfalls from Iraq or Kuwait. More importantly, OPEC's share of world production was only 38 percent in 1990, compared with 56 percent in 1973.[11] All of these factors helped to offset any real shortfall and to cushion the blow to the American consumer during the present crisis.

Even though the United States was better prepared for this energy crisis than any other that preceded it, the looming threat of an uncertain oil future sent the energy markets into what seems to be an unavoidable panic. The phrase "energy crisis" reappeared in American newspapers.[12] Fear and speculation resulted in stockpiling of additional supplies, and the sudden, high demand for oil drove up prices. Again, anticipated supply loss, this time from an embargo on Iraqi oil, market speculation driven by fear, and anticipation of conflict colluded to cause a spike in prices similar to previous crises. In October of 1990, when Hussein threatened to destroy petroleum supply systems, prices on future markets more than doubled to $40 per barrel. Bruce Beaubouef writes, "The supply disruption had not reached the market as yet, but purchasers were willing to pay higher prices than before to ensure supply."[13]

In January of 1991, as the UN deadline for Iraq to withdraw from Kuwait passed, the United States and its allies launched a counterattack. The Persian Gulf War was short lived due to the US led coalition's dominance in missile and warplane strikes. While the initial US coalition air strikes briefly caused a spike in the price of oil to $30 per barrel, within a few days it had dropped to $20 per barrel. The Iraqi army, the third largest and most powerful in the world, collapsed before the combined might of the United States and its allies.[14] By the end of February 1991, Saddam Hussein ordered his troops out of Kuwait. However, before they surrendered, the Iraqi army damaged 710 Kuwaiti oil wells, setting fire to 610 of them and releasing 4.6 million barrels of oil per day totaling over 1.5 billion barrels of oil by the time the last well was extinguished.[15]

The Kuwaiti oil fires remain the largest oil spill in human history. For perspective, the recent Deepwater Horizon oil spill in the Gulf of Mexico in 2010 poured out an estimated 4.9 million barrels over the course of eighty-seven days, slightly more than the amount of oil burned in just one day in 1990 in Kuwait. The Kuwaiti oil fires raged on for over nine months and required technologically advanced firefighting efforts from multiple countries and organizations before the last well was extinguished in November 1990. Even after most of the oil combusted, 25 to 40 million barrels remained strewn about the Kuwaiti land and in the Persian Gulf, requiring a massive international cleanup effort.

Amid the 1990 Gulf War, the energy-crisis cycle played out in full. The Iraqi invasion of Kuwait escalated concern about Middle Eastern politics and energy supply, creating for Americans the perception of an energy crisis, and therefore citizens acted as though it crisis was indeed real. As with previous energy crises, Americans were fueled by concern about future energy security and started panic-buying to stock up on gas and oil out of fear that prices would continue to climb and supplies would fall. The public grew outraged at the rising costs of oil and gas and started to call on the government to investigate the oil industry for price gouging and to pass legislation easing the price crunch at the pumps. Specifically, heavy debate ensued around the intention and use of the Strategic Petroleum Reserve: should it be used to ease prices, or should it only be used in the presence of a true oil shortage (which never really occurred for the United States during this crisis)? Nevertheless, the 1990–1991 energy-crisis cycle helped to open a policy window, which resulted in legislation that helped to clarify the SPR as a tool to protect consumers by broadening the identified conditions under which the SPR should be drawn down.

Public Reaction to the Third Energy Crisis

A key element in the energy-crisis cycle is that an energy crisis must exist in the eyes of the public in order for the energy-crisis cycle to occur. While there may be an energy crisis according to various experts and government officials, if the public perception of the energy crisis is not as severe, then in effect there is no actual crisis—at least from a policy standpoint. Since 1978, a number of surveys showed that the "perceived seriousness [of the national energy situation] has remained somewhat high."[16] More importantly, a Gallup poll taken toward the end of the Gulf War in 1991 revealed that 84 percent of Americans judged the energy situation as "very serious" or "fairly serious" compared to only 73 percent in August of 1990.[17] In addition, 66 percent of Americans did not believe that oil prices would drop by the next year.[18] This is a strong indicator for just how serious and long-term the public believed the situation was. Following Hussein's invasion of Kuwait, oil prices started to rise as public concern started to grow. In the months that followed, public opinion about the severity of the energy problem also intensified. It is safe to say that there was a perceived crisis among the American people.

The public's reaction to rising gas prices was immediate and similar to the previous crises. In spite of the evidence that only 6 percent of Americans could correctly identify how much oil the United States imported in 1990, the public still held strong opinions about the effects of the crises once it occurred.[19] In general, the oil industry is not highly trusted among the American public: "The seeds for this mistrust seem to have been planted during the mid to late seventies, when the oil embargo strained the adaptive capacity of the nation's oil production and delivery infrastructure."[20] Since the 1970s or perhaps even earlier, privately owned oil companies have lost their unique strength, but they still have a strong impact because of their sheer size and wealth.[21] However, oil companies still face intense "scrutiny, suspicion, and mistrust."[22] Polls show that in 1988 slightly over 20 percent of Americans found oil companies "moderately to highly favorable," but by 1990 only slightly over 10 percent of Americans held the same opinion.[23]

The ongoing distrust of oil companies is exacerbated when oil prices rise and lack of trust translates into outright blame for oil crises. One American, Bill Boehmer of St. Louis, Missouri, expressed such concerns to his local paper when asked about the price of gasoline: "This is just a rip off . . . plain old price gouging."[24] Another outraged consumer stated, "It rankles most of us who realize the cost of that gasoline we're buying at the pump now really hasn't been affected [by the invasion]."[25] Similar sentiments were held by a majority of Americans during this time; a Harris Poll revealed that 86 percent believed that oil companies deliberately tried to overcharge the American motorist after Iraq invaded Kuwait.[26]

The results of these polls are similar to the trends across all energy crises. The American public is quick to blame the oil industry for exacerbating the high prices at the pump. In turn, media headlines such as "Fight Hits the Home Front, Gas Prices Strike Well of Outrage" drove home the public's distrust of oil companies as well.[27] It is easier to report isolated events than to place current circumstances in the broader context of foreign affairs and the overall oil industry, and as a result there is generally more negative media attention put on oil companies.[28] Most Americans do not have a good understanding of what oil profits actually are, as they often confuse oil markups with profits.[29] Oil companies attempt to fight negative exposure through public relations efforts; however, such efforts are often futile because they are assumed to be motivated by the companies' own self-interest.[30]

While oil companies and their advocates were blaming the Iraqi invasion of Kuwait and the unpredictable volatility of the oil market for increased gas prices, consumer groups were quick to point out the weakness in such an argument. Consumer groups argued that the current gasoline supply was produced "weeks before the invasion and that by selling at higher prices, gasoline wholesalers and retailers were using the political upheaval as an excuse and to reap unconscionable profits."[31] One consumer group, Citizens Actions, charged that the price hikes were blatant acts of economic aggression and urged motorists to identify and boycott gas stations with the highest prices.[32] Messages from the consumer activist groups resonated with the public; just days after Iraq invaded Kuwait, 86 percent answered "yes" when asked, "Do you feel that the oil suppliers are just using the situation in the Middle East to make more money?"[33]

The public holds strong opinions about government regulation over oil supply and oil prices—particularly when prices are high; the higher the price of gasoline, the more respondents call for greater regulation.[34] While the American public learned in the past that market forces would balance the prices of oil eventually, when crises hit that lesson is quickly forgotten. Compared to 1988, the percentage of respondents who believed that there was not enough government regulation of oil and gasoline pricing rose by 25 percent, marking the highest point of public concern in this arena since 1980.[35] A Harris Poll in 1990 also shows that 60 percent of Americans were in favor of the federal government creating a government-owned and operated oil corporation to keep the private oil companies honest in their pricing and operations.[36] Such opinions are not as strong during non-crisis years; thus, in times of crises it is hard for politicians not to intervene.[37]

The public also begins to pay more attention to energy sources outside of petroleum when oil prices spike. Public acceptance of coal, the third most-used energy source falling slightly under natural gas, spiked between 1990 and 1991. Perhaps even more significant is the increased acceptance of nuclear power among the public. Since the late seventies, nuclear power had very low approval rates due to the perception of its high risks based on events such as the Three Mile Island partial nuclear meltdown. However, during crisis years, nuclear power tends to receive a slight reprieve from its infamy. In a Cambridge poll, the percentage of Americans who agreed with the statement, "We should use the nuclear plants we have now, and build more nuclear plants," increased nine points between May 1990 and November 1990 (24 percent and 33 percent respectively). This is quite a dramatic increase in just a six-month period. The effects of the Iraq invasion in Kuwait and the impending US military intervention can partially explain this increase. Figure 7.1 shows the pointed surge in public concern about all topics that fall broadly under the topic of "energy" surrounding the invasion of Kuwait in 1990.

Among the possible solutions to the problem of rising prices that was garnering increasing public attention was to draw down on the SPR to increase oil supply and lower costs. The SPR was established to protect domestic markets from oil crises such as these, but the conditions under which the SPR was to be used to offset market fluctuations were still unclear. The crisis the public perceived was largely constructed out of concern and insecurity combined with rising prices, not an actual loss in oil supply. Assistant Energy Secretary for International

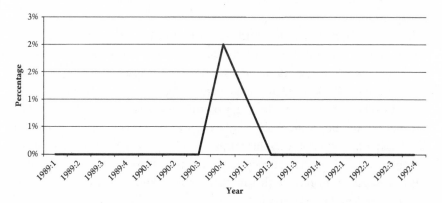

Figure 7.1 Quarterly Proportion of Respondents Who Identify "Energy" as "Most Important Problem," 1989-1992.

The data used here were originally collected by Frank R. Baumgartner and Bryan D. Jones, with the support of National Science Foundation grant numbers SBR 9320922 and 0111611, and were distributed through the Department of Government at the University of Texas at Austin. Neither NSF nor the original collectors of the data bear any responsibility for the analysis reported here.

Affairs, John J. Easton, testified in front of the House Subcommittee on Energy and Power that while he believed the current crisis would qualify for a drawdown under the 1975 Energy Policy and Conservation Act requirements, he added that "presently, there is not a significant shortfall of crude on the market."[38] Drawing down on the SPR and pushing supply into the market at the beginning of the crisis could help to avoid a deeper crisis in the long-term. However, the Bush Administration was reluctant to deploy an early-use strategy, as many within the administration argued against using it early without a significant reduction in supply.

Government Response: The George H. W. Bush Administration

Prior to Iraq's invasion of Kuwait, President Bush requested a national energy strategy from the Department of Energy in the summer of 1990. However, the events in Iraq and Kuwait altered the sense of urgency and strategy of the developing plan. With growing pressure from Congress and the public for the president to take action to help assuage the economic pressures of high-energy prices, Bush was quick to respond to the issue. In an address before a joint session of the Congress on September 11, 1990, Bush laid out the steps that needed to be taken to stabilize oil prices and reduce the nation's economic and political vulnerability due to national dependence on foreign oil. Bush's proposal focused heavily on promoting domestic development and growth through "growth-oriented tax measures," including extending incentives for research and experimentation and "creating incentives for the creation of enterprise zones and initiatives to encourage more domestic drilling."[39]

The Bush Administration's short-term solution to the energy crisis rested largely on steps to expand oil and gas production and on conservation rather than using reserves held in the SPR to increase supply. Taking a pro-development position, President Bush called on Congress to create initiatives to encourage more domestic oil exploration and drilling, particularly in Alaska.[40] While the call for research and development of alternative energy was not completely ignored by the President, it was not a significant part of his agenda. Even though various members of Congress had already requested the release of oil from the SPR, Bush was hesitant to rely on that method while acknowledging that it was an option if the "conditions warrant."[41]

The president's decision to put off use of the SPR raised a debate about the function and use of the SPR more generally. While the Bush Administration opted not to engage in an early drawdown of the reserve, many in Congress opposed this tactic. On August 7, 1990, House Subcommittee on Energy and Power Chairman Philip Sharp (D-IN) said, "We have spent $15 billion of the taxpayers' money to buy an insurance policy called the Strategic Petroleum Reserve. . . . Now is the time to use it."[42] However, many in and around the executive administration viewed early use of the SPR as an unnecessary attempt to influence oil prices and intervene in the market. In a mid-September briefing, Bush stated, "You're seeing the fluctuation driven not by market forces, not by supply and demand today, but by speculation as to what it might be in the future, and I just don't think that that would entirely be offset by an SPR drawdown."[43]

Congress became increasingly frustrated with the Bush Administration's failure to immediately lower domestic oil and gas prices and quickly voted to expand SPR drawdown authority. It was believed that according to the 1975 Energy Policy and Conservation Act (EPCA) that the SPR could only be released with presidential approval and in instances where there was a severe energy supply interruption or to meet US obligations under the International Energy Program. However, with swift and unanimous Congressional approval, Congress passed amendments to the EPCA, which widened appropriate drawdown circumstances to include domestic and international supply disruptions, regional disturbances in supply, and in advance of a suspected oil supply disruption. Though Bush was not pleased with the legislation, which helped to facilitate non-emergency drawdowns to help correct steep market fluctuations, he signed the EPCA amendments into law on September 15, 1990.

It is worth noting that this is clearly a case of Congress and the president responding to public opinion long after the Iraqi invasion that started this crisis. As we argued in chapter 2, public opinion plays a role throughout a focusing episode, not just in the beginning by drawing attention to an issue. Here we see sustained public concern forcing specific policy changes that otherwise would have failed to garner the attention of Congress and approval of the president.

While increasing public concern and media attention brought the need for action on energy policy to the forefront, the administration continued to delay sending an energy proposal to Congress. There were several reasons for the delay, but a large part was the uncertainty of the situation. A statement made by Professor Henry Lee of Harvard's Kennedy School of Government summarized the situation this administration was facing: "We are going to have a very different oil regime in the world after this war, and I'm not sure we know what this implies for U.S. energy policy."[44] From the political perspective, Senator Gore issued a strong statement condemning the Bush administrations delay, stating:

[The delay] is an attempt to save Mr. Bush the embarrassment of releasing an energy strategy that doesn't do very much about conservation and renewable energy while Washington is the site of the first rounds of international talks on a try to reduce global warming. The administration is ducking the hard decisions on energy and the environment.

They are engaged in a shell game, pretending not to act while behind
the scenes preventing action, even by others.[45]

President Bush released his long-awaited National Energy Strategy on February
19, 1991. Free-market advocates in the administration were successful in keeping
measures that sought to increase domestic production, including streamlining
licensing procedures from nuclear and electricity plants and drilling in ANWR.
The conservation measures, which were only a small part of the overall proposal,
required private fleets to acquire alternative-fuel vehicles, and efficiency rebates for
consumers were only a small portion of the overall proposal. Environmentalists
immediately criticized the plan, calling it the "Drain America First" policy.[46]
Democrat Philip Sharp of Indiana and chairman of the House Subcommittee
on Energy and Power said the plan was "seriously flawed" because it lacked more
aggressive steps to promote conservation and renewable energy sources. Members
from coal-producing states were also disappointed in the lack of funding for developing "clean coal" technologies. An editorial in the Washington Post read, "Just
Tinkering with Energy; Bush's plan avoids the tough steps."[47]

However, not everybody reacted negatively to the administration's plan.
Several members of Congress found it encouraging seeing a Republican administration put forth a comprehensive energy plan.[48] Senator Bennett Johnston and
Senator Malcolm Wallop's legislation, proposed roughly at the same time, had
many similarities to the administration's plan only it contained additional conservation efforts that would help it pass the Senate. On the House side, Energy
and Commerce Chairman John D. Dingell (D-MI) called it a "good beginning."[49]

As the year progressed, President Bush moved beyond pushing his own
agenda through Congress and endorsed the Johnston-Wallop bill. The legislation had many similarities to the administration's agenda. President Bush held a
pep rally to push for its enactment in July 1991, stating that the "energy strategy
'relies on the magic of the marketplace,' rather than on mandates to do most of
the work."[50] At the time of the endorsement, the bill did not require higher gasoline mileage. Johnston made it clear that the mileage issue would be at play and
would tie it to arctic drilling. During the "endorsement pep rally," Bush stated
that he would veto the bill if it did not open up drilling in ANWR.[51]

Congressional Response

When an energy crisis occurs, such as it did in the summer of 1990, the number
of hearings held in Congress sharply increases as well. As the Iraq-Kuwait war
developed during the summer of 1990, politicians were preparing to defend
their constituents' economic stability as well as their own political positions.

Though Congress was in recess, committees in both chambers conducted numerous hearings concerning the prices of oil and energy policy. As the crisis faded and oil prices dropped, so did the number of hearings. There were thirty-nine energy-related hearings in both 1990 and 1991 (figure 3). This is compared to only twenty-two in 1989 and a decline to only nineteen hearings by 1992, when oil prices had dropped and stabilized. Congress members generally react swiftly to energy crises and specifically to their constituents' anger over the rising oil prices. The following sections describe in detail the actions of House and Senate during the 1990–91 energy crisis.

Senate Action

Consistent with previous energy crises and with the energy crisis cycle, the public reliably puts blame for high gas prices on the oil companies, who the public perceives to be unscrupulous and looking to profit from the public during a crisis. Also consistent with the energy crisis cycle, members of Congress must respond to the concern of their constituents. During the summer of 1990, Congressional Democrats, led by Senator Joseph Lieberman, urged President Bush to act against price gouging by the oil companies. Just a day before the oil executives were summoned to Congress, the National Associations of Attorneys General and the Department of Justice's Antitrust Division announced investigations into oil companies' pricing decisions. While most of the criticism against the oil companies came from the Democratic members, the Republicans also voiced their suspicions. Senator Robert Dole asked that the DOJ begin antitrust investigations and suggested that Congress might "enact a windfall profits tax on oil, comparable to what was levied in the 1970s."[52] Senator John Kerry implied that the American public was being scammed by the oil industry, saying, "Someone is making a killing," during one of the hastily arranged hearings.[53]

Members of Congress called for a release of some of the oil stockpiled in the Strategic Petroleum Reserve to alleviate prices. President Bush was urged by Congress to tap into the nation's never-used strategic oil reserves led by Representative Sharp (D-IN), the chairman of the House Subcommittee on Energy and Power. Bills were introduced to increase the reserve to one billion barrels, compared to the 750-barrel cap proposed by the Bush administration earlier in the year. The DOE, which was in the midst of preparing a comprehensive energy plan for the administration, cautioned Congress that they would advise the President to veto any bill that expanded the SPR;[54] this did not thwart efforts in Congress to expand the reserve, however. Under strong pressure from the American public to alleviate high gas prices and prevent further increases, Congress passed the EPCA amendments on September 13 and sent them to

Bush to sign, which he did under duress from the public, on September 15. This was the first of several moves Congress would make in the next eighteen months to address the energy crisis.

While Congress previously had several energy proposals at varying stages of progress, the crisis in Iraq brought the issue to the forefront of the national agenda. However, the 101st Congress did little more than pass a small number of targeted energy-related proposals and left the debate over a comprehensive national energy policy for 1991. With a midterm election in progress, the Gulf crisis did little to raise the debate beyond sharpened rhetoric. The debate over energy policy revolved around two main arguments for how to reduce US dependence on foreign oil. Pro-industry advocates argued for increased exploration of domestic oil sources, while environmentalists contended that the crisis gave reason for the United States to wean itself from fossil fuels through alternative energy sources and conservation.[55] The most significant change in energy policy during the 101st Congress was the adoption of a bill that expanded the SPR to one billion barrels and created a second reserve for refined products. Prior to the crisis, President Bush threatened to use a veto to stop any such legislation from becoming law. However, in the wake of the rising gas prices and increased public awareness, Bush was forced to accept the measure despite the fact that he found it too "expensive and unnecessary."[56] Again, public opinion was heard and obeyed. The president felt that his options were limited by the people's demands.

In a surprise announcement, just two weeks after signing the bill, President Bush stated that he would be releasing five million barrels of oil from the SPR as a "test sale" of SPR crude to demonstrate readiness of the SPR. This did not stave off the already-mounting pressure from members of Congress and the Department of Energy Secretary Watkins, who argued that fifteen million barrels was the amount necessary to stabilize gas prices. However, the measure faced strong opposition from Office of Management and Budget Director Richard Darman, Treasury Secretary Nicholas Brady, and National Security Advisor Brent Scrowcroft. On September 28 the House passed HR 5731, mandating the President to sell off an additional ten million barrels of oil. The Senate Energy Committee approved the House passed bill on October 11; however the full Senate did not take the measure up before adjournment, and the bill was delayed until the next Congress.

The Iraqi invasion of Kuwait served to bolster support of the Motor Vehicle Fuel Efficiency Act (S. 1224), which had been previously dropped from the Clean Air Act package to be considered separately. Heavy lobbying from the automotive industry and the Bush Administration prevented the Senate's attempt to raise federal fuel efficiency standards prior to the crisis. Lobbyists for the auto industry argued that the measure would require further downsizing, which would lead to small, unsafe cars. During a September 13 hearing, both Energy Secretary James D. Watkins and Transportation Secretary Samuel K. Skinner told the committee that they would recommend a veto on the grounds that the legislation was "not economically sound or technically feasible."[57] On September 25, eleven senators—including eight Republicans—switched their votes on the motion to cut off debate on the bill from the previous cloture vote invoked on the motion to proceed to the bill eleven days earlier, killing the energy-conservation bill. In this particular instance, the environmentalists lost, and the ramifications were felt throughout the environmental movement. Dan Becker of the Sierra Club said, "Today the gas guzzler won, and they're popping the champagne corks in Saddam Hussein's palace."[58]

The Persian Gulf Crisis also strengthened the debate over domestic oil drilling, particularly in the Arctic National Wildlife Reserve (ANWR) and offshore. President Bush announced an offshore drilling ban off much of the East and West coasts in June of 1990 in hopes that Congress would allow drilling elsewhere. However, Congress used the annual Interior spending bill to not only continue but also expand the existing moratorium against drilling offshore in the wake of increasing pressure from other state lawmakers.[59] Representative W. J. "Billy" Tauzin (D-LA), a pro-development oil-statesman, spoke out against the moratoriums using an argument often invoked by the other side: "The environmental movement is still too strong. It is going to take long lines again; it's going to take shortages; it's going to take people getting cold."[60] Opening up the ANWR for oil drilling was what the Bush Administration was seeking in exchange for supporting offshore drilling bans.

While the crisis did increase support for drilling in ANWR, on October 11 the Senate Energy Committee decided against an end-of-the-session bid to persuade Congress to open up the wilderness area. Representative Frank H. Murkowski wanted the committee to include the ANWR-drilling bill (S. 684) in the deficit-cutting reconciliation bill. However, he retreated when it was made clear that both Senate and House Democratic leaders would oppose the move. Senator Richard Bryan (D-NV) also introduced legislation (S. 279) to increase CAFE levels by 20 percent in 1995 and 40 percent in 2001. The Senate killed the measure by filibuster on September 25 after heavy industry lobbying. While there was increased support for energy legislation, there was also strong opposition on both sides, and a midterm election that prevented such controversial legislation from being quickly decided upon even during a crisis.

There was some significant legislation passed during the 101st Congress despite the otherwise rhetorical and slow debate. Legislation to refine national energy conservation goals and promote state energy-efficiency programs was passed by both the chambers in the first week of October and signed into law by President Bush October 18. The measure (S. 247) encouraged the efficient use of available energy sources by updating and widening the scope of the Department of Energy programs that funded state energy-conservation initiatives. Supporters viewed the bill as a stepping-stone in helping the nation become less dependent on foreign oil, a situation made more precarious by the Persian Gulf Crisis.[61] In late October, both chambers approved a bill that established an Energy Department research program to develop hydrogen as an alternative fuel. The bill was named after a late Senator, Spark M. Matsunaga, whose fifteen-year push for alternative energy research had fallen on deaf ears.

The beginning of the 102nd Congress in January of 1991 was marked by the looming deadline for Iraq to pull out of Kuwait. As the war against Iraq appeared ever more certain, it created an inexorable push in Congress to write a new comprehensive energy bill. In the Senate Energy and Natural Resources Committee, Chairman J. Bennett Johnston (D-LA) and ranking minority member Malcolm Wallop (R-WY) introduced sweeping legislation (S. 1220) that sought to create a broad coalition for energy legislation by including the top energy producers (those with access to ANWR) along with a proposal to increase CAFE standards. Johnston proposed to pay for a host of energy conservation and research programs with federal revenues from ANWR drilling.

The Gulf War was brief and drawing to a close in February of 1991. In light of waning public concern and Bush's impending national energy proposal, Johnston put his committee on a hectic back-to-back hearing schedule through March in order to advance his bill. The debate, much to the surprise of many, moved quickly despite heavy disagreements. Johnston, mindful of the fading attention to energy policy after the Gulf War, quickly began the revision process during the week of April 15. In hopes of streamlining the process even further, the committee provided DOE officials with a table at the front of the committee room where markups took place. Deputy Energy Secretary W. Henson Moore attended most of the sessions and was often called upon to clarify administration policy or react to proposals.[62]

Despite the bipartisan legislative efforts of Johnston and Wallop, committee members on both sides of the party line opposed various aspects of the bill. Democrats in the committee opposed many of the provisions, especially the opening of ANWR to oil and gas drilling and easing regulation of the nuclear industry.[63] The bill also faced competition from proposals that ranked higher with environmental groups, including Senator Bryan's CAFE legislation (S. 279), which was reintroduced on the same day as the Johnston-Wallop bill. Environmentalist lawmakers and lobbyists preferred Senator

Bryon's higher standard of 40-mpg, which had been defeated during the previous Congressional session.

Other lobbying efforts also helped stall the legislation. The Mendocino Environmental Center called for the public action against the legislation.

The Sierra Club spearheaded a huge attack on the proposition to open up ANWR to drilling. Republicans on the committee obstructed Johnston's attempts to add a proposal that would impose CAFE standards of 34 mpg by 2001. Facing opposition from pro-industry and pro-environment interests, Johnston offered a compromise on May 14 to set mileage targets to 30.2 mpg for 1996 and 37 mpg for 2001. Johnston's hope to find a middle ground and compete with Senator Bryan's bill was defeated as both sides once again could not reach a compromise. Bryan's bill also faced heavy opposition and found difficulty getting past Representative John Dingell (D-MI), chairman of the House Energy and Commerce Committee and an ally of the Detroit auto industry.

The proposal in the Johnston-Wallop bill to open ANWR to oil and gas drilling faced heated debate from both sides. Senator Tim Wirth (D-CO) lost his battle in committee to strike the ANWR drilling measure from the bill in an 8–11 vote. Senator John Seymour (R-CA), who was the deciding swing vote, backed the drilling proposal, explaining that unlike Californians, many Alaskans were eager to open ANWR to oil and gas exploration. The committee also upheld offshore drilling bans in California and New Jersey until 2000.

Several other aspects of the bill faced significant opposition as well. A proposal that required importers to set aside 9 percent of imports to fill the SPR faced heavy opposition. Subsequently, the bill was amended during markup to reduce the import set-aside requirement to only 3 percent. The nuclear power provision and ensuing debate centered on the streamlining of licensing for plant operations. The loudest opposition was voiced by a freshman senator, Paul Wellstone (D-MN), who spoke against his chairman in defense of environmental interests. Senator Wellstone's proposal to delete one-step licensing and ensure that states could regulate low-level radioactive waste was defeated in the committee. Considerable debate also centered on streamlining licensing of hydroelectric plants, including federal environmental reviews and state regulation. Once again, Wellstone objected stating that the measure would "gut the Clean Air Act."[64] Outside of hydroelectric power, renewable energy proposals went largely unchallenged as committee members agreed to boost energy production through authorizing millions in federal research to promote renewable energy sources.

After much debate and dramatic final markup, the Johnston-Wallop bill was reported to the Senate floor on May 23, 1991. The end result was a mixed bag: an import set-aside was included but at a much lower percentage, offshore drilling was banned but opening ANWR was included, CAFE standards were set aside while alternative-fuel vehicle requirements for federal agencies remained. In addition, the committee amended the bill to include deregulation of the wholesale electricity business.

Environmental groups found something to dislike in almost every title of the bill, especially aid to coal and nuclear industries and ease of hydroelectric dam regulations. Even the pro-environment measures were criticized for not going far enough. While the ambitious Johnston-Wallop bill moved quickly through the Energy and Natural Resources Committee, that was not the last of the markup. The bill faced additional challenges and changes as it moved through two other Senate committees—Environment and Public Works and Commerce, Science, and Transportation—both of which planned to make major changes in the legislation.

Over the summer of 1991, both sides of the aisle waged publicity campaigns on the bill even though floor action seemed unlikely and distant.[65] In late June, eight senators, represented in person or through a press release, used the Senate TV gallery to attack the bill. On the offensive, Johnston maintained that the bill provided ample conservation and efficiency measures sought by environmentalists. In July, while speaking to a group of energy executives, President Bush praised the Senate bill and urged it to go to the floor after the August recess. However, three freshman senators, in opposition to ANWR oil and gas drilling, threatened a filibuster. The threat led Majority Leader George J. Mitchell to delay scheduling on the floor until late 1991. When the bill hit the floor, the three freshman senators—Richard Bryan (D-NV), Paul Wellstone (D-MN), and Tim Wirth (D-CO)—led the filibuster as promised. On November 1, the Senate fell ten votes short of being able to invoke cloture, officially halting the legislation from further action. Johnston, while being dealt the blow, talked of reintroducing the energy legislation after the New Year.

The debate over fuel mileage standards was far from over as well. One day after Johnston's bill was defeated, Senator Bryan declared plans to push ahead with the legislation he sponsored by the beginning of the year.[66] An onslaught of new testimony and lobbying softened some support for Bryan's proposal, leading many to prefer Johnston's bill that did not prescribe specific mileage standards but rather directed the Transportation secretary to set standards and increase them if feasible.[67] The Persian Gulf War provided momentum for comprehensive energy-policy reform, but competing interests prevented much change from the status quo. Now nine months after the end of the Gulf War, impetus gave way to the customary regional and ideological gridlock. Prices were too low by this time to cause great public concern or pressure on lawmakers.

As promised, Senator Johnston resurrected the energy legislation that was denied at the end of 1991 via filibuster. This time around, however, Johnston jettisoned two of the bills more controversial elements—opening drilling in ANWR and forcing higher CAFE standards on domestic automakers—in hopes of ushering it past the opposition. The main thrust behind the bill was reliance on pro-development measures such as speeding up construction on nuclear power plants and natural gas pipelines, along with pro-environment measures such as mandating the use of non-gasoline fuels and other energy-efficient technologies.[68] Senator Johnston felt totally confident that the bill would pass this time around. While a major hurdle was cleared on February 4, with a Senate vote of 90–5 to begin working on the bill, there were still major criticisms regarding the bill's provisions. In the first week of debate, pro-environment senators sought to strengthen the conservation and energy-efficiency sections, and to restore certain environmental protections relating to hydroelectric power plants and natural gas pipelines. Such measures were approved by the Senate, which also overwhelmingly approved an amendment by Al Gore (D-TN) urging the administration to speed up the phase-out of ozone-depleting chemicals.[69]

Pro-development senators agreed to drop drilling in ANWR in order to get the bill moving forward. However, drilling advocates "vowed to try to attach the proposal to other legislation, probably a jobs bill."[70] Environmentalists also lost key battles to soften provisions aimed at boosting nuclear power and to provide more support for non-gasoline transportation fuels—both of these issues could have jeopardized Republican support for the bill and drew strong opposition from the administration.[71] The Bush Administration won a key battle through the Senate when senators rejected efforts to abandon some streamlining of federal licensing of nuclear power plants. Despite some hefty opposition to the provision from both sides, the Senate overwhelmingly passed the energy bill on February 19 with a 94–4 vote. The significant support for the bill largely had to do with the fact that it no longer included the most controversial provisions of the bill introduced during the previous Congress, such as oil drilling in ANWR, increasing gas mileage standards, and easing power-plant emission standards. Public cries for reform and relief subsided after the end of the Gulf War, and without strong public opinion, these significant policy reforms lacked the necessary support. While both sides of the debate lost some battles, the environmentalists suffered the heaviest defeat. Since it was an election year, many representatives found it helpful to their campaigns to pass legislation for purpose of credit-claiming.

House Action

Simultaneously, the House of Representatives also developed energy legislation; however, it proceeded at a much slower and less controversial course. Much of this had to do with the institutional characteristics of the House and the fact that the legislation was split up between nine different committees. Early in 1991, Representative Philip R. Sharp (D-IN), chairman of the Energy and Commerce Subcommittee, introduced five bills concerning energy issues and promised to offer a more comprehensive proposal. However, Sharp did not move quickly enough, conducting hearings at a methodical pace, and House Republicans presented a wide-ranging energy bill in March (HR 1543). As Representative Norman Lent (R-NY) and members of a House Republican energy task force unveiled their bill in late March, Lent goaded Democrats: "Here's our comprehensive bill; where's yours?"[72] The Republican-authored legislation resembled the Johnston-Wallop bill and the Bush administration's proposal, but aimed to satisfy a broader spectrum of interests.

The measure contained elements aimed at pleasing both environmental and pro-industry interests, such as tax credits for energy produced from renewable sources and tax incentives for domestic oil and natural gas producers. Taunts and competitive bills from the Republican side of the House showed just how much the issue was still very politically charged even as time lapsed. The House Democrats were in a tough place: trying to produce a bill to the liking of the environmentalist contingency would come at an electoral cost to the party and face presidential veto. Democratic members from oil-producing states went as far as to criticize the administration's and the Senate's plans for not doing enough to promote oil and gas production. Many Democrats were also unwilling to face political fallout by supporting major energy taxes to boost prices.[73]

As promised, however, Representative Sharp developed an expansive energy bill in his Energy and Commerce Subcommittee over the summer and fall of 1991. Sharp's legislation contained many of the same proposals as the Johnston-Wallop bill but gave greater consideration to environmental and consumer groups. Sharp circumvented the highly contested issues, such as gas mileage standards and drilling in ANWR, in hopes of successfully pushing through the legislation. At the close of 1991, Sharp's bill was on track to go to the full Energy Committee at the beginning of the year.

Representative Leon Panetta (D-CA) also introduced an energy bill (HR 560) that mandated higher fuel-efficiency standards, established a floor price for domestic oil, and a contingency gas tax to counter price drops and increase federal spending on conservation grants and research into alternative fuels. At this time, hearings were already underway in the Senate Energy Subcommittee of the Energy and Power Committee under Chairman Phillip Sharp.

The House finally passed a bill equivalent to the Senate's three months later. The bill passed through nine committees before being brought to the floor on May 27, where it passed 381–37. The conference committee process delayed the final passage of the bill until October. During conference committee, President Bush threatened to veto the bill unless offshore drilling was expanded and nuclear power regulations were eased. However, on October 24, President Bush signed the Energy Policy Act of 1992, finalizing what turned out to be an eighteen-month process. The final legislation looked dramatically different than what the original sponsors had intended. Much of this had to do with the legislative process in general, which tends to be deliberative and intentionally conflict-ridden. However, much of the reason the energy bill did not end up being as comprehensive and effective as originally intended is that the energy crisis and price hikes at the pump had waned long before the passage, and with that so did the media and public attention to the issue. When Congress members are not pressured by their constituents to make a significant change, the end result is much closer to the status quo, especially during an election year where accountability will matter even more.

Interest Group Activity in Response to the Third Energy Crisis

Times of energy crisis not only prompt calls for action from politicians and the public; other political actors, such as interest groups, use the window of opportunity to advance their agendas as well. Crises tend to bring out both sides of the given argument. Consumer and environmental groups called for investigations and conservation, while development groups placed the need for domestic drilling back onto the agenda. Major oil companies and the state of Alaska had high-powered lobbying campaigns to promote drilling in ANWR. Both sides had a heavy presence on the Hill, in the media, and in advertisements.

Interest groups also partake in heavy criticism of the oil industry during energy crises. The consumer group, Citizens Action, charged that the price hikes were "blatant acts of economic aggression" and urged motorists to identify and boycott gas stations with the highest prices.[74] Environment and energy-interest groups also formed a major coalition in order to provide a joint political campaign for fuel-efficient transportation. The Coalition for Fuel Efficient Transportation, composed of eight different interest groups, announced its nationwide television and radio advertising campaign concerning Middle East troop deployment and national energy policy at a press conference in Washington, DC on November 1, 1990. While each of these groups had been working independently toward similar goals, they used the Persian Gulf crisis and subsequent price hikes as a window of opportunity to consolidate their voices.

On August 23, 1990, just a few weeks after the Iraq invasion of Kuwait and subsequent price hikes, a national press conference was held by a coalition of environmental groups aimed at redirecting the nation's energy strategies. The topics covered at the conference echoed the sentiments of environmental interest groups during the Persian Gulf Crisis. The coalition focused on national energy-policy issues such as incentives for conservation, energy efficiency to increase competitiveness in the world market, limiting oil drilling, non-nuclear alternative fuels, energy taxes, and renewable sources.[75]

Criticism of the Bush administration's energy and environmental policies also came under heavy attack from environmental groups. An international co-alition of environmental groups published a statement in opposition to the war in the Middle East, proclaiming that the administration was "holding fast to the very policy that has brought the world to the brink of war."[76] The coalition argued that big oil and energy companies were exploiting the Persian Gulf Crisis to promote harmful policies such as nuclear power and oil drilling in protected wilderness areas.

The coal industry also used the opportunity to try to convince Congress that coal was a viable and readily available alternative to oil.[77] The president of the National Coal Association, Richard Larson, suggested that coal could accom-modate great amounts of the economic pressure felt during the crisis. Larson ac-knowledged that the attention to the advancement of coal production increases immediately during crises, but argued that the industry had made advancements even when the cries for alternatives faded.

Representatives of the major oil companies in turn blamed the higher prices on the United States' dependence on imported oil and the Persian Gulf War, which triggered a sharp increase in replacement costs due to shortages in sup-ply. Oil companies, while denying any charges of price gouging, responded to President Bush's call for restraint. A week after the Iraqi invasion, Philips Petroleum Company and Atlantic Richfield Company froze their prices. However, other companies, such as Mobil, responded to Bush's statement by insisting that they had not increased prices unfairly.[78] Whether by addressing accusations of scam and profiteering publically, or by capping price increases, the oil lobby felt prompted to defend their perspective in light of increasingly critical public opinion.

The Coalition for Vehicle Choice unveiled a national TV and radio ad cam-paign against Senator Bryan's bill, stating it would force smaller unsafe cars from manufacturers during the week of June 3, 1991. The debate around increas-ing fuel standards prompted increased activities among lobbyists and interest groups. The fundamental arguments between environmental and industry inter-ests were vested in a safety-versus-size debate. Opponents contended that auto-motive manufacturers would have to make cars smaller to meet standards, thus lowering safety standards. The Coalition for Vehicle Choice even took out tele-vision and print ads featuring a government crash test between a Ford Crown Victoria and a Subaru Justy. In the head-on crash test, the front of the Subaru was totally crushed. "Fuel efficiency is important, but safety is vital," the ads warned.[79] The response by proponent groups reverberated through studies and statistics that cars did not need to be smaller to be efficient and that smaller cars are necessarily less safe.

Conclusion

Similar to the previous cases, the 1990–1991 energy crisis was initiated by a focusing episode, in this case the Iraqi invasion of Kuwait and the destabilization of Persian Gulf politics. Public concern about future energy shortages and price increases quickly bubbled up and created a perceived energy crisis, even if a real oil shortage had not occurred yet. Heightened public concern in response to the events in the Gulf placed upward pressure on politicians to respond and gave energy-related interest groups impetus to take action.

The combination of a focusing episode and growing public concern created incentives for politicians to take action on energy-related policies. The combination of the problem stream with the political stream facilitated significant policy changes, most notably the clarification and expansion of conditions under which the president may draw down the Strategic Petroleum Reserve through the EPCA Amendments Act of 1990. While more comprehensive energy policy eventually came to the table with the 102nd Congress, the hearings began after the short-lived Gulf War had ended, and the policy window was quickly closing. As a result, the most significant and controversial energy-policy issues, domestic oil drilling in ANWR and auto-emission standards, failed to garner strong political attention lacking the public concern necessary to justify controversial politics.

The advocacy coalitions activated by the 1990–1991 energy crisis were clear: pro-industry and pro-environment. The coal industry and the oil industry both used the opportunity to introduce or reintroduce proposals that they believed suited the times: if there was less oil to import, then we should grow domestic production, including in the ANWR. Citizens groups and environmental organizations also used the opportunity to advocate for energy conservation efforts and more fuel-efficient vehicles. The energy-related advocacy groups had all made similar proposals previously, but the crisis gave them a window to push them under different political circumstances with greater public attention.

Compared to the other energy crises we address, the 1990–1991 crisis was brief and did not incur real oil shortages compared to the previous two crises. This case is an exemplary instance of a socially constructed crisis. The public was quick to call to mind the crises of the 1970s and 1980s with long lines at the pump, rationing, and prolonged real shortages. However, in this case, the reality was far less of a crisis than the public perceived. Between the release of oil from the SPR and the willingness of other countries to make up for shortfalls from Iraq and Kuwait, the oil supply in the United States was largely uninterrupted. However, panic still ensued, which led to energy stockpiling, less supply, and higher prices. The price spike served to confirm public suspicion that there was an energy shortage and therefore a crisis that demanded governmental response and relief.

Public opinion played a critical role in the crisis from start to finish. When the public learned of the Iraqi invasion of Kuwait and disruption of oil exports from this region, their concern began to grow. Elected officials were called on to guard the public against any price gouging by oil companies and to introduce legislation that would offer relief to the consumer. The Bush Administration was pushed to justify when and under what conditions the SPR would be used to alleviate consumers. Under heavy pressure from the public, the Administration released oil in a "test run" even though they argued it was unnecessary to do so without a real shortage in oil. Congress responded by passing specific legislation to broaden the conditions under which the SPR could be used—making it easier to draw on the SPR and avoid future crises. As the war drew to a close and the price spike abated, public attention drifted away—just as comprehensive energy-policy reform was being introduced to Congress. Lacking public attention and concern, the most significant energy proposals during this period were cut from the major legislation and left on the floor in committee hearings.

8

The Era of Peak Oil Energy Prices

The Oil Shocks of 1999–2000 and 2007–8

The 1990s ended with another energy price shock to the United States, albeit one that crept up more quietly. The cause was not a physical disruption of supply or conflict in Middle Eastern countries as in earlier crises, but a series of OPEC price hikes starting in 1999 in response to falling oil prices. In December 1998, oil prices had fallen to less than $11 per barrel[1] because of overproduction by OPEC, warm winter weather, and stagnant Asian oil demand resulting from the Asian economic crisis. Oil-producing countries responded with oil-production cutbacks, and prices more than tripled. In September 2000 oil prices peaked at $37 per barrel. The steep climb in the price of oil during this period made it one of the most critical issues in the 2000 presidential election.

The price of oil in the years following the 1999–2000 crisis was characterized by volatility. Oil prices declined after the presidential election in November and in the wake of the September 11, 2011 terrorist attacks, but then began to climb steadily in early 2002. Prices edged past $50 per barrel in the spring of 2005, not long before Hurricanes Katrina and Rita roared into the Gulf of Mexico. Prices continued to rise, then dropped briefly at the end of 2006, dipping to $55 per barrel in January 2007. But then oil prices began rising again, not as a result of supply shortages as in earlier crises and price shocks, but as a result of stagnant global production and increased global demand.[2] In March 2008 the price crept past $100 per barrel, and on July 3, 2008 it peaked at a record high of $145 per barrel, leaving consumers paying $4.17 for a gallon of gasoline.[3] As in the presidential election of 2000, the price of oil was a critical campaign issue in the 2008 presidential election. The price run-up of 2007–8 contributed to the financial crisis that was underway, sending the economy into recession.[4] By the end of 2008, prices had fallen to $41 per barrel.

The twenty-first century appears to have ushered in a new era of permanently high oil prices (figure 8.1). The energy crises of 1999–2000 and 2007–8 are distinct from the earlier crises we discussed in two ways. First, their causes

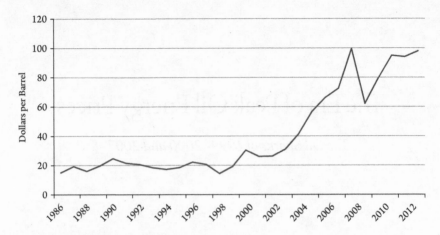

Figure 8.1 Annual Crude Oil Prices, 1986–2013.[1]
Energy Information Administration[1]Annual average price of West Texas Intermediate crude.

differ from the previous price shocks. The physical supply disruptions or conflicts in Middle Eastern countries were absent in the two most recent energy crises. In the case of the 1999–2000 crisis, OPEC countries restricted production in response to falling oil prices. In the case of the 2007–8 crisis, stagnant production and increasing global demand drove up oil prices. Second, while the earlier crises were characterized by a temporary spike in oil prices and then a return to prices at or slightly above the baseline, after the 1999–2000 and 2007–8 peaks, prices fell but remained significantly higher than they had been before the spike.

Although the causes of the 1999–2000 and 2007–8 energy crises differ from those of the earlier crises we discussed, the sequence of events that follows in both cases is similar to previous crises and is consistent with the energy crisis cycle. Both crises served as focusing episodes, with the sharp and significant increase in the price of oil in both 1999–2000 and 2007–8 leading to windfall profits for the domestic oil industry. With American drivers feeling the pinch at the pump, media attention to the issue of oil prices soared. The high oil and gas prices and massive profits made the oil industry the target of politicians' and the public's accusations of pricing manipulation. Interest groups on both sides of the issue mobilized, feeding sound bites to the media and lobbying policy makers in favor of solutions to the high price of oil that best served their interest. Public concern about the price of oil and gas and distrust of the oil industry led to demands that the government take action to reduce prices. In both crises, the government responded with proposals to address the problem. In 2000, President Clinton released oil from the Strategic Petroleum Reserve, allowing prices to dip slightly and temporarily in the weeks before the presidential election. In the 2007–8 crisis, however, prices began to decline as a result of exogenous factors before policy makers were able to take remedial steps that had the effect of prolonging the shortage by allowing consumers to continue using oil at the same rate, although it is important to note that many of the policy proposals would have had this effect had they been enacted. The following will describe the energy crisis cycle in detail as it applies to the 1999–2000 and 2007–8 energy crises.

The 1999–2000 Oil Shock
Oil Prices Fall to a Twenty-Five Year Low

With the exception of a few temporary spikes in oil and gasoline prices (including the 1991 price spike caused by the first US–Iraq War), the price of oil remained low between the mid-1980s and the beginning of the twenty-first century. By late 1998, the price of oil had fallen to a twenty-five year low[5] because of over-production by OPEC, two unusually warm winters, and a decrease in Asian oil consumption resulting from the East Asian economic crisis. In December 1998, a barrel of oil cost less than $11, and a gallon of gasoline cost less than a dollar. As the price of oil declined, the percentage of the population who believed we were spending too little on improving and protecting the environment climbed (see figure 3.1 in chapter 3). While American drivers and auto manufacturers rejoiced at the low price of oil, oil producers struggled as profits dropped. At the same time, an article appeared in *Scientific American* warning that peak oil—the point at which we have pumped half the world's oil supply—would be reached no later than 2010.[6] Once we had reached that tipping point, the authors argued, oil prices would rise sharply and permanently unless demand for oil dropped.

As Oil Prices Climb, So Does Public
Pressure on Elected Officials

When the price of oil bottomed out in December 1998, OPEC responded by reducing oil production, ending the era of low gas prices that had lasted for two decades. OPEC members met in March and agreed to cut production by more than two million barrels of oil per day for what remained of 1999. By the middle of April, the price of oil had jumped to $17 per barrel. American drivers were squeezed as gas prices inched up. Newspaper headlines announced, "Local Drivers Feel Pinch at Pumps,"[7] and wondered "Will Oil Prices Ruin Vacations?"[8] Drivers were suspicious. In California, where the rise in gas prices was sharpest, driver Robert Arias told a reporter as he fueled up his pickup truck, "I think somebody just wants more money in their pocket."[9] He was not alone in his suspicion—75 percent of Americans believed that oil companies were making too much profit.[10]

In September the price of oil edged past $24 per barrel, and gas prices exceeded $1.30. The members of OPEC agreed to continue cutting oil production through March 2000. With prices continuing to climb, the Clinton Administration and Democrats in the Senate sought to make oil companies pay royalties based on the market price of oil rather than on a lower price set by the oil companies themselves. Senator Boxer (D-CA) denounced the oil industry's history of paying royalties based on an industry-established oil price as a plot intended to "rob this Treasury of millions and millions of dollars"[11] and "an intentional defrauding of the United States taxpayer."[12] Although the effort to increase the basis for royalties to market value was unsuccessful, the concern among the public and politicians about the windfall profits earned by the oil industry as the price of oil climbed is typical during this stage in energy crisis cycle.

The price of oil continued to climb as the twentieth century ended and the new century began. In January 2000, the price topped $30 per barrel, and consumers were pressed as gasoline and heating oil prices increased. At the New England Heating Oil Summit in February, politicians, truckers, industry representatives, and consumers puzzled over the question of whether "the price spikes [were] solely the work of the market, or [whether there] was some manipulation afoot."[13] Senator John Kerry (D-MA) expressed concern that the price increases were not "a pure reflection of market forces."[14]

In protest of the high fuel prices, hundreds of truck drivers formed a convoy from Baltimore to Washington, DC. A procession of 18-wheelers and semi-trucks stretching five miles long slowly made its way to the nation's capital. One of the truckers told a reporter, "The price of fuel has really brought everything to a head. If they don't do something about it, the country's going to find out what it's like to have 200,000 truckers on vacation for two weeks."[15] Public demands on the government to take steps to reduce the price of oil are typical during an energy crisis, and the case of the 1999–2000 energy crisis was no different. The frustration expressed by members of the public and by elected officials continued to grow as prices increased.

A Window of Opportunity Opens

Rising oil prices served as a focusing episode and created an opportunity for competing interests to lobby in favor of policy options that had previously received less support among the public. In the first quarter of 2000, the percent of Americans who named energy as the most important problem for lawmakers to address in the Gallup Poll rose slightly from zero (see figure 8.2). The percent who thought we were spending too little on protecting the environment

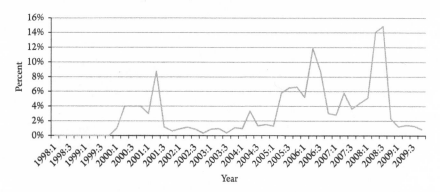

Figure 8.2 Quarterly Proportion of Respondents Who Identify "Energy" as "Most Important Problem," 1998-2009.

declined slightly (see figure 3.1 in chapter 3), and the percent of Americans who thought that protection of the environment should be given priority dropped more than ten points (see figure 3.3 in chapter 3). Among Californians, support for offshore oil drilling increased by more than twenty points (see figure 3.5 in chapter 3), a shift that signaled an opening for oil development.

Under pressure to release oil from the Strategic Petroleum Reserve (SPR), Energy Secretary Richardson appeared before the House International Relations Committee in March and asked lawmakers to "let the results of our energy diplomacy work."[16] Committee member Representative Sam Gejdenson (D-CT) replied, "I don't understand your hesitance. We're being held hostage [by OPEC]."[17] Advocates of drawing oil from the SPR believed it would reduce oil prices and compel OPEC to increase production. President Clinton had said the option was on the table, but his administration intended to continue talks with oil-producing countries before releasing oil from the emergency reserve.

As we would expect during the energy crisis cycle, Congress kept busy when it came to energy policy, with action on both sides of the aisle. In 1999, Congress held 65 hearings on the subject of energy, up from 36 hearings in 1998 (see figure 8.3). The number remained high in 2000, as gas prices continued to climb. Furthermore, 172 bills having to do with energy were introduced in the House and the Senate in 1999, up from 74 in 1998.

Among the pieces of legislation introduced by Republicans was a bill proposed by the chairman of the House International Relations Committee, Representative Benjamin Gilman (R-NY), that would "reduce, suspend, or terminate" military assistance and arms exports to any oil-exporting country involved in price manipulation.[18] The bill was stripped as it moved through the legislative process, and the version that the House overwhelmingly passed at the end of March instructed the president to prepare a report on the international oil situation and to pursue diplomatic actions to compel OPEC members to

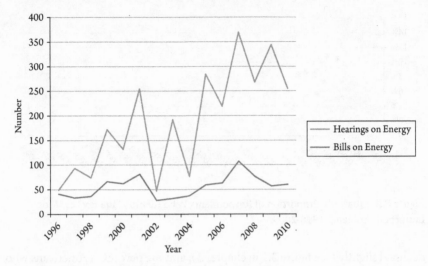

Figure 8.3 Congressional Action Related to Energy, 1996–2010.
The Policy Agendas Project (http://policyagendas.org/page/trend-analysis)

increase production, which the administration was already doing. In the end, the vote was largely symbolic.

The rising costs of oil and gasoline prompted Republican presidential candidate Governor George W. Bush and Democratic presidential candidate Vice President Al Gore to add energy policy to their list of campaign issues. In March, Governor Bush announced his support for the legislation introduced by Senate Energy Committee Chairman Frank Murkowski (R-AK) that would allow oil drilling in the Arctic National Wildlife Refuge (ANWR). Although support for offshore oil drilling increased, at least among Californians, Americans were divided about whether ANWR should be opened for drilling.[19]

Governor Bush also supported the idea of reducing or repealing the federal gas tax, a proposal that 74 percent of Americans also supported at the time.[20] He and Vice President Gore held starkly different positions on both the issue of issues, with Gore opposing both a gas tax holiday and drilling in ANWR. The Senate took up both issues, but Republicans were not able to garner enough support to pass either.

President Clinton also kept busy when it came to energy policy. By the end of 2000, he had issued twenty-seven written and oral statements about energy and petroleum, up from six in 1999. He also issued a total of three executive orders related to energy in 1999 and 2000. Two sought to green the government by increasing energy efficiency in federal buildings and the federal fleet of vehicles. A third sought to reduce dependence on petroleum by promoting the development of biofuels.

In advance of the March 27, 2000 meeting of OPEC, President Clinton presented potential options for addressing the high cost of gasoline. Among them was a proposal to stop exporting Alaskan crude oil and instead use that oil domestically. As he had previously announced, releasing oil from the SPR was also on the table. Removing the moratorium on offshore oil drilling was another option.[21] Each of these proposals, along with the proposals by Senate Republicans to reduce or remove the federal gas tax and to increase oil production on public lands, would discourage the natural response to a supply crunch—conservation. The high price of oil had already brought with it changes in consumer behavior, and economists worried that these changes would slow economic growth.[22] At the end of the month, it was announced that OPEC would increase production, but in the months that followed, prices continued to climb.

Throughout this period, oil company profits soared as gas prices increased (see figure 3.9 in chapter 3). In April, some of the nation's largest oil companies reported windfall profits. Texaco's first-quarter net income increased nearly six times compared with the same quarter the previous year. Conoco's net income rose four times, and ExxonMobil doubled its net income.[23] The public responded with outrage. The president of the interest group Public Citizen, Joan Claybrook, called on Congress to reenact the Crude Oil Windfall Profit Tax Act,[24] which had been repealed in 1988.

The same month, drivers took to the Internet to call for a three-day boycott of gas stations to protest gas prices.[25] A California driver who participated in the boycott wrote that the national movement was "testimony to the power of the Internet and the helplessness and outrage people feel when they are paying too much. It's a way to speak out and make that rage tangible."[26] Despite the increase in production by OPEC, prices continued to rise, as did public outrage.

As drivers prepared for the summer travel season, Kevin Lindemer, senior director at Cambridge Energy Associates, warned, "It's going to be a summer of volatility."[27] In May, the price of gas exceeded $1.70 per gallon, and in June the price of oil reached $34. Energy Secretary Bill Richardson announced that the Clinton administration was investigating the oil industry for "potential price fixing."[28] President Clinton said there was "no economic explanation" for the increase in gas prices since June 1, and he indicated that the source of the high prices was price manipulation by oil companies.[29] Senator Chuck Schumer (D-NY) warned that the United States could face the most serious energy crisis since the 1970s and called on President Clinton to establish a commission to study energy production and consumption in the United States.[30] With the presidential election only five months away, the energy crisis offered Democrats an opportunity to point the finger at Republicans for their cozy relationship with the oil industry and lack of support for conservation and alternative-energy

policies. Conversely, Republicans accused Democrats of hampering energy production and independence with environmental regulations.

In July, the Federal Trade Commission subpoenaed a number of oil companies and owners and operators of pipelines and terminals in its investigation of
whether price fixing caused the sharp increase in gas prices in the Midwest. At
the same time, ExxonMobil and Chevron reported record profits. ExxonMobil's
earnings increased 123 percent from the same quarter the previous year, while
Chevron's earnings jumped 140 percent.[31] Energy industry profits captured the
headlines, and accusations flew about which energy actor was benefiting the
most at the expense of the American public. Headlines reported, "Small Gas
Stations Struggle as Big Oil Producers Profit,"[32] and "Texas Drillers Enjoy High
Oil Prices, For Now."[33]

The energy industry tried to disassociate itself from the pain drivers were feeling at the pump, standing by statements such as the one made by an analyst at
investment bank CIBC World Markets that "the majority of the profits did not
come from the gas pumps. Earnings were really driven by the refining, or wholesale end of the business."[34] Independent oil and gas producer David Fleischaker
of Oklahoma wrote in an essay that appeared in USA Today that "the federal
government and the media are on a witch hunt. Guess who's the bad guy: Big
Oil."[35] It is not "Big Oil" that is the culprit, he argued, but the American public,
whose addiction to cheap oil got us in to this mess. An analyst at the stock bro-
kerage firm PaineWebber told reporters that blame for the sharp rise in gas prices
should not be attributed to oil companies, but to OPEC's decision to cut production and to the EPA's requirement that cleaner gas be distributed to several
states during the summer months.[36]

Meanwhile, the price of oil bounced back and forth in the low to mid-$30
range, and candidates for elected office threw jabs back and forth across the aisle
at one another, assigning blame for the oil shock and touting their solutions as
the ones that would bring oil and gas prices back down. The volatility of the
oil and gas market was reflected in the newspaper headlines—a July 2 headline
declared, "Gas Prices Fall in Time for Holiday,"[37] while a headline the next month
announced, "Oil Prices Spike Back Up; Pump Prices May Follow."[38] Media attention to the energy crisis had climbed dramatically during this period—by the
end of 2000, the number of articles on the subject had increased by 486 percent
over the previous year, from 44 to 214 (see figure 8.4).

The Price of Oil Peaks at $37 per Barrel

At this point in the energy crisis cycle, the increase in oil prices had focused the
attention of the public, the media, interest groups, and policymakers on the issue
of energy. Policymakers responded with proposals to address high gas prices. As

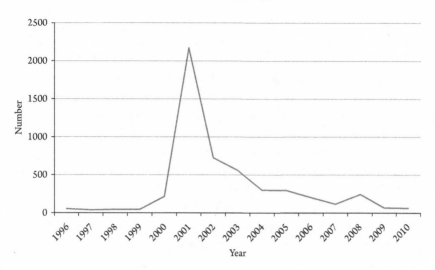

Figure 8.4 Articles Related to Energy Crisis in *New York Times* Index and US Newspapers, 1996–2010.
Wall Street Journal, Los Angeles Times, New York Times, USA Today

in the earlier crises we discussed, the final stage in the energy crisis cycle is for the government to take steps that lower oil prices without reducing demand or increasing supply in the long-term.

As the presidential election approached, the price of oil continued to climb, peaking at $37 per barrel on September 20, 2000. US oil inventories had dropped to twenty-four-year lows. Economists predicted that the natural gas shortage, soaring gasoline prices, and record-breaking electricity demands would send the country into an energy crisis that would peak in the middle of the winter, when temperatures were at their lowest. Energy Secretary Bill Richardson said oil prices were "dangerously high"[39] and reported that the president was still considering releasing oil from the SPR and was urging OPEC to do its part to avoid global recession by increasing output.

On September 22, with the presidential election less than two months away, Vice President Gore announced a proposal to release a small amount of oil—five million barrels—from the SPR in order to bring prices down. The next day, President Clinton ordered the release of thirty million barrels of oil from the nation's emergency reserve over a one-month period. The order authorized companies to borrow crude oil and refine it into heating oil, then replace the oil later when the market had improved. Energy Secretary Bill Richardson said it was expected that thirty million barrels would produce three to five million barrels of heating oil.[40] Republican presidential nominee George W. Bush denounced the move as "bad policy" and accused Clinton and Gore of using the emergency oil reserves "as an attempt to drive down oil prices right before an election."[41]

He called for heavy-handed diplomacy and domestic oil production to address the high price of oil. If Bush was right about Clinton, of course, this would be a clear-cut case of public policy being made in direct response to public opinion.

The release of oil from the SPR had a temporary impact on oil prices—they dropped from $37 to $30 per barrel in the weeks following the issue of the order—but they climbed again following a terrorist attack on the USS Cole in a Yemeni port in October. At the end of the month, OPEC announced that it would increase production, but there was skepticism that its members would be able to deliver because they had already increased production over the past several months, and analysts suspected they would be hard pressed to increase production any further. However, in November OPEC declared that it would not increase production to five hundred thousand barrels per day as it had announced in November, allowing for continued uncertainty in the market.

Prices remained above $30 in the weeks following the November 7 presidential election, which remained contested until the US Supreme Court announced its decision in the case of Bush v. Gore on December 12, ending the recount of votes in Florida and handing the victory to George W. Bush. In early December, prices slid below $30 per barrel, marking the end of the 1999–2000 oil price shock.

The Oil Price Shock Ends, but Prices Remain High

Although prices dropped below $30 per barrel, they did not return to their pre-oil shock levels, as was the case in the previous energy crises we have discussed. The International Energy Agency declared in its December 2000 monthly oil market report that, even though prices had fallen, we were "not out of the woods yet."[42] Prices declined gradually over the next year, bottoming out at $18 per barrel in January 2002. The terrorist attacks on September 11, 2001 caused a very brief bump in oil prices, but then prices dropped below $20 per barrel until March 2002 because analysts worried that the aftermath of the terrorist attacks might trigger a recession that would reduce energy demand.[43] Geopolitics in the years following September 11, 2001 had a much greater impact on the price of oil, as political instability in oil-producing countries limited production. Concern about peak oil also resurfaced. Cal Tech physicist David Goodstein reminded the public that "nature is not making any more oil."[44] He and a number of others echoed Colin Campbell and Jean Laherrere's 1998 prediction[45] that we would reach peak oil by 2010.

The gradual increase in the price of oil between the twenty-first-century bottom in 2002 and the summer of 2006 seemed to support the peak-oil hypothesis. The price of oil climbed from $18 to $77 over the four-and-a-half-year period. A number of factors seemed to indicate that America had entered a new energy era—one in which the price of oil would remain high. First, oil prices never returned to pre-shock levels, even after the 1999–2000 oil shock had ended. Second, prices did not stabilize after the oil shock. Finally, the causes of the high oil prices differed from early price shocks. In the case of the 1999–2000 oil shock, OPEC responded to falling oil prices by limiting production. In previous energy crises, supply was limited because of war or crisis in oil-producing countries. Although the 1999–2000 oil shock was characteristically different from earlier energy crises, it nonetheless followed the pattern of the energy crisis cycle, as we have seen in this chapter.

First, the sharp and significant increase in the price of oil in 1999 led to windfall profits for the domestic oil industry. As a result of the high prices and huge profits, the energy industry was targeted by politicians and interest-group advocates who made claims that the energy industry manipulated prices in an effort to increase their own profits. The public's outrage at the belief that they had been duped by the oil industry led to demands that the government take remedial steps without any additional cost to consumers. The government released oil from the emergency reserves, which temporarily brought oil and gas prices down, effectively subsidizing America's addiction to oil. The same pattern can be seen in the next American oil shock, which began in 2007.

The 2007–8 Oil Shock

2002–7: Volatility in the Oil Market

The second oil shock of the twenty-first century was triggered by stagnant production and increasing global demand. In 2002, Goldman Sachs analysts warned that the low oil prices of the late 1990s had stopped the flow of investment into global energy infrastructure, and that it would be difficult to maintain or expand energy production in order to meet demand in the coming years. Oil prices, they said, were "likely to rise sooner, and to a higher level, than is typical."[46] Their predictions were born out—the price of oil bottomed out at $18 per barrel in December 2002 and began a steady climb, reaching $77 per barrel in the summer of 2006. The rate of increase jumped slightly in the run-up to the US invasion of Iraq in March 2003, and then prices fell below $30 per barrel until June, when they began climbing again.

According to Blake Clayton, a member of the Integrated Oil and Gas Equity Research Team at Citigroup, underdeveloped energy infrastructure and instability in oil producing countries "were setting the stage for a boom. But it was demand that lit the fuse."[47] The period between 2002 and 2007 was marked by rapid growth in the world economy. Global demand for oil grew at an incredible rate, and oil consumption was greatest in the developing economies in China, India, the Middle East, Eastern Europe, and Latin America. The Chinese economy grew at a rate of 12 percent between 2003 and 2008,[48] and with it, the demand for oil. However, OPEC could not keep up with demand, and countries outside of OPEC struggled to close the gap.

The price of oil bounced up and down between 2002 and 2007 in response to instability in oil-producing nations and domestic disruptions, including Hurricane Ivan in September 2004, which caused the price of oil to edge past $50 per barrel temporarily. In February 2005, the price of oil passed the $50 mark and continued to climb, reaching $60 per barrel in July. In April 2006, the price of oil soared to $70 per barrel and kept going. Then, at the beginning of September 2006, the price of oil began to drop, and after a six-month decline, fell below $60 per barrel.

The Race to Assign Blame for Rising Oil Prices

The drop in the price of oil was followed by a steep and dramatic climb that began in 2007, marking the beginning of the 2007–8 oil price shock. Initially, it seemed that the rising price of gas was just the "spring ritual" of "price increases and congressional outrage" that had begun in 2004.[49] However, prices quickly passed the peaks that had been reached earlier in the decade. In April, gas prices reached $2.90 per gallon, and ExxonMobil posted record profits in the first quarter. Profit climbed 10 percent, from $8.4 billion in the first quarter of 2006 to $9.28 billion in the same quarter of 2007. Chevron also reported a first-quarter increase—profits had increased by 18 percent compared to the same quarter in the previous year. In response, eight Democratic senators introduced legislation to re-establish a windfall profits tax. The measure would have imposed a 50 percent tax on profits when oil prices exceeded $50 a barrel.[50]

In May, gas prices nearly reached the inflation-adjusted record set in the wake of the 1979–80 energy crisis. In March 1981, the adjusted price of unleaded regular gas was $3.22; in May 2007, it reached $3.22. At this point, the price of gasoline was rising at a faster rate than the price of oil, in large part because of domestic refinery problems. While analysts blamed refinery accidents and maintenance closings for the dramatic slowing of gasoline production that forced gas prices up, the media, elected officials, and the public blamed oil companies. On May 7, a headline in the New York Times read, "Profits Climb 5.7% at Shell Despite Falling Oil Prices."[51] Warren Brown, a columnist for the Washington Post, wrote, "What the oil companies are doing isn't moral. Nor is it illegal. But it is business. Crises usually are profitable for people positioned to exploit them; and they usually are costly for those who aren't."[52]

Brown's words reflected public sentiment about the soaring profits earned by oil companies, and they reflected the reality that drivers faced. A May report published by two consumer-advocate groups revealed that the average US household spent $2,277 on gas in 2006, an increase of 78 percent since 2001, and a figure that was rising as the price of gas climbed in 2007.[53] According to a poll conducted in April, 67 percent of Americans reported that the recent price increases in gas caused financial hardship, up from 57 percent the previous year.[54] Another poll found that nearly half had to make adjustments to their usual spending and saving habits in significant ways, while the rise in gas prices had created a financial hardship for nearly one in five people.[55] Americans attributed the increase in gas prices to oil companies. When asked why they thought the price of gasoline was so high, 34 percent said oil companies were gouging the public, more than any other explanation given.[56]

Democrats in Congress also pointed the finger at oil companies. Representative Rahm Emanuel (D-IL) wrote, "The oil companies have two words to say about the new record high gas prices: mission accomplished."[57] In a call to investigate price gouging by oil companies, Senator Byron Dorgan (D-ND) wrote, "It's odd, isn't it, how the need to shut refineries for maintenance coincides with peak demand?"[58] And Representative Bart Stupak (D-MI) told the House Energy and Commerce Subcommittee on Oversight and Investigations that "Big Oil companies are reaping record profits" and that "across our nation, people are struggling to pay to fill up their gas tank and their frustration with gas prices is boiling over."[59] He pointed out that Royal Dutch Shell's profits in the first three months of 2007 were $7.3 billion, Chevron's were $4.7 billion, ConocoPhillips were $3.5 billion, and ExxonMobil's were $9.2 billion.

Several Democrats in Congress who were distrustful of the oil industry even spread their message beyond the walls of the Capitol. On May 9, six Senators rallied in front of an Exxon station near the Capitol, promoting legislation aimed at regulating the oil industry. Senator Chuck Schumer (D-NY) said Congress would investigate the possibility of breaking up the oil giants.[60] Earlier in the week, he accused oil companies of limiting gas inventories because of lack of investment into the maintenance of refineries and said the Government Accountability Office would investigate.[61] Senator Maria Cantwell (D-WA) promoted a bill she had introduced that would make gas-price gouging a federal crime. Senator Bernie Sanders (D-VT) endorsed the windfall-profits tax legislation proposed in the Senate.

Washington Responds to Public Pressure

With public and media attention focused on rising oil prices, the executive and legislative branches responded with policy action. President George W. Bush issued two executive orders related to energy in 2007, compared with zero in

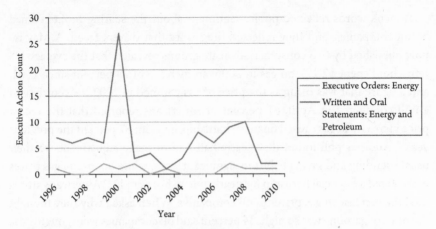

Figure 8.5 Executive Action Related to Energy, 1996–2010.
The Policy Agendas Project (http://policyagendas.org/page/trend-analysis) and the American
Presidency Project (www.presidency.ucsb.edu)

2006 (see figure 8.5). One of them—E.O. 13423—addressed energy production and consumption and was aimed at improving energy management in
the federal government.[62] The period between 2005 and 2008—during which
President Bush campaigned in support of his energy policy package—witnessed
an increase in the number of oral and written statements issued by the president.
Congress also kept busy when it came to energy policy. In 2007, 369 bills related
to energy were introduced in the House and the Senate, compared with 219 in
2006 (see figure 8.3).[63] The number of congressional hearings also increased,
jumping from 63 in 2006 to 107 in 2008.

By the end of May, the centerpieces of the Democrats' short-term response
to rising energy prices were the anti-price-gouging legislation introduced in
both chambers of Congress and a proposed increase in Corporate Average Fuel
Economy (CAFE) standards. Republicans also seized on the opportunity to
address the issue of energy with proposals to expand domestic energy production. On May 1, the Bush administration announced a proposal to expand oil
and gas drilling off the coasts of Alaska and Virginia. Dirk Kempthorne, secretary of the Department of the Interior, said, "The outer continental shelf is a vital
source of domestic oil and natural gas for America, especially in light of sharply
rising energy prices."[64]

Gas prices remained above $3 per gallon through July 2007. Expensive gas
did little to dampen demand, and oil inventories were having trouble keeping
up because of refinery outages, bad weather, unimpressive production in developed countries, and instability in Nigeria and Middle Eastern nations.[65] The
quality of oil that was being produced by OPEC members like Saudi Arabia
also put a strain on inventory. Refineries required certain types of oil based on

their operating arrangements, and new environmental regulations in the United States and other countries required fuel that was lower in sulfur. By the end of July, the price of oil began to climb, exceeding $70 per barrel.

In fall of 2007, the high price of gas and the beginning of the financial crisis reduced demand for oil temporarily, but the debate over a policy solution continued. After extensive debate in the House and the Senate and the threat of a presidential veto, both chambers of Congress passed and in December 2007 President Bush signed the Energy Independence and Security Act (EISA). The energy bill required the first fuel-economy mandate in thirty-two years—a new Corporate Average Fuel Economy (CAFE) standard of 35 mpg for cars and light trucks by 2020. It also required a substantial increase in ethanol production by 2022, new efficiency standards for lighting and household appliances, and new standards in energy use in federal buildings.

Earlier versions of the EISA debated in the House and the Senate included Democratic provisions involving the regulations of greenhouse gas emissions, increased taxes on the oil, coal, and gas industries, and the requirement that electric utilities use renewable sources of energy. Such measures were controversial and did not make it into the final version of the bill that became law. In the end, what was initially labeled as an ambitious energy bill was referred to as a "weaker," "pared-down" energy bill once it was approved.[66]

In February 2008, the price of oil soared past $100 per barrel for the first time ever. In March, it reached $110 per barrel. In April, the price of oil approached $120 per barrel. Even still, record-high prices could not drive production to keep up with global demand. The chief economist of the International Energy Agency, Fatih Birol, told reporters that economic theory and the history of oil tell us that rising oil prices have two major effects: they reduce demand and they increase oil production. Referring to the price shock of 2007–8, he said, "Not this time."[67] The primary difference between the 2007–8 price and earlier shocks was that global production simply could not keep up with growing demand, and speculation on commodity markets nudged prices past previous records. Robert Mabro of the Oxford Institute for Energy Studies cautioned, "We're in a bubble right now. Prices are rising because everyone expects them to do so. We've seen the same thing in the real estate market."[68]

An overwhelming majority of Americans reported that the rise in gas prices caused them financial hardship,[69] and demand for gasoline dropped as drivers changed their behavior. A driver in Cleveland, who started taking the bus to work instead of driving, told a reporter that she could no longer afford the high gas prices. "They're insane," she said. A nursing assistant in Chicago started working extra shifts in order to make ends meet. "The whole gas price situation makes me so angry. Rising gas prices end up hurting working, lower class people like me, who can't afford it anymore," she told a reporter.[70]

In the years following the 1999–2000 oil price shock, the number of Americans who believed we should focus on protecting the environment as opposed to focusing on economic growth had begun to climb again, reaching 55 percent in 2007. Then, with the 2007–8 oil price shock well underway, support for environmental protection fell more than ten percentage points (see figure 3.3 in chapter 3). The trend was similar for support for offshore oil drilling among Californians—after the 1999–2000 oil price shock, support fell, and then began to climb again as gas prices climbed during the 2007–8 price shock (see figure 3.5 in chapter 3).

With gas prices reaching record highs, consumer confidence fell to its lowest level since 1980. In May, ExxonMobil posted its second-best quarterly profit in its history,[71] while the Ford Motor Company announced production cuts because of decreased demand for gas-guzzling vehicles.[72] The public believed that oil companies were making too much profit[73] and that they deserved most of the blame for the country's energy problems.[74] "There's too many politicians' hands in our pockets, and too many crooks in the oil companies. I'm all for helping other countries, but we need to help our people here in the U.S. first," an Army veteran tending bar in Des Plaines, Illinois reported.[75]

With the 2008 presidential election campaign well underway, Republican presidential hopeful Senator John McCain and Democratic presidential hopeful Senator Hillary Clinton responded to the public's frustration with rising gas prices with proposals to suspend the federal excise tax on gas for the summer travel season. A number of candidates for state-level offices also joined the call for a gas tax holiday. Governor Charlie Crist, then-Republican of Florida, sought to cut the state's gas tax for a two-week period, saying, "I'm supposed to respond to the people and try to make them happy."[76] Critics of the gas tax, including President Bush and Democratic presidential hopeful Senator Barack Obama, argued that it was a political ploy that would do little to save drivers money. Americans, who believed that the high price of gas represented a permanent change rather than a temporary fluctuation,[77] were also skeptical about a gas tax holiday. About half of registered voters nationwide thought that eliminating the federal gas tax for the summer was a bad idea, compared with 41 percent who thought it was a good idea.[78] The majority of Americans agreed with President Bush and Senator Obama that the proposed gas tax holiday was a political ploy—70 percent thought that some candidates had proposed eliminating the gas tax mainly to help themselves politically.[79]

President Bush's energy agenda continued to focus primarily on the expansion of domestic production. In April 2008, he held a press conference in which he addressed the economic downturn. President Bush spoke to Americans' concern about the high price of gas, referring to it as a "tax increase on the working people."[80] He attributed the high gas prices to the failure of global oil production to keep up with growing demand and to the lack of refining capacity. President Bush proposed expanding domestic oil production and opening ANWR to oil development, expanding refinery capacity, and expanding the use of nuclear power in order to address the root causes of high gas prices. Congress, he said, had blocked each of his proposals and was instead supporting legislation that would "raise taxes on domestic energy production, impose new and costly mandates on producers, and demand dramatic emissions cuts that would shut down coal plants and increase reliance on expensive natural gas."[81]

The Price of Oil Peaks and the Bubble Bursts

The price of oil peaked at a record $145 on July 3, 2008. Drivers were paying more than $4 for a gallon of gas. Then, the oil speculation bubble burst. On July 15, in the face of a global economic crisis and reduced oil demand, the price of oil began to drop as quickly as it had climbed, marking the end of the 2007–8 oil price shock. By the end of July, the price of oil had fallen from $145 to $124.

The decline in the price of gas was much more gradual—it was not until mid-October 2008 that it dropped below $3.50 per gallon—and the high cost of gas remained at the top of the public's list of concerns. Public opinion polls conducted in August and September found that energy and the cost of gas ranked among the top issues that registered voters thought should be the highest priority for the federal government or presidential candidates to address.

With voters still expressing concern about gas prices and the general election only four months away, elected officials continued to seek policy solutions that would bring down the price of gas. At the end of July, House Democrats attempted to force the Bush Administration to release oil from the SPR in order to bring gas prices down, but they were held up by Republican demands for a vote on an expansion of offshore drilling. When Congress adjourned for a five-week summer recess in August, several dozen Republican members of Congress refused to leave, demanding a special summer session be called to address high gas prices. Republicans favored the expansion of domestic oil production, particularly offshore, while Democrats insisted that the government should focus on limiting speculation in the oil futures market and developing renewable energy sources.[82]

Economic Collapse: A Quick Fix for High Oil Prices

Typically at this stage in the energy crisis cycle, the government takes steps to alleviate the pressure on consumers by implementing policy that temporarily lowers gas prices. However, gas prices came down before policymakers could implement price-reducing policies. In the summer of 2008, US Treasury

Secretary Henry Paulson told reporters that "there's no quick fix" for high oil prices.[83] It turns out there was a quick fix, as Blake Clayton points out: economic collapse. Although it would bring down oil prices, "it was a cure worse than the disease."[84] By October, the global economy had weakened as a result of the credit crisis, and demand for oil was down. The price of oil had dropped by half since July, and OPEC members discussed a sharp cut in production to stabilize prices. Iran's oil minister told reporters, "The era of cheap oil is finished."[85] However, the price of oil continued to plummet. Prices dropped below $70 per barrel in the weeks before the presidential election in November, and below $50 per barrel in December. The price of oil bottomed out at $30.28 the week of Christmas.

It began climbing again in the spring of 2009 and has bounced around between $70 and $110 ever since, validating the declaration by Iran's oil minister that "the era of cheap oil is finished." With only two brief exceptions, the price of oil has remained well-above $50 per barrel since 2005, making the $20 oil of the twentieth century seem like a distant memory.[86]

Conclusion

The two most recent oil price shocks follow the stages of the energy crisis cycle, and they fit well into the framework of focusing episodes that we adapted from Thomas Birkland's framework. In both the 1999–2000 and the 2007–8 oil price shocks, rising gas prices led to consumer suspicion of the oil industry, as profits soared. With media and public attention focused on the issue of energy, the window of opportunity opened for interest groups and elected officials to pursue energy policies that were in line with their political goals, and that would please voters. In the 1999–2000 crisis, the government responded with action that temporarily lowered gas prices, but did not address energy problems in the long-term. In the 2007–8 crisis, economic collapse caused a drop in gas prices before the proposed gas tax holiday could be passed or implemented.

These two crises follow the patterns that we saw in their earlier energy crisis cycles, and they show the continuing influence of public opinion as the crises unfold, but they also make it clear that we have entered a new era of peak-oil energy prices. Since the beginning of the twenty-first century, prices have never returned to the low baseline that consumers enjoyed for two decades at the end of the twentieth century. In fact, the predictions of the economists who forecasted that oil would peak by 2010 seem to have been born out. Even with the increased domestic energy production that has taken place during the Obama administration, oil prices remain higher that they were in the 1990s. As we have seen in all of the cases that we have examined here, energy crises can open windows of opportunity for policy change, but an open window is not enough to produce long-term policy solutions to our energy problems.

9

Conclusion

This study began with two broad purposes. First, we sought to explore and to explain the political dynamics during energy crises. When energy crises strike, how do the public, policy advocates, and politicians respond? Are there repeated patterns that appear in each crisis? Second, we sought to pay particular attention to public opinion because we believed its role in the policymaking process has been understated in past research. We want to close by briefly reflecting on those two themes.

Energy Crises

We began by asking if there were patterns that occur in energy crises. There are indeed. The patterns can be explained by the agenda-setting and punctuated-equilibrium theories developed by John Kingdon, Frank Baumgartner and Byron Jones, Thomas Birkland, and others.[1] Energy crises present almost the perfect cases of situations in which policy change is highly likely.

In energy crises, we can predict that Kingdon's three streams will come together. The policy stream, consisting of the accumulated knowledge and policy proposals from experts, is well developed. Policy advocates on all sides have proposals. What should we do when oil prices skyrocket? The oil and gas industry has a set of off-the-shelf policy proposals. Build the Keystone XL pipeline. Open up oil drilling in the arctic. Prevent state and local governments from banning hydrofracking. Repeal the ban on exporting oil. Environmental groups have their preferred policies as well. Increase the CAFE automobile fuel-efficiency standards. Pass a carbon tax. Make the federal Production Tax Credit to subsidize renewable energy permanent. Invest in research on electric cars. No one has to spend time to develop new ideas. They are already sitting on the shelf waiting for the right time.

The policies do not all have to address rising oil prices directly. Other than releasing oil from the Strategic Petroleum Reserve, little can be done by the government to lower oil prices quickly. Most policy changes would only begin to have some effect years after they were adopted. Indeed, some policy proposals would be unlikely ever to affect oil prices. Yet if wind-power advocates can successfully frame an oil-price shock as a broader energy crisis, then producing more alternative energy (electricity) might gain attention and support.

The problem stream consists of the energy crisis itself. Rapidly rising oil prices focus the public's attention on energy policy. In the first two energy crises of 1973–74 and 1979–80, focusing events that triggered the public's attention slowly evolved into focusing episodes as continually rising prices plus the associated ongoing political events continued to hold the public's gaze. In the final energy crisis we examined, which began in 1999, there was no single focusing event, but the steadily rising gasoline prices drew the public's attention anyway in a focusing episode.

Because most of the energy crises, including the first one in 1973, started with wars, they were immediately framed as political problems. The 1973 Arab boycott of Western nations that supported Israel in the Arab-Israeli War was a political act. It demanded a political response from the White House and Congress. The next two energy crises were also started by Middle Eastern wars and were, therefore, automatically framed as political problems. By the time the most recent energy crisis began to build with the run-up of oil prices starting in 1999, seeing surging oil prices as a political problem was routine.

The political stream consists of the public's response along with the reactions of interest groups and politicians. Kingdon wrote about the "public mood."[2] In the case of energy crises, *public anger* is more accurate. Polls showed that a high percentage of Americans reported changing their behavior because of rising gasoline prices. No one liked it. These are conditions that elected officials cannot ignore. Public anger forces politicians to respond.

The rising oil prices activate a wider group of participants and groups than in normal times, when policy changes are incremental. Over fifty years ago, E. E. Schattschneider labeled these situations "issue expansion," an idea more fully developed by Baumgartner and Jones.[3] Instead of leaving policymaking to routine congressional adjustment, presidents and other influential political actors respond to the crisis. This sets the stage for potential policy punctuations.

In short, during energy crises, Kingdon's three streams do come together. Surging oil prices have predictable effects. A policy window opens, policy advocates put forward their proposals, and Congress and the White House respond.

Jones and Baumgartner are pessimistic about the likelihood of making much progress in developing theories to predict policy change. They write,

> No one simple causal theory can explain policy change across all areas.
> This difficulty in generalization is one reason that policy studies has

relied so heavily on case analysis. The clear and present danger of case studies is that a different causal theory will have to be deployed for each policy area, with no mechanism for resolving the contradictions among these various theories.[4]

We do not dispute their claim, but we caution against exaggerating it. The punctuated-equilibrium theory we are using allows us to predict that when oil prices surge, the public will demand that something be done, and the policy advocates and elected official will respond by seeking to enact substantial policy changes. We expect that there are other policy areas in which similar predictions can be made.

What we cannot predict is what specific policy changes will occur or whether they will occur at all. The difficulty stems from the fact that there is more than just the crisis and public opinion driving policy changes. At the simplest level, which party or parties control the White House, the House, and the Senate can make all the difference in the world. When the first energy crisis hit the nation in 1973, both houses of Congress were controlled by the Democratic Party, and Richard Nixon, although a Republican, was politically moderate and open to strengthening environmental controls early in his administration. The result was significant policy change. Imagine the same crisis striking the United States today, when a pro-environment Democrat sits in the White House and both houses of Congress are controlled by conservative Republicans with little tolerance for environmental regulation. Under such conditions—even in the face of an energy crisis—significant energy policy change would be unlikely. We would have had gridlock.[5] As a result, we think that it is far easier to predict when policies will come to the top of the political agenda and become the focus of attempts to change them than to predict the actual nature and scope of policy change.

Public Opinion and Energy Crises

Public opinion plays an influential role in policymaking. When a triggering event or episode draws the public's attention to a problem, the media begin covering it, policy advocates push their policy proposals, and Congress begins to hold hearings. But the role of public opinion does not end once the process starts. Interest groups try to frame their proposals to gain popular support throughout their efforts to change the law. Elected officials always monitor public opinion to avoid running afoul of it.

Over the years, a recurring question that scholars have addressed is, how well does our system of democracy establish the laws and public policies that the public wants? No one expects public opinion completely to determine public policy. When the president and members of Congress make policy decisions, they take into account a wide array of considerations—the views of their party and committee leaders, their fellow legislators, interest groups, major donors, their own personal preferences, as well as what their constituents think.[6] Yet public opinion on high-profile issues stands out as an important factor. Scholars have sought to find out how much it matters.

Most researchers who study the impact of public opinion on policy have concluded that public opinion is an important cause of policy on high-profile issues.[7] When public opinion moves in a direction, public policy generally follows. Paul Burstein points out that to some extent this pattern is a result of sampling. The issues on which we have public-opinion survey data are high-profiles issues that get a lot of media coverage.[8] Which is to say, we have survey data only on high-profile issues but not on a representative sample of issues with all levels of salience. It is not the case, he argues, that the public always gets what it wants, but rather that the public generally gets what it wants on the big issues to which people pay attention. On most issues, he argues, the public neither pays attention nor cares.

For our purposes, what matters is that a substantial number of studies claim that on major issues, public policy follows the lead of public opinion. They do not examine policy change using the theoretical lenses of agenda-setting and punctuated-equilibrium theory, but they are nevertheless looking at the same policy changes studied in the agenda-setting literature. We interpret this as further evidence, albeit indirect evidence, that public opinion matters.

In our view, the role of public opinion in studies of agenda setting and punctuated equilibrium has not been sufficiently explored. No one suggests that public opinion is only relevant at the very beginning of the policy change process, but by and large, most studies ignore public opinion after the initial focusing event. There is more to public opinion than Gallup's most important problem question. The public's policy preferences and their assessments of who should get the blame when things go wrong are important. We believe that looking at the role of public opinion throughout the policy process is a promising direction for agenda-setting and policy-change research.

Appendix A

ENERGY MOOD QUESTIONS

Items listed below are the subset identified in the text as "energy mood" queries. The series are identified by the originating survey house.

Cambridge Reports/Research International

I'm going to read you several proposals for dealing with the energy crisis, and I'd like you to tell me whether you generally favor or oppose each one.... Expanding offshore drilling for oil and natural gas. [1976–1994]

I'm going to read you some proposals for dealing with the country's energy needs, and I'd like you to tell me whether you generally favor or oppose each one.... Developing oil and natural gas reserves in the Arctic North-Slope region of Alaska. [1991–1994]

The Arctic National Wildlife Refuge in northern Alaska is a publicly owned wilderness area that may be one of the country's largest untapped sources of oil and gas. Some people say development of this area should begin right away to help reduce our dependence on foreign oil. They say this development can be controlled in a way that protects the wildlife and wilderness character of the area. Other people say it is not yet clear how much oil and gas exist in the Arctic National Wildlife Refuge, and they say any development would cause irreparable harm to one of the nation's great wilderness areas. In general, do you favor or oppose development of the Arctic National Wildlife Refuge? [1987–1994]

Gallup

Next I am going to read some specific environmental proposals. For each one, please say whether you generally favor or oppose it. How about—Opening up the Arctic National Wildlife Refuge for oil exploration? [2001–2003]
Do you think the Arctic National Wildlife Refuge in Alaska should or should not be opened up for oil exploration? [2002–2005]

ABC/*Washington Post*

Do you think the federal government should or should not allow oil drilling in the Arctic National Wildlife Refuge in Alaska? [2001–2007]

CBS/*New York Times*

Currently, drilling for oil and natural gas is prohibited in Alaska's Arctic National Wildlife Refuge. Do you approve or disapprove of the proposal to open up the Arctic National Wildlife Refuge in Alaska for oil and natural gas drilling? [2001–2006]

Associated Press (AP)

Do you favor or oppose opening up part of the Arctic National Wildlife Refuge in Alaska for oil exploration? [2002]

Fox

Do you favor or oppose opening a small amount—less than 10 percent—of the Alaskan wilderness areas for oil exploration as a way to reduce the country's dependence on foreign oil? [2002–2004]

Los Angeles Times

George W. Bush said that he would consider opening up part of the Alaskan Arctic Wildlife Refuge to oil and gas exploration. Do you approve or disapprove of Bush's proposal? [2003]

Appendix B

SURVEY DATA INFORMATION

Data from the public opinion surveys of Californians listed below were used in chapters 3 and 4. All of the surveys were conducted by the Field Institute (http://field.com/). Ten of the surveys are Field Polls, which are publicly available from the University of California, Berkeley's UCDATA (http://ucdata. berkeley.edu/). The Field Polls are identified by the year in which the survey was conducted and the number of the poll (e.g., 7703 is the third survey conducted in 1977 by the Field Institute). One of the surveys, COODEPS, was conducted by the Field Institute for Eric Smith. The COODEPS survey is archived at the Inter-University Consortium for Social and Political Research (https://www. icpsr.umich.edu/).

The COODEPS survey was funded by a grant from the Minerals Management Service, U.S. Department of the Interior, under MMS Agreement No. 1435-01-00-CA-31063. The views and conclusions contained in this document are those of the authors and should not be interpreted as necessarily representing the official policies, either express or implied, of the U.S. Government.

Survey	Dates	Sample Size
7703	6/17–7/2/77	1,034
7801	1/7–15/1978	1,003
7902	5/3–15/1979	485 (random half; total sample n = 979)
8002	4/2–8/1980	501 (random half; total sample n = 1,012)
8006	10/15–18/1980	506 (random half; total sample n = 1,018)
8104	10/26–11/1/1981	1,102
8401	2/1–9/1984	743 (random half; total sample n = 1,511)

Survey	Dates	Sample Size
8903	7/12–23/1989	993
9004	8/17–27/1990	614 (random half; total sample n = 1,235)
COODEPS*	3/5–18/1998	810
0102	5/11–20/2001	448 (random half; total sample n = 1,015)

*California Offshore Oil Drilling and Energy Policy Survey

Survey Questions used in the California Surveys
Table 3.4

Income

"Now, we don't want to know your exact income, but just roughly, could you tell me if your annual household income before taxes is under $20,000, $20,000 to $40,000, $40,000 to $60,000, $60,000 to $80,000, or more than $80,000?" 1= Under $20,000; 2=$20,000 - $40,000; 3 = $40,000 - $60,000; 4 = $60,000 – $80,000; 5 = More than $80,000.

Financial Status

"During the last few years, has your financial situation been getting better, getting worse, or has it stayed the same." 1 = Worse; 2 = Same; 3 = Better.

Age

"What is your age?" Actual age coded; 97 = 97 or older.

Party identification

"Generally speaking, do you usually think of yourself as a Republican, a Democrat, an Independent, or what?"

If Republican or Democrat: "Would you call yourself a strong or not very strong (Republican) (Democrat)?"

If independent: "Do you consider yourself as closer to the Republican or the Democratic Party?" 0 = Strong Democrat; 1 = Weak Democrat;

2 = Independent-leaning Democrat; 3 = Independent; 4 = Independent-leaning Republican; 5 = Weak Republican; 6 = Strong Republican.

Ideology

"Generally speaking, in politics do you consider yourself as conservative, liberal, middle-of-the-road?"

If conservative: "Do you consider yourself a strong or not very strong conservative?"

If liberal: "Do you consider yourself a strong or not very strong liberal?"
If middle-of-the-road: "If you had to choose, would you consider yourself as being conservative, liberal, or middle-of-the-road?" 0 = Strong Liberal; 1 = Weak Liberal; 2 = Liberal-leaning Middle-of-the-road; 3 = Middle of the Road; 4 = Conservative-leaning Middle-of-the-road; 5 = Weak Conservative; 6 = Strong Conservative.

Ethnicity

"Are you a Latino or of Hispanic origin, such as Mexican-American, Latin American, South American, or Spanish-American?" 0 = Not Latino or Hispance; 1 = Latino or Hispanic.

Figure 4.4

Oppose Nuclear Power

"I'd like you to tell me whether you agree strongly, agree slightly, disagree slightly, or disagree strongly with each of the statements as I read it....

"The building of more nuclear power plants should be allowed in California." 0 = Strongly Disagree; 1 = Slightly Disagree; 2 = Slightly Agree; 3 = Strongly Agree.

Cut Standard of Living

"I would prefer to cut back on my standard of living in order to conserve energy rather than to go on using up natural resources at the present rate." 0 = Strongly Disagree; 1 = Slightly Disagree; 2 = Slightly Agree; 3 = Strongly Agree.

Slow Population Growth

"Population growth and housing development in California should be slowed down to reduce energy needs." 0 = Strongly Disagree; 1 = Slightly Disagree; 2 = Slightly Agree; 3 = Strongly Agree.

Slow Industrial Growth

"The growth of industries requiring large amounts of energy should be slowed down to reduce energy needs." 0 = Strongly Disagree; 1 = Slightly Disagree; 2 = Slightly Agree; 3 = Strongly Agree.

Trust People

"Generally speaking, would you say that most people can be trusted, or that you can't be too careful in dealing with people?" 0 = You Can't Be Too Careful; 1 = Most People Can Be Trusted.

Trust Government

"How much of the time do you think you can trust the government in Washington to do what is right--just about all of the time, most of the time, or only some of the time?" 0 = Only Some of the Time; 1 = Most of the Time; 2 = All of the Time.

Big Interests Run Government

"Would you say that the government is pretty much run by a few big interests looking out for themselves or that it is run for the benefit for all people?" 0 = Run by a Few Big Interests; 1 = Run for the Benefit for All People.

Smart People Run Government

"Do you feel that almost all the people running the government are smart people who usually know what they are doing or do you think that quite a few don't seem to know what they are doing?" 0 = Quite a Few Don't Seem to Know What They Are Doing; 1 = Run by Smart People.

Oil Companies Allowed to Drill

"I'd like you to tell me whether you agree strongly, agree slightly, disagree slightly, or disagree strongly with each of the statements as I read it. . . . Oil companies should be allowed to drill more oil and gas wells in state tidelands along the California seacoast.." 0 = Strongly Disagree; 1 = Slightly Disagree; 2 = Slightly Agree; 3 = Strongly Agree.

Favor Offshore Oil Development

"Do you generally favor or oppose increasing oil and gas drilling along the California coast?" 0 = Oppose; 1 = Favor.

Confidence in Government Scientists

"How much confidence do you have in statements made by government scientists about potential health risks associated with living near an oil drilling site? Do you have a great deal of confidence, a moderate amount of confidence, only some confidence, or almost no confidence at all?" 0 = Almost None; 1 = Only Some; 2 = A Moderate Amount; 3 = A Great Deal."

Confidence in Environmental Group Scientists

"How much confidence do you have in statements made by government scientists about potential health risks associated with living near an oil drilling site? Do you have a great deal of confidence, a moderate amount of confidence, only some confidence, or almost no confidence at all?" 0 = Almost None; 1 = Only Some; 2 = A Moderate Amount; 3 = A Great Deal."

Confidence in Oil Industry Scientists

"How much confidence do you have in statements made by government scientists about potential health risks associated with living near an oil drilling site? Do you have a great deal of confidence, a moderate amount of confidence, only some confidence, or almost no confidence at all?" 0 = Almost None; 1 = Only Some; 2 = A Moderate Amount; 3 = A Great Deal."

NOTES

Chapter 1

1. Elizabeth Douglass, "Gas Dealers Say They Aren't Guzzling Profits," *Los Angeles Times*, March 11, 2003.
2. Elizabeth Douglass, "Davis Orders State Agencies to Probe Soaring Cost of Gas," *Los Angeles Times*, March 14, 2003.
3. David E. Nye. *Consuming Power* (Cambridge, MA: MIT Press, 1998), 187.
4. *Population data source: Population Reference Bureau; World Population Data Sheet, 2012. Accessed May 10, 2016 at http://www.prb.org/pdf12/2012-population-data-sheet_eng.pdf*
   Energy data source: U.S. Energy Information Administration, International Energy Statistics: Total Primary Energy Consumption, 2012. Accessed May 10, 2016 at http://www.eia.gov/cfapps/ipdbproject/iedindex3.cfm?tid=44&pid=44&aid=2&cid=regions&syid=2012&eyid=2012&unit=QBTU
5. US Energy Information Administration, Annual Energy Review 2012, Figure 1.0, accessed July 31, 2012, http://www.eia.gov/totalenergy/data/annual/pdf/sec1_3.pdf.
6. US Energy Information Administration, Annual Energy Review 2012, Figure 2.0, accessed July 31, 2012, http://www.eia.gov/totalenergy/data/annual/pdf/sec2_3.pdf.
7. Joseph J. Bozell, "Connecting Biomass and Petroleum Processing with a Chemical Bridge," *Science* 3299 (July 2010): 522–23.
8. Congressional Quarterly, *Energy & Environment: The Unfinished Business* (Washington, DC: Congressional Quarterly Press, 1985), 19.
9. Nye, *Consuming Power*; James C. Wilson, *Energy and the Making of Modern California* (Akron, OH: University of Akron Press, 1997).
10. R. Douglas Arnold, chap. 9 in *The Logic of Congressional Action* (New Haven, CT: Yale University Press, 1990).
11. William Freudenburg and Robert Gramling, *Blowout in the Gulf* (Cambridge, MA: MIT Press, 2011).
12. Al Richman, "The Polls: Public Attitudes Toward the Energy Crisis," *Public Opinion Quarterly* 43 (1979): 576–85.
13. Adapted from Eric R. A. N. Smith, *Energy, the Environment, and Public Opinion* (Boulder, CO: Rowman & Littlefield, 2002).
14. Anthony Downs, "Up and down with ecology—the issue-attention cycle," *Public Interest* 28 (1972): 38–50; John W. Kingdon, *Agendas, Alternatives, and Public Policies* (Boston: Little, Brown, 1984); Frank R. Baumgartner and Bryan D. Jones, *Agendas and Instability in American Politics* (Chicago: University of Chicago Press, 1993); Bryan D. Jones and Frank R. Baumgartner, *The Politics of Attention* (Chicago: University of Chicago Press, 2005).
15. Baumgartner and Jones, *Agendas and Instability in American Politics*; Frank R. Baumgartner and Bryan D. Jones, eds, *Policy Dynamics* (Chicago: University of Chicago Press, 2002); Jones

and Baumgartner, *Politics of Attention*; Repetto, *Punctuated Equilibrium and the Dynamics of U.S. Environmental Policy* (New Haven, CT: Yale University Press, 2006); Thomas A. Birkland, *After Disaster: Agenda Setting, Public Policy, and Focusing Events* (Washington D.C.: Georgetown University Press, 1997).

16. Charles D. Elder and Roger W. Cobb, *The Political Uses of Symbols* (New York: Longman Publishing Group, 1983); John W. Kingdon, *Agendas, Alternatives, and Public Policies*, 2nd ed. (New York: Harper Collins, 1995); Thomas A. Birkland, *After Disaster: Agenda Setting, Public Policy, and Focusing Events* (Washington, DC: Georgetown University Press, 1997).

17. Jones and Baumgartner, *The Politics of Attention*, 92.

Chapter 2

1. Sir Winston Churchill, date unknown

2. See Frank R. Baumgartner and Bryan D. Jones, *Agendas and Instability in American Politics* (Chicago: University of Chicago Press, 1993); and Bryan D. Jones and Frank R. Baumgartner, *The Politics of Attention* (Chicago: University of Chicago Press, 2005); as well as Robert Repetto, ed., *Punctuated Equilibrium and the Dynamics of U.S. Environmental Policy* (New Haven, CT: Yale University Press, 2006); George J. Busenberg, *Oil and Wilderness in Alaska* (Washington, DC: Georgetown University Press, 2013). See also Maxwell E. McCombs and Donald L. Shaw, "The Agenda-Setting Function of Mass Media," *Public Opinion Quarterly* 36, no. 2 (1972): 176–87; Anthony Downs, "Up and Down with Ecology—the Issue-Attention Cycle," *The Public Interest* 28 (Summer 1972): 38–50; John W. Kingdon, *Agendas, Alternatives, and Public Policies* (New York: Longman, 2003).

3. Repetto, *Punctuated Equilibrium and the Dynamics of U.S. Environmental Policy*, 25.

4. Walter, Lippmann. *Public Opinion* (New York: MacMillan, 1922).

5. McCombs and Shaw, "The Agenda-Setting Function of Mass Media," 176.

6. Anthony Downs, "Up and Down with Ecology—the Issue-Attention Cycle," *The Public Interest* 28 (Summer 1972): 38-50.

7. Ibid. 39.

8. Ibid. 40.

9. Sharon Wrobel and David Connelly, "Revisiting the Issue-Attention Cycle: New Perspectives and Prospects" (paper presented at the annual meeting of the American Political Science Association, Boston, MA, August 28, 2002).

10. Roger W. Cobb and Charles D. Elder, "The Politics of Agenda-Building: An Alternative Perspective for Modern Democratic Theory," *The Journal of Politics* 33, no. 4. (November 1971): 905.

11. E. E. Schattschneider, *The Semi-Sovereign People* (New York: Holt, Rinehart and Winston, 1960).

12. Cobb and Elder, "The Politics of Agenda-Building: An Alternative Perspective for Modern Democratic Theory, 914.

13. Charles D. Elder and Roger W. Cobb, *The Political Uses of Symbols* (New York: Longman Publishing Group, 1983).

14. John W. Kingdon, *Agendas, Alternatives, and Public Policies*, 2nd ed. (New York: Harper Collins, 1995).

15. Thomas A. Birkland, *After Disaster: Agenda Setting, Public Policy, and Focusing Events* (Washington, DC: Georgetown University Press, 1997).

16. John W. Kingdon, *Agendas, Alternatives, and Public Policies* (Ann Arbor: University of Michigan Press, 1984; 2nd ed., 1995), 94–96.

17. Kingdon, John W. *Agendas, Alternatives, and Public Policies* (Boston: Little, Brown, 1984).

18. John W. Kingdon, *Agendas, Alternatives, and Public Policies* (New York: Longman, 1995; 2nd ed., 2003), 17.

19. Ibid. 19.

20. Ibid. 19.

21. Ibid. 202.

22. Niles Eldredge and Stephen J. Gould, "Punctuated Equilibria: An Alternative to Phyletic Gradualism," in *Models in Paleobiology*, ed. T. J. M. Schopf (San Francisco: Freeman, Cooper and Company, 1972), 82–115.

23. Baumgartner and Jones, *Agendas and Instability in American Politics*; see also Repetto, *Punctuated Equilibrium and the Dynamics of U.S. Environmental Policy*.

24. Baumgartner and Jones, *Agendas and Instability in American Politics*, 236.

25. Ibid.; Kingdon, *Agendas, Alternatives, and Public Policies*, 96; and Birkland, *After Disaster: Agenda Setting, Public Policy, and Focusing Events*.

26. Baumgartner and Jones, *Agendas and Instability in American Politics*, 100.

27. Frank R. Baumgartner and Bryan D. Jones, eds., *Policy Dynamics* (Chicago: University of Chicago Press, 2002), 8–9.

28. Ibid. 7. See also Jones and Baumgartner, *Politics of Attention*.

29. Birkland, *After Disaster: Agenda Setting, Public Policy, and Focusing Events*.

30. Ibid. 22.

31. Paul A. Sabatier, "An Advocacy Coalition Framework of Policy Change and the Role of Policy-Oriented Learning Therein," *Policy Sciences* 21 (1988): 129–68; Paul A. Sabatier, "Political Science and Public Policy," *PS: Political Science and Politics* 24 (1991): 61–69.

32. Thomas A. Birkland, "Focusing Events, Mobilization, and Agenda Setting," *Journal of Public Policy* 18, no. 1 (1998): 67.

33. Baumgartner and Jones, *Agendas and Instability in American Politics*.

34. Eric R. A. N. Smith, *Energy, the Environment, and Public Opinion* (Lanham, MD: Rowman & Littlefield), 24.

35. Birkland, *After Disaster: Agenda Setting, Public Policy, and Focusing Events*, 26.

36. See for example, Larry M. Bartels, *Unequal Democracy* (Princeton, NJ: Princeton University Press, 2008); Thomas Piketty, *Capital in the Twenty-First Century* (Cambridge, MA: Harvard University Press, 2014).

37. Birkland, *After Disaster: Agenda Setting, Public Policy, and Focusing Events*, 11.

38. US Department of Commerce National Oceanic and Atmospheric Administration, "California Drought: 2014 Service Assessment," http://www.nws.noaa.gov/om/assessments/pdfs/drought_ca14.pdf.

39. Ibid.

40. According to our LexisNexis count, stories including both keywords "California" and "drought" in the *New York Times* and *San Jose Mercury News* jumped significantly in 2014 from 2013 and all years dating back to 2009. We could not include counts from the *Los Angeles Times* because LexisNexis only maintains a rolling count from the previous six months.

41. Governor of California, Executive Order B-29-15, Executive Department for the State of California (April 1, 2015).

42. Roger E. Kasperson and Pieter Jan M. Stallen, *Communicating Risks to the Public: International Perspectives*, vol. 4. Dordrecht, The Netherlands: Springer Science & Business Media, 1991).

43. Thomas E. Mann, *Unsafe at Any Margin: Interpreting Congressional Elections* (Washington, DC: American Enterprise Institute for Public Policy Research, 1978); R. Douglas Arnold, *The Logic of Congressional Action* (New Haven, CT: Yale University Press, 1990).

44. Birkland, *After Disaster: Agenda Setting, Public Policy, and Focusing Events*, 30.

45. McCombs and Shaw, "The Agenda-Setting Function of the Mass Media"; Maxwell E. McCombs, *Setting the Agenda*, 2nd ed. (Cambridge: Polity Press, 2003); Iyengar, Shanto, and Donald R. Kinder. *News that Matters: Television and American Opinion*. (Chicago, IL: University of Chicago Press, 1987).

46. Kimberly Gross and Sean Aday, "The Scary World in Your Living Room and Neighborhood," *Journal of Communication* 53 (2003): 411–26; Christine Ader, "A Longitudinal Study of Agenda Setting for the Issue of Environmental Pollution," *Journalism and Mass Communication Quarterly* 72 (1995): 300–311.

47. Harold Zucker, "The Variable Nature of News Media Influence," in *Communication Yearbook 2*, ed. Brent Ruben (New Brunswick, NJ: Transaction Books, 1978), 225–40;

James Winter, Chaim Eyal, and Ann Rogers, "Issue-Specific Agenda Setting," *Canadian Journal of Communication* 8, no. 2 (1982): 1–10; David Weaver, Doris Graber, Maxwell McCombs, and Chaim Eyal, *Media Agenda Setting in a Presidential Election* (Westport, CT: Greenwood, 1981).

48. McCombs, *Setting the Agenda*, 26–27; Douglas R. Bohi and Joel Darmstadter, "The Energy Upheavals of the 1970s," in *The Energy Crisis: Unresolved Issues and Enduring Legacies*, ed. David Lewis Feldman (Baltimore, MD: Johns Hopkins University Press, 1996), 25–61.

49. Paul L. Joskow, "California's Electricity Crisis," *Oxford Review of Economic Policy* 17, no. 3 (2001): 365–88; US Congressional Budget Office, "Causes and Lessons of the California Electricity Crisis," September, 2001, accessed July 26, 2015, http://www.cbo.gov/sites/default/files/californiaenergy.pdf.

50. Baumgartner and Jones, *Agendas and Instability in American Politics*; and Jones and Baumgartner, *The Politics of Attention*. See also Repetto, *Punctuated Equilibrium and the Dynamics of U.S. Environmental Policy*.

51. Sabatier, "An Advocacy Coalition Framework of Policy Change and the Role of Policy-Oriented Learning Therein"; Birkland, *After Disaster: Agenda Setting, Public Policy, and Focusing Events*.

52. Birkland, *After Disaster: Agenda Setting, Public Policy, and Focusing Events*, 5.

53. This account is primarily drawn from Thomas R. Wellock, *Critical Masses: Opposition to Nuclear Power in California, 1958–1978* (Madison, WI: University of Wisconsin Press, 1998), chap. 4.

54. Joseph G. Morone and Edward J. Woodhouse, *The Demise of Nuclear Energy?* (New Haven, CT: Yale University Press, 1989), 86; David Okrent, *Nuclear Reactor Safety: On the History of the Regulatory Process* (Madison, WI: University of Wisconsin Press, 1981), 220, 231.

55. Baumgartner and Jones, *Agendas and Instability in American Politics*, chap. 7; Jones and Baumgartner, *The Politics of Attention*.

56. Frank R. Baumgartner, "Punctuated Equilibrium Theory and Environmental Policy," in Repetto, *Punctuated Equilibrium and the Dynamics of U.S. Environmental Policy*, 24–46.

57. Robert J. Duffy, *The Green Agenda in American Politics: New Strategies for the Twenty-first Century* (Lawrence: University Press of Kansas, 2003).

58. Sarah B. Pralle, *Branching Out, Digging In: Environmental Advocacy and Agenda Setting* (Washington, DC: Georgetown University Press, 2006); Sarah B. Pralle, "Agenda Setting and Climate Change," *Environmental Politics* 18, no. 5 (2009): 781–99; Sheldon Ungar, "The Rise and (Relative) Decline of Global Warming as a Social Problem," *The Sociological Quarterly* 33, no. 4 (1992): 483–501; and C. Trumbo, "Longitudinal Modeling of Public Issues: An Application of the Agenda-Setting Process to the Issue of Global Warming," *Journalism and Mass Communication Monographs* 152 (1995): 1–57.

59. Birkland, *After Disaster: Agenda Setting, Public Policy, and Focusing Events*.

60. Bradford H. Bishop, "Focusing Events and Public Opinion: Evidence from the Deepwater Horizon Disaster," *Political Behavior* 36, no. 1 (2014): 1–22.

61. Michael E. Kraft and Sheldon Kamieniecki, eds., *Business and Environmental Policy: Corporate Interests in the American Political System* (Cambridge, MA: MIT Press, 2007).

62. Birkland, *After Disaster: Agenda Setting, Public Policy, and Focusing Events*, 14.

63. Bruce A. Beaubouef writes about this disagreement between analysts regarding whether or not the 1990 oil-supply disruption was a "shock" or not in *The Strategic Petroleum Reserve: US Energy security and Oil Politics, 1975–2005* (Texas University Press, 2007), 279n.2. Beaubouef writes how Vito Stagliano, DOE Senior Energy Analyst during the Bush administration, characterizes what occurred not as a "shock" but merely an oil-supply disruption. However, M. A. Adelman, an MIT oil economist, and Phillip K. Verleger, Jr. both view the 1990 crisis similarly to previous crises. Beaubouef also cites New York-based oil consultant Dimitrious Koutsomitis, who was quoted in a *New York Times* article as saying, "There has been a price shock, but so far there hasn't really been a demand shock." Matthew L. Wald, "Oil Prices Up Despite Bush Move," *New York Times*, September 28, 1990, D-1, accessed May 2, 2016, (http://www.nytimes.com/1990/09/28/business/oil-prices-up-despite-bush-move.html)

64. Deborah A. Stone, "Causal Stories and the Formation of Policy Agendas," *Political Science Quarterly* (1989): 281.

65. James W. Dearing and Everett Rogers, *Agenda-Setting* (Thousand Oaks, CA: Sage Publishing, 1996), 71.

66. Robert S. Wood, "Tobacco's Tipping Point: The Master Settlement Agreement as a Focusing Event," *Policy Studies Journal* 34, no. 3 (2006): 423.

67. James E. Akins remarked, "Oil experts, economists and government officials who have attempted in recent years to predict future demand and prices for oil have had only marginally better success than those who foretell the advent of earthquakes or the second coming of the Messiah. . . . Oil shortages were predicted again in the 1920s, again in the late thirties, and after the Second World War. None occurred, and supply forecasters went to the other extreme: past predictions of shortages had been wrong, they reasoned, therefore all such future predictions must be wrong and we could count on an ample supply of oil for as long as we would need it." See James E. Akins, "The Oil Crisis: This Time the Wolf is Here" *Foreign Affairs* 51, no. 3 (1973): 462–64.

68. Daniel Yergin, *The Prize: The Epic Quest for Oil, Money & Power* (New York: Simon and Schuster, 2011), 752.

69. Ibid. 751.

70. Colin Campbell and Jean Laherrere, "The End of Cheap Oil," *Scientific American* 278, no. 3 (March 1998): 78–83.

71. US Energy Information Administration, "Annual Energy Review," last modified August 2012, http://www.eia.gov/totalenergy/data/annual/index.cfm.

72. Paul Light, *The President's Agenda: Domestic Policy Choice from Kennedy to Clinton* (Baltimore, MD: John Hopkins University Press, 1999), 85.

73. US Energy Information Agency, "Petroleum & Other Liquids," accessed May 12, 2016, http://www.eia.gov/dnav/pet/hist/LeafHandler.ashx?n=PET&s=F000000__3&f=M.

74. US Department of Transportation, Office of the Assistant Secretary for Research and Technology, Bureau of Transportation Statistics, "5-8 Motor Vehicle Gas Prices: Jan. 1980– Sept. 2013 (Table)," http://www.rita.dot.gov/bts/sites/rita.dot.gov.bts/files/publications/pocket_guide_to_transportation/2014/5_Economy/table5_8_table.

75. Sources: EIA, 2010. Annual Energy Review 2010. Report DOE/EIA-0384 (2010). Energy Information Administration, 175, accessed May 13, 2016 https://www.eia.gov/totalenergy/data/annual/archive/038410.pdf; GDP: Bureau of Economic Analysis, http://www.bea.gov/national/—the data were on the main page under "Current-dollar and 'real' GDP (Excel)."

76. James D. Hamilton, "Oil and the Macroeconomy since World War II," *Journal of Political Economy* 91 (1983): 228–48; James D. Hamilton, "This is What Happened to the Oil Price-Macroeconomy Relationship," *Journal of Monetary Economics* 38 (1996): 215–20; Gert Peersman, "What Caused the Early Millennium Slowdown? Evidence Based on Vector Autoregressions," *Journal of Applied Econometrics* 20 (2005): 185–207. For an alternative view, see Robert B. Barsky and Lutz Kilian, "Oil and the Macroeconomy since the 1970s," *Journal of Economic Perspectives*, 18, no. 4 (2004): 115–34.

77. Gallup's wording of the question, which first appeared in 1946, is as follows: "What do you think is the most important problem facing this country today?" see Policy Agendas Project, "Gallup's Most Important Problem," accessed May 13, 2016, http://policyagendas.org/page/datasets-codebooks#gallups_most_important_problem

78. Pew Research Center, "Rising Price of Gas Draws Most Public Interest in 2000," press release, December 25, 2010, http://www.people-press.org/2000/12/25/rising-price-of-gas-draws-most-public-interest-in-2000/.

79. James A. Stimson, *Public Opinion in America: Moods, Cycles, and Swings*, 2nd ed. (Boulder, CO: Westview Press, 1991).

80. Walter Lippmann, *Public Opinion* (MacMillan: New York, 1922).

81. Stimson, *Public Opinion in America: Moods, Cycles, and Swings*, 18.

82. See Appendix A for item content. While the Policy Agendas Project (http://www.policyagendas.org) calculated our energy policy mood for us, an algorithm for estimating

mood is provided in Appendix 1 of Stimson's book, p. 129–131; Stimson, *Public Opinion in America: Moods, Cycles, & Swings.*

83. Frank R. Baumgartner and Bryan D. Jones in, *Agendas and Instability in American Politics*, 2nd ed. (Chicago: University of Chicago Press, 2009), 103

84. Ibid. chap. 6.

85. Michelle Wolfe, Bryan D. Jones, and Frank R. Baumgartner, "A Failure to Communicate: Agenda Setting in Media and Policy Studies." *Political Communication* 30, no. 2 (2013): 179.

86. Ibid.

87. Our count of newspaper articles was conducted using LexisNexis. Policy Agendas Project (http://www.policyagendas.org) also provides a count of *New York Times* coverage of "energy" issues. Our count of *New York Times* articles conducted via LexisNexis is significantly different (more inflated) than that of Policy Agendas Project. However, the movement of the trend lines accord with one another.

88. Our search via LexisNexis includes the terms related to the energy crisis, including "energy crises," "oil," "profits," "energy bill," "energy legislation," "energy policy."

89. See http://ww.presidency.ucsb.edu.

90. A manifest content analysis was conducted for us by Gerhard Peters of The American Presidency Project, http://www.presidency.ucsb.edu/.

91. http://www.policyagendas.org/page/trend-analysis.

92. These four laws are classified as *major legislation* by Congressional Quarterly (CQ) Almanac *CQ Almanac 1973*, 29th ed., 788, Washington, DC: Congressional Quarterly, 1974.. Initially, we had hoped to rely on the classifications of the CQ Almanac for our counts of major legislation, but in 1979 the publication omitted the "box score" and thus its list of major legislation. Incidentally, only one of the four pieces of legislation included in the CQ Almanac are also included in both Sarah A. Binder's and David R. Mayhew's counts of major legislation, which is the Trans-Alaskan Pipeline Authorization Act of 1973 (PL 93–153).

93. *CQ Almanac 1973*, 29th ed., 788, Washington, DC: Congressional Quarterly, 1974.

94. Figure 2.10 contains data from both Sarah A. Binder, *Stalemate: Causes and Consequences of Legislative Gridlock* (Washington, DC: Brookings Institution Press, 2003); and David R. Mayhew, *Divided We Govern: Party Control, Lawmaking and Investigations, 1946–2002* (New Haven, CT: Yale University Press, 2005). Mayhew's data are available on his website, http://campuspress.yale.edu/davidmayhew/datasets-divided-we-govern/, and Binder shared hers with us upon request. Please note, some legislation included in Binder's list of major legislation is ostensibly included in Mayhew's list, but the authors of this book could not reconcile the two lists perfectly. That is, of the passed major energy legislation, Binder's list included some that was coded by her as also being on Mayhew's, but we could not find them on Mayhew's list.

95. Sarah A. Binder creates a measure for the systematic agenda by extracting issues from the editorial pages of the New York Times. In doing so, she codes the legislative content of each editorial that mentioned Congress, the House, or the Senate and then uses the issues mentioned to compile a list of agenda items for each Congress, also tallying the number of editorials the Times ran on each issue. Our count of issues included in Figure 2.10 is determined by extracting energy related issues from the data that she shared with us.

96. Light, *The President's Agenda: Domestic Policy Choice from Kennedy to Clinton*, 162.

97. See chapter 5 for a discussion on the role of environmental and public interest groups in energy-related policy change resulting from the 1973–74 energy crisis.

Chapter 3

1. John W. Kingdon, *Congressmen's Voting Decisions*, 3rd ed. (Ann Arbor, MI: University of Michigan Press, 1989); R. Douglas Arnold, *The Logic of Congressional Action* (New Haven, CT: Yale University Press, 1990); Kristina Miler, *Constituency Representation in Congress* (New York: Cambridge University Press, 2014).

2. Paul Burstein, *American Public Opinion, Advocacy, and Policy in Congress* (New York: Cambridge University Press, 2014); Robert S. Erikson, Gerald C. Wright, and John P. McIver, *Statehouse*

Democracy (New York: Cambridge University Press, 1993); Benjamin I. Page, "The Semi-Sovereign People," in *Navigating Public Opinion*, ed. Jeff Manza, Fay Lomax Cook, and Benjamin I. Page (New York: Oxford University Press, 2002); Robert Y. Shapiro, "Public Opinion, Elites, and Democracy," *Critical Review* 12 (1998): 501–28; Benjamin I. Page, "The Semi-Sovereign People," in Manza, Cook, and Page, *Navigating Public Opinion*; Robert Y. Shapiro, "Public Opinion, Elites, and Democracy," *Critical Review* 12 (1998): 501–28; James Stimson, Michael B. MacKuen, and Robert S. Erikson, "Dynamic Representation," *American Political Science Review* 89 (1995): 543–65.

3. Anthony Downs, "Up and Down with Ecology: The Issue-Attention Cycle," *Public Interest* 28 (1972): 38–50.

4. Robert C. Mitchell, "Silent Spring/Sold Majorities," *Public Opinion* 2 (August/September 1979): 55.

5. Robert C. Mitchell, "Public Opinion on Environmental Issues," in *Environmental Policy in the 1980s*, ed. Norman Vig and Michael Kraft (Washington, DC: Congressional Quarterly Press, 1984); Riley E. Dunlap, "Public Opinion and Environmental Policy," in *Environmental Politics & Policy*, ed. James P. Lester (Durham, NC: Duke University Press, 1995), 63–114.

6. Tom W. Smith, Peter Marsden, Michael Hout, and Jibum Kim, *General Social Surveys, 1972–2010: Cumulative Codebook* (Chicago: National Opinion Research Center, 2011).

7. Ted Nordhaus and Michael Shellenberger, *Break Through: From the Death of Environmentalism to the Politics of Possibility* (Boston: Houghton Mifflin, 2007), 31–33.

8. Eric R. A. N. Smith, *The Unchanging American Voter* (Berkeley: University of California Press, 1989), chap. 2; Daniel M. Wegner, *The Illusions of Conscious Will* (Cambridge, MA: MIT Press, 2002); Ruud Custers and Henk Aarts, "The Unconscious Will," *Science* 399 (2010): 47–50.

9. Frank L. Davis and Albert H. Wurth, "Voting Preferences and the Environment in the American Electorate," *Society & Natural Resources* 16 (2003): 729–40; Frank L. Davis, Albert H. Wurth, and John C. Lazarus, "The Green Vote in Presidential Elections: Past Performance and Future Promise," *Social Science Journal* 45(2008): 525–45.

10. Deborah Lynn Guber, *The Grassroots of a Green Revolution* (Cambridge, MA: MIT Press, 2003), chap. 3.

11. Benjamin I. Page and Robert Y. Shapiro, *The Rational Public* (Chicago, IL: University of Chicago Press, 1992), 385.

12. http://www.gallup.com/poll/1615/Environment.aspx

13. Stephan J. Goetz, Richard C. Ready, and Brad Stone, "U.S. Economic Growth vs. Environmental Conditions," *Growth and Change* 3 (1996): 209–23; Paul Hawken, Amory Lovins, and L. Hunter Lovins, *Natural Capitalism* (New York: Little, Brown, & Co., 1999).

14. Felix K. Yeboah, Michael Kaplowitz, Frank Lupi, and Laurie Thorp, "Exploring the Middle Ground between Environmental Protection and Economic Growth," *Public Understanding of Science* 22 (2013): 413–26.

15. We tested all the other variables that Guber used both individually and in combinations, and none came close to statistical significance.

16. Data from Cambridge Research International quoted by William Mayer, *The Changing American Mind* (Ann Arbor: University of Michigan Press, 1992), 489.

17. Data from the Field Research Corporation and the Field Institute (http://field.com/fieldpollonline/subscribers/Rls2380.pdf). The Field Poll has not asked about offshore oil drilling since June 2011.

18. The gasoline price data are for the average price of gasoline in real 1996 dollars. The data are from the US Department of Energy, *Annual Energy Review 2000*, table 5.22. These data are available on the web at https://www.eia.gov/totalenergy/data/annual/archive/038400.pdf.

19. In one of the alternative specifications we tested, we discovered that omitting the *Exxon Valdez* variable lowered the p-value of gas prices to just p < .06.

20. Richard F. Fenno, *Homestyle* (Boston: Little, Brown, 1978); Paul Burstein, *American Public Opinion, Advocacy, and Policy in Congress* (New York: Cambridge University Press, 2014).

21. The two surveys are the California Offshore Oil Drilling and Energy Policy Survey, which was conducted March 5-18, 1998 and Field Poll 0102, which was conducted May 11-20, 2001.

Both surveys were conducted by the Field Institute. The California Offshore Oil Drilling and Energy Policy Survey is archived at the Inter-university Consortium for Political and Social Research (www.icpsr.umich.edu) and the Field Poll is archived at UCData (http://ucdata.berkeley.edu/).

22. More precisely, at the time of the March 1998 survey, the average price of unleaded regular was $1.04 per gallon. It dropped to $0.955 per gallon in February 1999, and then shot up to $1.729 by the time of the second survey in May 2001. We refer to the 81 percent increase from February 1999 to May 2001 because that increase is what drew the reaction from the public and politicians. If one only looks at the March 1998 to May 2001 increase, it was 66 percent. The data are from the US Energy Information Administration, http://205.254.135.7/forecasts/steo/realprices/.

23. Frank Bruni, "Bush, in Energy Plan, Endorses New U.S. Drilling to Remedy Oil Prices," *New York Times*, September 30, 2000; Alison Mitchell, "The 2000 Campaign: The Vice President; Gore Says Bush Plan Will Cause Lasting Damage to the Environment," *New York Times*, September 30, 2000.

24. Pew Research Center for the People & the Press, "Rising Price of Gas Draws Most Public Interest in 2000," press release, December 25, 2000, http://www.people-press.org.

25. John Sivacek and William D. Crano, "Vested Interest as a Moderator of Attitude– Behavior Consistency, *Journal of Personality and Social Psychology* 43 (1982): 210–21; David O. Sears and Carolyn L. Funk, "Self-Interest in Americans' Political Opinions," in *Beyond Self-Interest*, ed. Jane J. Mansbridge (Chicago: University of Chicago Press, 1990), 147–70; David O. Sears and Carolyn L. Funk, "The Role of Self-Interest in Social and Political Attitudes," in *Advances in Experimental Social Psychology*, vol. 24, ed. Mark P. Zanna (New York: Academic Press, 1991), 2–91; Dale T. Miller, "The Norm of Self-Interest," *American Psychologist* 54 (December 1999): 1053–60; Rebecca K. Ratner and Dale T. Miller, "The Norm of Self-Interest and its Effects on Social Action," *Journal of Personality and Social Psychology* 81 (July 2001): 5–16.

26. Richard J. Bord and Robert E. O'Connor, "The Gender Gap in Environmental Attitudes: The Case of Perceived Vulnerability to Risk," *Social Science Quarterly* 78 (1997): 830–40; Guber, *The Grassroots of a Green Revolution*, chap. 3.; Robert Emmet Jones and Riley E. Dunlap, "The Social Bases of Environmental Concern: Have They Changed Over Time?," *Rural Sociology* 57 (1992): 28–47; Eric R. A. N. Smith, *Energy, the Environment, and Public Opinion* (Boulder, CO: Rowman & Littlefield, 2002), chap. 3.

27. Smith, *Energy, the Environment, and Public Opinion*; John R. Zaller, *The Nature and Origins of Mass Opinion* (New York: Cambridge University Press, 1992).

28. Pew Research Center for the People & the Press, "Rising Price of Gas Draws Most Public Interest in 2000."

29. Bruni, "Bush, in Energy Plan, Endorses New U.S. Drilling to Remedy Oil Prices"; Mitchell, "The 2000 Campaign: The Vice President; Gore Says Bush Plan Will Cause Lasting Damage to the Environment."

30. Paul R. Abramson, *Political Attitudes in America* (San Francisco: W. H. Freeman, 1983); William G. Mayer, *The Changing American Mind: How and Why American Public Opinion Changed Between 1960 and 1988* (Ann Arbor: University of Michigan Press, 1993); Smith, *Energy, the Environment, and Public Opinion*; Alison G. Keleher and Eric R. A. N. Smith, "Explaining the Growing Support for Gay and Lesbian Equality since 1990," *Journal of Homosexuality* 59 (2012): 1307–27.

31. Thomas Brambor, William R. Clark, and Matt Golder, "Understanding Interaction Models: Improving Empirical Analyses," *Political Analysis* 14 (2006): 63–82.

32. We tried looking at income and financial status separately. We tried dropping the two interaction terms. We also created a dummy variable so that we could measure people with the lowest incomes versus those with moderate or high incomes. None of these variations revealed any effects.

33. When both party identification and ideology are included in the equation, we have a multicollinearity problem. Neither coefficient is statistically significant. The ideology results are not presented here to save space.

34. Harold Zucker, "The Variable Nature of News Media Influence," in Brent Rubin, ed., *Communication Yearbook 2* (New Brunkswick, NJ: Transaction Books, 1978), 225–40; Maxwell E. McCombs, *Setting the Agenda*, 2nd ed. (Cambridge: Polity Press, 2003), 71–77.

35. ABC News/Washington Post Poll. June 12-15, 2008, reported at http://pollingreport.com/energy3.htm.

36. http://field.com/fieldpollonline/subscribers/Rls2277.pdf

37. These data are annual averages from the Department of Energy, Energy Information Administration, *Annual Energy Review 2010*, tables 3.12 and 5.24, https://www.eia.gov/totalenergy/data/annual/archive/038410.pdf. The profit data are for return on investment, measured as net income divided by net investment in place. The gasoline prices are in real 2005 dollars. The Energy Information Administration discontinued its publication of oil-industry profits after 2010.

38. Ronald White, "Big Oil Firms Profit on Slim Output," *Los Angeles Times*, April 29, 2011; Clifford Krauss, "Oil Industry Hums as Higher Prices Bolster Quarterly Profits at Exxon and Shell," *New York Times*, October 28, 2011.

39. The full question was, "Here is a list of groups who have been mentioned in one way or another as being to blame for the current energy crisis in the United States. Would you go down that list and for each one tell me whether you think they deserve major blame for the energy crisis, some blame, or no blame at all?" Barbara C. Farhar, "Trends in U.S. Perceptions and Preferences on Energy and Environmental Policy," *Environment and Resources* 19 (1994): 211–39.

40. Al Richman, "The Polls: Public Attitudes toward the Energy Crisis," *Public Opinion Quarterly* 43 (1979): 577.

41. Pew Research Center, "Public Worried about Iran but Wary of Military Action." 16 May 2006, http://www.people-press.org/2006/05/16/public-worried-about-iran-but-wary-of-military-action/.

42. Page and Shapiro, *The Rational Public.*

Chapter 4

1. Paul R. Ehrlich and Anne H. Ehrlich, *Betrayal of Science and Reason* (Washington, DC: Island Press, 1996); Ross Gelbspan, *Boiling Point* (New York: Basic Books, 2004); Albert Gore, *An Inconvenient Truth: The Crisis of Global Warming* (New York: Viking, 2007); Richard Wolfson and Stephen H. Schneider, "Understanding Climate Science," in *Climate Change Policy: A Survey*, ed. Stephen H. Schneider, Armin Rosencranz, and John O. Niles (Washington, DC: Island Press, 2002).

2. Ralph J. Cicerone, "Ensuring Integrity in Science," *Science* 327 (2010): 624; Kathy Sykes, "The Quality of Public Dialogue," *Science* 318 (2007): 1349.

3. Naomi Oreskes and Erik M. Conway, *Merchants of Doubt* (New York: Bloomsbury Press, 2010); Eric Pooley, *The Climate War* (New York: Hyperion, 2010); James L. Powell, *The Inquisition of Climate Science* (New York: Columbia University Press, 2011).

4. Carl I. Hovland, Irving L. Janis, and Harold H. Kelly, *Communication and Persuasion: Psychological Studies of Opinion Change* (New Haven, CT: Yale University Press, 1953), 13.

5. Richard E. Petty and John T. Cacioppo, "Central and Peripheral Routes to Persuasion: Applications to Advertising," in *Advertising and Consumer Psychology*, ed. Larry Percy and Arch G. Woodside (Lexington, MA: Heath, 1983), 3–23; Richard E. Petty and John T. Cacioppo, *Communication and Persuasion: Central and Peripheral Routes to Attitude Change* (New York: Springer-Verlag, 1986); Richard E. Petty and John T. Cacioppo, "The Elaboration Likelihood Model of Persuasion," in *Advances in Experimental Social Psychology 19*, ed. L. Berkowtiz (New York: Academic Press, 1986), 123–205; Richard E. Petty and Duane T. Wegener, "The Elaboration Likelihood Model: Current Status and Controversies," in *Dual-Process Theories in Social Psychology*, ed. L. Berkowtiz (New York: Guilford Press, 1999), 41–72; Shelly Chaiken, "Heuristic versus Systematic Information Processing and the Use of Source versus Message Cues in Persuasion," *Journal of Personality and Social Psychology* 39 (1980): 752–66; Shelly A. Chaiken, A. Liberman, and Alice H. Eagly, "Heuristic and Systematic Information Processing within and beyond the Persuasion Context," in

Unintended Thought, ed. James S. Uleman and John A. Bargh (New York: Guilford Press, 1989), 212–52; Serena Chen and Shelly Chaiken, "The Heuristic-Systematic Model in Its Broader Context," in *Dual-Process Theories in Social Psychology*, ed. Shelly Chaiken and Yaacov Trope (New York: Guilford Press, 1999), 73–96.

6. Elizabeth J. Wilson and Daniel L. Sherrell, "Source Effects in Communication and Persuasion Research: A Meta-Analysis of Effect Size," *Journal of the Academy of Marketing Science* 21 (2009): 101–12.

7. Timothy C. Earle and George T. Cvetkovich, *Social Trust: Toward a Cosmopolitan Society* (Westport, CT: Praeger, 1995); Timothy C. Earle and George Cvetkovich, "Social Trust and Culture in Risk Management," in *Social Trust and the Management of Risk*, ed. George Cvetkovich and Ragnar E. Löfstedt (London: Earthscan, 1999), 9–21; William R. Freudenburg, "Risk and Recreancy: Weber, the Division of Labor, and the Rationality of Risk Perceptions," *Social Forces* 71 (1993): 909–32; Roger E. Kasperson, Dominic Golding, and Jeanne X. Kasperson, "Risk, Trust, and Democratic Theory," in *Social Trust and the Management of Risk*, ed. George Cvetkovich and Ragnar E. Löfstedt (London: Earthscan, 1999); Paul Slovic, "Perceived Risk, Trust, and Democracy," in *Social Trust and the Management of Risk*, ed. George Cvetkovich and Ragnar E. Löfstedt (London: Earthscan, 1999), 42–52.

8. Stephen E. Binney, Robert Mason, Steven W. Martsolf, and John H. Detweiler, "Credibility, Public Trust, and the Transport of Radioactive Waste through Local Communities," *Environment and Behavior* 28 (1996): 283–301; Richard J. Bord and Robert E. O'Connor, "Risk Communication, Knowledge, and Attitudes: Explaining Reactions to a Technology Perceived as Risky," *Risk Analysis* 10 (1990): 499–506; Hank C. Jenkins-Smith, "Culture, Trust, Ideology, and Perceptions of the Risks of Nuclear Wastes: A Causal Analysis" (paper prepared for the annual meeting of the Society for Risk Analysis, San Diego, CA, December 6–9, 1992); Frank N. Laird, "The Decline of Deference: The Political Context of Risk Communication," *Risk Analysis* 4 (1989): 543–50; John C. Pierce, Mary Ann E. Steger, Brent S. Steel, and Nicholas P. Lovrich, *Citizens, Political Communication, and Interest Groups* (Westport, CT: Praeger, 1992).

9. Kasperson, Golding, and Kasperson, "Risk, Trust, and Democratic Theory."

10. Blair T. Johnson, Gregory R. Maio, and Aaron Smith-McLallen, "Communication and Attitude Change: Causes, Processes, and Effects," in *The Handbook of Attitudes*, ed. Dolores Albarracin, Blair T. Johnson, and Mark P. Zanna (Mahwah, NJ: Lawrence Erlbaum, 2005), 617–69.

11. Carolyn W. Sherif, Muzafer Sherif, and Roger E. Nebergall, *Attitude and Attitude Change: The Social Judgment-Involvement Approach* (Philadelphia: Saunders, 1965); Carolyn W. Sherif, Muzafer Sherif, and Carl I. Hovland, *Social Judgement: Assimilation and Contrast Effects in Communication and Attitude Change* (New Haven, CT: Yale University Press, 1961); Muzafer Sherif and Carolyn W. Sherif, "Attitude as the Individual's Own Categories: The Social Judgment-Involvement Approach to Attitude and Attitude Change," in *Attitude, Ego-Involvement and Change*, ed. Carolyn W. Sherif and Muzafer Sherif (New York: Wiley, 1967), 105–39.

12. Muzafer Sherif, Daniel Taub, and Carl I. Hovland, "Assimilation and Contrast Effects of Anchoring Stimuli on Judgments," *Journal of Experimental Psychology* 55 (1958): 150–55; Sherif et al., *Social Judgment*, 1961.

13. Dolores Albarracín and Robert S. Wyer, "The Cognitive Impact on Past Behavior: Influences on Beliefs, Attitudes, and Future Behavioral Decisions," *Social Psychology Bulletin* 27 (2000): 691–705; Martin Fishbein and Ajzen Icek, "Acceptance, Yielding, and Impact: Cognitive Processes in Persuasion," in *Cognitive Responses in Persuasion*, ed. Richard E. Petty, Thomas M. Ostrom, and Timothy C. Brock (Hillsdale, NJ: Erlbaum, 1981), 339–59; Anthony G. Greenwald, "Cognitive Learning, Cognitive Responses to Persuasion and Attitude Change," in *Psychological Foundations of Attitudes*, ed. Anthony G. Greenwald, Timothy C. Brock, and Thomas M. Ostrom (New York: Academic Press, 1968), 147–70; Robert J. MacCoun and Susannah Paletz, "Citizens' Perceptions of Ideological Bias in Research on Public Policy Controversies," *Political Psychology* 30 (2009): 43–65.

14. Craig A. Anderson, "Abstract and Concrete Data in the Perseverance of Social Theories: When Weak Data Lead to Unshakable Beliefs," *Journal of Experimental Social Psychology* 19 (1983): 93–108; Charles C. Lord, Lee Ross, and Mark R. Lepper, "Biased Assimilation and Attitude Polarization: The Effects of Prior Theories on Subsequently Considered Evidence," *Journal of Personality and Social Psychology* 37 (1979): 2098–109; Charles G. Lord, Lee Ross, and Mark R. Lepper, "Biased Assimilation and Attitude Polarization: The Effects of Prior Theories on Subsequently Considered Evidence," *Journal of Personality and Social Psychology* 37 (1979): 2098–109.

15. R. Shelly Chaiken, Giner-Sorolla, and Serena Chen, "Beyond Accuracy: Defense and Impression Motives in Heuristic and Systematic Information Processing," in *The Psychology of Action: Linking Cognition and Motivation to Behavior*, ed. Peter M. Gollwitzer and John A. Bargh (New York: Guilford Press, 1996), 553–78; Eva M. Pomerantz, Shelly Chaiken, and Rosalind S. Tordesillas, "Attitude Strength and Resistance Processes," *Journal of Personality and Social Psychology* 69 (1995): 408–19; Tom Pyszczynski and Jeff Greenberg, "Toward an Integration of Cognitive and Motivational Perspectives on Social Inference: A Biased Hypothesis-Testing Model," in *Advances in Experimental Social Psychology 20*, ed. Leonard Berkowitz (New York: Academic Press, 1987), 297–340; Lord et al., "Biased Assimilation and Attitude Polarization."

16. Dolores Albarracín, "Cognition in Persuasion: An Analysis of Information Processing in Response to Persuasive Communications," *Advances in Experimental Social Psychology* 34 (2002): 61–130.

17. Howard Margolis, *Dealing with Risk* (Chicago: University of Chicago Press, 1996).

18. Sharon Arad and Peter J. Carnevale, "Partisanship Effects in Judgments of Fairness and Trust in Third Parties in the Palestinian-Israeli Conflict," *Journal of Conflict Resolution* 38 (1994): 423–51; Slovic, "Perceived Risk, Trust, and Democracy."

19. Riley E. Dunlap and Araon M. McCright, "A Widening Gap: Republican and Democratic Views on Climate Change," *Environment: Science and Policy for Sustainable Development* 50, no. 5 (2008): 26–35; Arield Malka, Jon A. Krosnick, and Gary Langer, "The Association of Knowledge with Concern about Global Warming: Trusted Information Sources Shape Public Thinking," *Risk Analysis* 29 (2009): 633–47; Peter J. Jacques, Riley E. Dunlap, and Mark Freeman, "The Organization of Denial: Conservative Think Tanks and Environmental Skepticism," *Environmental Politics* 17 (2008): 349–85.

20. Mark Baldassare, *California in the New Millennium: The Changing Social and Political Landscape* (Berkeley: University of California Press, 2000), 17.

21. The survey was conducted in March, 1998 by the Field Institute, located at 550 Kearny Street, Suite 900, San Francisco, CA 94108. The sample is a representative sample of 810 adult residents of the state. Respondents were selected by random digit dialing. Interviews were conducted in either English or Spanish, as appropriate. The Field Institute is a nonpartisan, not-for-profit public opinion research organization established by the Field Research Corporation. The dataset is archived at the University of California's UCDATA, located at the UC Berkeley campus.

22. The model in figure 4.4 was estimated using LISREL 8.8.

23. The data for this analysis come from a telephone survey of 1,475 California adults conducted in July and October, 2002. The survey was conducted by the University of California, Santa Barbara Survey Research Center. Respondents were selected by random-digit dialing. Interviews were conducted in English or Spanish, as appropriate. The response rate (RR2) was 27 percent; the cooperation rate (COOP2) was 55 percent.

24. This analysis first appeared in "The Public's Trust in Scientific Claims Regarding Offshore Oil Drilling." It is available online at http://pus.sagepub.com/content/19/5/514. The final, definitive version of this paper has been published in *Public Understanding of Science* 19, no. 5 (2010): 514–27. © Juliet E. Carlisle, Jessica T. Feezell, Kristy E. H. Michaud, Eric R. A. N. Smith, and Leeanna Smith.

25. The ANOVA yielded F = 30.2, p < .0001.

26. Nancy Kraus, Torbjörn Malmfors, and Paul Slovic, "Intuitive Toxicology: Expert and Lay Judgments of Chemical Risks," *Risk Analysis* 12, no. 2 (1992): 215–32; Slovic, "Perceived Risk, Trust, and Democracy."

27. The source effect was insignificant (F = .5, n.s.); the interaction was significant (F = 3.6, p < .03).

28. An ANOVA analysis shows the differences are statistically significant (F = 8.9, p < .003).

29. Our survey found that 24 percent of Californians described themselves as liberal, and 44 percent said they were middle-of-the-road, for a total of 68 percent

30. The number of undecided respondents on the question about offshore oil drilling was too small to allow us to examine them separately.

31. (F = 243.0, p < .0001).

32. Gordon Gauchat, "Politicization of Science in the Public Sphere," *American Sociological Review* 77 (2012): 167–87.

33. Congressional Budget Office, "Causes and Lessons of the California Electricity Crisis," <is this address correct? I thought it might be useful to your readers to have this information><Yes it is correct. Good idea!> https://www.cbo.gov/publication/13292; Paul L. Joskow, "The California Electricity Crisis," *Oxford Review of Economic Policy* 17 (2001): 365–88; James L. Sweeney, *The California Electricity Crisis* (Stanford, CA: Hoover Institution Press, 2002).

Chapter 5

1. "Annual Energy Review," last modified August 2012, http://205.254.135.24/totalenergy/data/annual/showtext.cfm?t=ptb0103.

2. "World Population Prospects: The 2010 Revision," http://esa.un.org/unpd/wpp/index.htm.

3. "Annual Energy Review," last modified August 2012, http://205.254.135.24/totalenergy/data/annual/showtext.cfm?t=ptb0103.

4. Eric R. A. N Smith, *Energy, the Environment, and Public Opinion* (Lanham, MD: Rowman & Littlefield Publishers, Inc., 2002), 23.

5. Daniel Yergin, *The Prize: The Epic Quest for Oil, Money & Power* (New York: Simon & Schuster, 1991), 604.

6. Ibid. 607.

7. Ibid. 608.

8. Michael Harvey and Roger Kerin, "Perspectives on Demarketing During the Energy Crisis," *Journal of the Academy of Marketing Science* 5, no. 4 (1977): 329.

9. Yergin, *The Prize: The Epic Quest for Oil, Money & Power*, 791.

10. Ibid. 615.

11. US Energy Information Agency, "25th Anniversary of the 1973 Oil Embargo," accessed May 17, 2016, http://www.osti.gov/scitech/servlets/purl/663603

12. Yergin, *The Prize: The Epic Quest for Oil, Money & Power*, 567.

13. Contraband oil refers to oil that was overproduced and in violation of state and federal regulations and quotas.

14. Douglas Arnold, *The Logic of Congressional Action* (New Haven, CT: Yale University Press, 1990), 227.

15. Ibid. 232.

16. Smith, *Energy, the Environment, and Public Opinion*, 24.

17. Don E. Kash and Robert W. Rycroft, *U.S. Energy Policy: Crisis and Complacency* (Norman: University of Oklahoma Press, 1984), 8.

18. Yergin, *The Prize: The Epic Quest for Oil, Money & Power*, 591.

19. "Gasoline: The Shortage Hits Home," *Time*, June 25, 1973, 85.

20. "Gas Shortage Shuts 562 Stations in U.S.," *Los Angeles Times*, May 10, 1973.

21. Yergin, *The Prize: The Epic Quest for Oil, Money & Power*, 616.

22. "Energy and the Environment, " *Congressional Quarterly Almanac, 93rd Congress, 1st Session* (Washington, DC: Congressional Quarterly Inc., 1973), 589.

23. "The Fuel Crisis Begins to Hurt," *Time*, December 17, 1973, 33.

24. "The Pinch at the Pumps," *Time*, November 12, 1973, 107.

25. Ibid.

26. "America's Mood," *U.S. News & World Report*, October 15, 1973, 20.

27. "The Harris Poll," *Sarasota Herald-Tribune*, February 7, 1974, https://news.google.com/news papers?nid=1755&dat=19740207&id=Wz0gAAAAIBAJ&sjid=1WYEAAAAIBAJ&pg=69 60,2491138&hl=en.
28. "Gasoline: The Shortage Hits Home," 85
29. Ibid.
30. "America's Mood," 20.
31. "A Deep Investigation of Oil," *Time*, September 10, 1973, 84.
32. William D. Smith, "Industry Regrets Timing as Oil Earnings Climb," *New York Times*, October 25, 1973, L71.
33. Lester A. Sobel, ed., *Energy Crisis*, vol. 1, *1969–73* (New York: Facts on File, 1974), 212.
34. Yergin, *The Prize: The Epic Quest for Oil, Money & Power*, 658.
35. "The Whirlwind Confronts the Skeptics," *Time*, January 21, 1974, 24.
36. James R. Murray et al., "Evolution of Public Response to the Energy Crisis," *Science* 184, no. 4134 (April 1974): 260.
37. Al Richman, "The Polls: Public Attitude Toward the Energy Crisis," *Public Opinion Quarterly* 43, no. 4 (1979): 577.
38. "$270 Billion Suit Says Oil Crisis Was Rigged," *Los Angeles Times*, January 1, 1974.
39. Yergin, *The Prize: The Epic Quest for Oil, Money & Power*, 658–59.
40. Richard H. K. Vietor, *Energy Policy in America Since 1945: A Study of Business-Government Relations* (Cambridge: Cambridge University Press, 1984), 240.
41. Mark Kosmo, *Money to Burn: The High Costs of Energy Subsidies* (Washington, DC: World Resources Institute, 1987), available online at http://pdf.wri.org/moneytoburn_bw.pdf.
42. Charles O. Jones and Randall Strahan, "The Effect of Energy Politics on Congressional and Executive Organization in the 1970s," *Legislative Studies Quarterly* 10, no. 2 (May 1985): 154–55.
43. Ibid.
44. James Everett Katz, *Congress and National Energy Policy* (: Transaction Publishing, 1983), 19.
45. Richard Nixon, "Special Message to the Congress on Energy Policy," April 18, 1973, online by Gerhard Peters and John T. Woolley, American Presidency Project, http://www.presidency.ucsb.edu/ws/?pid=3817
46. Congressional Quarterly, *Congressional Quarterly Almanac, 93rd Congress, 1st Session*, 501-A.
47. Richard Nixon, "Special Message to the Congress on Energy Policy," April 18, 1973, online by Gerhard Peters and John T. Woolley, American Presidency Project, http://www.presidency.ucsb.edu/ws/?pid=3817.
48. Congressional Quarterly, *Congressional Quarterly Almanac, 93rd Congress, 1st Session*, 589.
49. Richard Nixon, "Address to the Nation about Policies to Deal with the Energy Shortages," November 7, 1973, online by Gerhard Peters and John T. Woolley, American Presidency Project, http://www.presidency.ucsb.edu/ws/?pid=4034.
50. Jones and Strahan, "The Effect of Energy Politics on Congressional and Executive Organization in the 1970s," 157.
51. William P. Bundy, *A Tangled Web: The Making of Foreign Policy in the Nixon Presidency* (New York: Hill and Wang, 1999), 458.
52. Yanek Mieczkowski, *Gerald Ford and the Challenges of the 1970s* (Lexington: The University Press of Kentucky, 2005), 201.
53. Sobel, *Energy Crisis*, vol. 2, *1974–75*, 85.
54. Vito Stagliano, *A Policy of Discontent: The Making of a National Energy Strategy* (Tulsa: PennWell Corporation, 2001), 27.
55. Ibid. 28.
56. Congressional Quarterly, *Congressional Quarterly Almanac, 93rd Congress, 2nd Session* (Washington, DC: Congressional Quarterly Inc., 1974), 723.
57. Ibid.
58. "Energy and Environment, 1975 Overview." In *CQ Almanac 1975*, 31st ed., 174. Washington, DC: Congressional Quarterly, 1976. http://library.cqpress.com/cqalmanac/cqal75-1213502.
59. Frank N. Laird, *Solar Energy, Technology Policy, and Institutional Values* (Cambridge: Cambridge University Press, 2004), 103.

60. Congressional Quarterly, *Congressional Quarterly Almanac, 93rd Congress, 1st Session*, 592.
61. "Unsheathing the Political Weapon," *Time*, October 29, 1973, 46.
62. "Demo Leaders Pledge Aid," *Daytona Beach Morning Journal*, January 26, 1974 .
63. Ibid.
64. Congressional Quarterly, *Congressional Quarterly Almanac, 93rd Congress, 1st Session*, 590.
65. The bill can be found under various monikers, including the Emergency Fuels and Energy Allocation Act (Thomas.gov); EPAA (Nixon's address to the nation on November 25, 1973); and Mandatory Fuel Allocation Act (Congressional Quarterly Almanac, 1973).
66. The three transportation measures included legislation that would open the Highway Trust Fund to help finance mass transit; legislation that established an independent federal agency to reorganize and upgrade railroad service in the Northeast and Midwest; and legislation that allowed Amtrak to manage and expand its transportation system.
67. Katz, *Congress and National Energy Policy*, 23–24.
68. S. 2652., 93rd Congress. (1973). Accesses May 19, 2016, https://www.congress.gov/bill/93rd-congress/senate-bill/2652.
69. Sobel, *Energy Crisis*, vol. 2, *1974–75*, 49.
70. "What Voters Are Telling Congress," *U.S. News & World Report*, January 21, 1974, 14–15.
71. Ibid.
72. Richman, "The Polls: Public Attitudes toward the Energy Crisis," 580.
73. Ibid. 577.
74. Sobel, *Energy Crisis*, vol. 2, *1974–75*, 63.
75. "The Whirlwind Confronts the Skeptics," 24.
76. Yergin, *The Prize: The Epic Quest for Oil, Money & Power*, 639.
77. Sobel, *Energy Crisis*, vol. 2, *1974–75*, 52.
78. Martha J. Mason, "Legislative Mandates for Energy Model Documentation and Access: A Historical Analysis" (MIT Energy Laboratory Working Paper no. MIT-EL 79-067WP, October 1979), http://dspace.mit.edu/bitstream/handle/1721.1/35239/MIT-EL-79-067WP-09253332.pdf?sequence=1.
79. Sobel, *Energy Crisis*, vol. 2, *1974–75*, 51.
80. "Miller Calls for Probe of Energy Conglomerates," *The Spartanburg Herald*, January 21, 1974.
81. "The Whirlwind Confronts the Skeptics," 24.
82. Sobel, *Energy Crisis*, vol. 2, *1974–75*, 50.
83. Katz, *Congress and National Energy Policy*, 26.
84. "Nixon Vetoes Energy Bill and Is Upheld," *New York Times*, March 7, 1974.
85. Katz, *Congress and National Energy Policy*, 28.
86. "Laws Blamed for Big Profits," *The Press-Courier*, April 24, 1974.
87. David Vogel, *Fluctuating Fortunes: The Political Power of Business in America* (Washington, DC: Beard Books, 2003), 127.
88. Mieczkowski, *Gerald Ford and the Challenges of the 1970s*, 234–35.
89. Grossman, Peter Z. *U.S. Energy Policy and the Pursuit of Failure.* (Cambridge: Cambridge University Press, 2013), 146.
90. Michael J. Graetz, *The End of Energy: The Unmaking of America's Environment, Security, and Independence* (Boston: MIT Press, 2011), 38.
91. According to Berry, Jeffrey M., *Lobbying for the People: The Political Behavior of Public Interests Groups* (Princeton, NJ: Princeton University Press, 1977), 7, a public interest group is one that lobbies for benefits that do "not selectively and materially benefit the membership and activists of the organization."
92. Jack L. Walker, Jr. "The Origins and Maintenance of Interest Groups in America." *American Political Science Review* 77 (1983): 390–406.
93. Kay Lehman Schlozman and John T. Tierney, *Organized Interests and American Democracy* (New York: Harper & Row, 1986), 75–76.
94. David S. Meyer and Douglas R. Imig, "Political Opportunity and the Rise and Decline of Interest Group Sectors," *The Social Science Journal* 30, no. 3 (1993): 258.

95. Thomas Raymond Wellock, *Critical Masses: Opposition to Nuclear Power in California, 1958–1978* (Madison: University of Wisconsin Press, 1998), 109.
96. Katz, *Congress and National Energy Policy*, 7.
97. Yergin, *The Prize: The Epic Quest for Oil, Money & Power*, 555.
98. Peter A. Coates, *The Trans-Alaska Pipeline Controversy: Technology, Conservation and the Frontier* (Cranbury, NJ: Associated University Presses, 1991), 240.
99. Katz, *Congress and National Energy Policy*, 21.
100. Wellock, *Critical Masses: Opposition to Nuclear Power in California, 1958–1978*, 110.
101. "The Whirlwind Confronts the Skeptics," 24.
102. Andrew S. McFarland, *Public Interest Lobbies: Decision Making on Energy* (Washington, DC: American Energy Institute, 1987), 83. Originally cited in Sierra Club pamphlet, "Why the Sierra Club."
103. The Sierra Club actually experienced an internal rift, where some of the leadership hoped nuclear energy would be a possible substitute to strip-mining and coal development while others remained opposed to it wholesale.
104. Congressional Quarterly, *Continuing Energy Crisis in America* (Washington, DC: Congressional Quarterly, Inc., 1975), 49.
105. Richard Nixon, "Address to the Nation about Policies To Deal with the Energy Shortages," November 8, 1973, online by Gerhard Peters and John T. Woolley, American Presidency Project, http://www.presidency.ucsb.edu/ws/?pid=4035.
106. Walter A. Rosenbaum, *The Politics of Environmental Concern* (Westport, CT: Praeger Publishers, 1977), 40.
107. Christopher Cubbison, "Gunter Opposes Drilling Pending Further Study," *St. Petersburg Times*, August 23, 1973.
108. Congressional Quarterly, *Congressional Quarterly Almanac, 93rd Congress, 2nd Session*, 725.
109. Congressional Quarterly, *Continuing Energy Crisis in America*, 82.
110. Ibid. 84.
111. Mieczkowski, *Gerald Ford and the Challenges of the 1970s*, 202.
112. Vietor, *Energy Policy in America Since 1945: A Study of Business-Government Relations*, 246.
113. Ibid.
114. Stan Luge, *Corporate Power, American Democracy, and the Automobile Industry* (Cambridge: Cambridge University Press, 2005), 91–92.
115. Ibid. 93.
116. David Vogel, "A Case Study of Clean Air Legislation 1967–1981," in *The Impact of the Modern Corporation*, ed. Betty Bock et al. (New York: Columbia University Press 1984), 344.
117. McFarland, *Public Interest Lobbies: Decision Making on Energy*, 94.
118. Ibid., 92.
119. Ibid., 69.
120. Ibid., 70.
121. D. K. Pinsonneault, "Nader Says Fuel Crisis 'Phony,'" *The Telegraph*, March 22, 1974.
122. McFarland, *Public Interest Lobbies: Decision Making on Energy*, 74.
123. Ibid. 57.
124. Ibid. 59.
125. Ibid. 60.
126. Ibid. 62.
127. Ibid. 63.
128. Kingdon, John W. *Agendas, Alternatives, and Public Policies* (Boston: Little, Brown, 1984).
129. Sobel, *Energy Crisis*, vol. 2, *1974–75*, 89.
130. The Energy Information Administration, "collects, analyzes, and disseminates independent and impartial energy information to promote sound policymaking, efficient markets, and public understanding of energy and its interaction with the economy and the environment." Energy Information Administrion, "About" http://www.eia.gov/about/, accessed May http://www.eia.gov/about/.

Chapter 6

1. Steve Isser, *The Economics and Politics of the United States Oil Industry, 1920–1990* (New York: Garland Publishing, 1996), 147.
2. Assiciated Press, "Popularity Drop? Carter Ends His Meet-The-People Trip With Poll Prediction," *Evening Independent*, March 18, 1977.
3. George Gallup, "Gallup Poll: Can Americans Give up their Love Affair with the Auto?," *Anchorage Daily News*, April 21, 1977.
4. James M. Naughton, "Carter Shaped Energy Plan with Disregard for Politics," *New York Times*, April 23, 1977.
5. Jimmy Carter, "The President's Proposed Energy Policy," April 18, 1977, *Vital Speeches of the Day* 43, no. 14 (May 1977): 418–20.
6. Isser, *The Economics and Politics of the United States Oil Industry, 1920–1990*, 146.
7. Isser, *The Economics and Politics of the United States Oil Industry, 1920–1990*, 146; James E. Katz, *Congress and National Energy Policy* (New Brunswick, NJ: Transaction Books, 1984), 97.
8. Associated Press, "President Proposes Department of Energy," *Sarasota Herald-Tribune*, March 2, 1977.
9. Seymour M. Lipset and William Schneider, *The Confidence Gap: Business, Labor and Government in the Public Mind* (New York: The Free Press, 1983), 181.
10. Lester A. Sobel, ed., *Energy Crisis*, vol. 4, *1977–79* (New York: Facts on File, 1980), 54.
11. Lipset and Schneider, *The Confidence Gap: Business, Labor and Government in the Public Mind*, 185.
12. Associated Press, "Carter Fights to Save Energy Bill," *The Bulletin*, October 13, 1977.
13. Tom Wicker, "Carter's Energy Program Suffering Credibility Crisis," *Star-News*, June 16, 1977.
14. Associated Press, "Deadlocked Conferees Shelve Energy Debate," *Toledo Blade*, December 23, 1977.
15. William Sweet and Sandra Stencel, "Public Confidence and Energy." In *Editorial Research Reports 1979, vol. I*, 381–400. Washington, D.C.: CQ Press, 1979.
16. W. Greider and J. P. Smith, "A Proposition: High Oil Prices Benefit U.S." *Washington Post*, July 3, 1977.
17. Ibid.
18. Ibid.
19. Katz, *Congress and National Energy Policy*, 113.
20. Philip George, *The Political Economy of International Oil* (Edinburgh: Edinburgh University Press, 1994), 62.
21. Dennis Mullin, "Tragedy for Iran—Meaning for U.S.," *U.S. News & World Report*, November 13, 1978, 36.
22. Lowell S. Feld, "Oil Markets in Crisis: Major Oil Supply Disruptions since 1973," in *The New Global Oil Market*, ed. Siamack Shojai (Westport, CT: Praeger, 1995).
23. Dennis Mullin, "Tragedy for Iran—Meaning for U.S.," *U.S. News & World Report*, November 13, 1978, 36.
24. Dennis Mullin, "Tragedy for Iran—Meaning for U.S.," *U.S. News & World Report*, November 13, 1978, 36.
25. Daniel Yergin, *The Prize: The Epic Quest for Oil, Money & Power* (New York: Simon & Schuster, 1991), 678.
26. Ibid. 679
27. Sobel, *Energy Crisis*, vol. 4, *1977–79*.
28. Joseph Fitchett and International Herald Tribune, "Industrial Nations Agree to Cut Oil Consumption," March 3, 1979.
29. Yergin, *The Prize: The Epic Quest for Oil, Money & Power*, 685–86.
30. Philip, *The Political Economy of International Oil*, 163.
31. Yergin, *The Prize: The Epic Quest for Oil, Money & Power*, 687.
32. Sobel, *Energy Crisis*, vol. 4, *1977–79*, 56.
33. Lawrence Martin, "Lawrence Martin in Washington: Chaos Ahead in Gas Pettiness," *Globe and Mail*, May 19, 1979.

34. Barbara C. Farhar, "The Polls—Poll Trends: Public Opinion about Energy," *Public Opinion Quarterly* 56 (1994): 603–32.
35. Barbara Farhar, Charles Unseld, Rebecca Voires, and Robin Crews, "Public Opinion About Energy," *Annual Review of Energy* 5 (1980): 144.
36. Al Richman, "The Polls: Public Attitudes Toward the Energy Crisis," *Public Opinion Quarterly* 43 (1979): 576–85.
37. Farhar et al., "Public Opinion About Energy," 161.
38. Sobel, *Energy Crisis*, vol. 4, *1977–79*, 54.
39. Richman, "The Polls: Public Attitudes Toward the Energy Crisis."
40. Fred Barbash, "Sen. Baker Hints at Oil Nationalization; Industry Warned: Beware Public's Fury," *Washington Post*, May 14, 1979.
41. Ibid.
42. Sobel, *Energy Crisis*, vol. 4, *1977–79*, 2.
43. Ibid. 65.
44. Ibid. 81.
45. Ibid. 82.
46. Katz, *Congress and National Energy Policy*, 134.
47. Ibid. 135.
48. Ibid. 135.
49. Hoyt C. Hottel and Carroll L. Wilson, "Clearing the Way for Synthetic Fuels," *Washington Post*, June 18, 1979.
50. Walter A. Rosenbaum, "Notes from No Man's Land: The Politics and Ecology of Energy Research and Development," in *Environment, Energy, Public Policy: Toward a Rational Future*, ed. Regina Axelrod (Lexington, MA: D. C. Heath and Company, 1981), 65.
51. Katz, *Congress and National Energy Policy*, 144.
52. Mark Steitz, "Oil Decontrol and the Windfall Profits Tax," in *Energy Policy Analysis and Congressional Action*, ed. Raymond C. Scheppach and Everett M Ehrlich (Lexington, MA: Lexington Books, 1982), 79.
53. Ibid. 80.
54. Ibid. 79.
55. Joseph A. Yager, "The Energy Battles of 1979," in *Energy Policy in Perspective: Today's Problems, Yesterday's Solutions*, ed. Craufurd D. Goodwin et al. (Washington, DC: The Brookings Institution, 1981), 632.
56. Katz, *Congress and National Energy Policy*, 135.
57. Ibid. 136.
58. Ibid. 137.
59. Ibid. 141.
60. Ibid. 142.
61. Ibid. 143.
62. J. P. Smith, "Powerful Hill Foes Flattened by Synfuels Bandwagon," *Washington Post*, November 16, 1979.
63. Steitz, "Oil Decontrol and the Windfall Profits Tax," 79.
64. Ibid. 80.
65. Katz, *Congress and National Energy Policy*, 147.
66. John E. Chubb, *Interest Groups and the Bureaucracy: The Politics of Energy* (Stanford, CA: Stanford University Press, 1983), 225.
67. Katz, *Congress and National Energy Policy*, 136.
68. Mary Russell, "Senate Votes 'Fast Track' Energy Unit," *Washington Post*, October 5, 1979.
69. Smith, "Powerful Hill Foes Flattened by Synfuels Bandwagon."
70. Katz, *Congress and National Energy Policy*, 144.
71. Yergin, *The Prize: The Epic Quest for Oil, Money & Power*, 714.

Chapter 7

1. Phil Kuntz, "Unstable Mideast Oil Supply Rocks the World Market," *Congressional Quarterly* 49 (January 1991): 21.

2. Bruce A. Beaubouef, *The Strategic Petroleum Reserve: U.S. Energy Security and Oil Politics, 1975–2005* (College Station: Texas A&M University Press, 2007).

3. Daniel Yergin. *The Prize: The Quest for Oil, Money & Power* (New York: Simon & Schuster, 1991), 771.

4. Ibid. 773.

5. Ibid. 173.

6. Kuntz, "Unstable Mideast Oil Supply Rocks the World Market," 22.

7. Yergin, *The Prize: The Quest for Oil, Money & Power*, 774.

8. Kuntz, "Unstable Mideast Oil Supply Rocks the World Market," 22.

9. David Lewis Feldman, ed., *The Energy Crisis: Unresolved Issues and Enduring Legacies* (Boulder, CO: Westview Press, 1982), 85.

10. Eric R.A.N. Smith, *Energy, the Environment, and Public Opinion* (Lanham, MD: Rowman & Littlefield Publishers, 2002), 35.

11. Feldman, *The Energy Crisis: Unresolved Issues and Enduring Legacies*, 85.

12. Steven Greenhouse, "Confrontation in the Gulf, No Oil Emergency Yet, Energy Experts Assert," *New York Times*, August 10, 1990; James Brook, "Caracas Asks US to Help on Oil Output," *New York Times*, September 21, 1990; Jim Hoagland, "A New Oil Order . . . ," *Washington Post*, October 11, 1990.

13. Beaubouef, *The Strategic Petroleum Reserve: U.S. Energy Security and Oil Politics, 1975–2005*, 152.

14. Smith, *Energy, the Environment, and Public Opinion*, 35.

15. Peter V. Hobbs and Lawrence F. Radke, "Airborne Studies of the Smoke from the Kuwait Oil Fires," *Science* 256, no. 5059 (1992): 987–91.

16. Barbara Farhar, "Public Opinion about Energy," *Public Opinion Quarterly* 58 (1994): 603–32.

17. Ibid. 605.

18. Louis Harris, "Few Believe Oil Companies, Polls Find," *San Francisco Chronicle*, September 10, 1990.

19. Smith, *Energy, the Environment, and Public Opinion*, 100.

20. Farhar, "Public Opinion about Energy," 605.

21. Yergin, *The Prize: The Quest for Oil, Money & Power*, 781.

22. Farhar, "Public Opinion about Energy," 608.

23. Farhar, "Public Opinion about Energy," 607.

24. John Curley, "Gas Debate: From Oval Office to Local Circles, Drivers Fume," *St. Louis Dispatch*, August 9, 1990.

25. Ibid.

26. Louis Harris, "Public Bitter Toward Oil Companies for Gasoline Price Hikes" *Harris Poll*, September 9, 1990, http://media.theharrispoll.com/documents/Harris-Interactive-Poll-Research-PUBLIC-BITTER-TOWARD-OIL-COMPANIES-FOR-GASOLINE-PRICE-HIKES-1990-09.pdf.

27. Judy Keen and Ellen Neuborne, "The Oil War: Fight Hits the Home Front; Gas Price Hikes Well of Outrage; Oil Companies Reject Charge of 'Ripoff,'" *USA Today*, August 7, 1990.

28. Steve Isser, *The Economics and Politics of the United States Oil Industry, 1920–1990: Profits, Populism, and Petroleum* (London: Routledge, 1996), 253.

29. Ibid. 253.

30. Ibid. 260

31. Curley. "Gas Debate: From Oval Office to Local Circles, Drivers Fume."

32. Ibid.

33. Paul Taylor and Rchard Morin, "Poll Finds that Americans Back U.S. Response, but Warily," *Washington Post* Poll, August 10, 1990, First section, A1.

34. Farhar, "Public Opinion about Energy," 607.

35. Ibid. 608.

36. Louis Harris, "Public Resents Oil Companies over Price Increases," *Harris Poll*, December 2, 1990, http://media.theharrispoll.com/documents/Harris-Interactive-Poll-Research-PUBLIC-RESENTS-OIL-COMPANIES-OVER-PRICE-INCREASES-1990-12.pdf.

37. Yergin, *The Prize: The Quest for Oil, Money & Power*.

38. Beaubouef, *The Strategic Petroleum Reserve: U.S. Energy Security and Oil Politics, 1975–2005*, 155.

39. George Bush, "Address before Joint Session of the Congress on the Persian Gulf Crisis and the Federal Budget Deficit," September 11, 1990, online by Gerhard Peters and John T. Woolley, American Presidency Project, http://www.presidency.ucsb.edu/ws/?pid=18820.
40. Ibid.
41. Ibid.
42. Beaubouef, *The Strategic Petroleum Reserve: U.S. Energy Security and Oil Politics, 1975–2005*, 155.
43. Ibid.
44. James Franklin, "Energy Plan Delay Sparks Speculation on Bush Proposals," *Boston Globe*, February 8, 1991.
45. James Franklin, "Oft-Postponed US Energy Plan is Delayed Again," *The Boston Globe*, February 7, 1991.
46. Holly Idelson, "Administration Plan Challenged as Too Weak on Conservation." *Congressional Quarterly Weekly*, Feb 23, 1991, 464.
47. Robert Samuelson, "Just Tinkering with Energy; Bush's Plan Avoids the Tough Steps," *Washington Post*, February 27, 1991.
48. Holly Idelson, "Administration Plan Challenged as Too Weak on Conservation." *Congressional Quarterly Weekly*, February 23, 1991, 464.
49. Ibid, 465.
50. Matthew Wald, "Bush Urges Congress to Pass Energy Plan," *New York Times*, July 25, 1991.
51. Ibid.
52. Louis Harris, "Few Believe Oil Companies, Polls Find," *San Francisco Chronicle*, Sept 10, 1990.
53. Associated Press, "The Iraqi Invasion: Democrats Urge Bush to Pressure Oil Companies on Price Increases," *New York Times*, August 8, 1990.
54. Yergin, *The Prize: The Quest for Oil, Money & Power*, 174.
55. "Little Action on Energy Policy in 1990." In CQ Almanac 1990, 46th ed., 312–13. Washington, DC: Congressional Quarterly, 1991, http://library.cqpress.com/cqalmanac/cqal90-1112661.
56. Ibid. 312.
57. Fuel-Efficiency Effort Defeated in Senate." In CQ Almanac 1990, 46th ed., 279–81. Washington, DC: Congressional Quarterly, 1991. http://library.cqpress.com/cqalmanac/cqal90-1112545.
58. Ibid..
59. "Little Action on Energy Policy in 1990." In CQ Almanac 1990, 46th ed., 312–13. Washington, DC: Congressional Quarterly, 1991. http://library.cqpress.com/.
60. Ibid. 312.
61. "Energy Conservation, Efficiency Programs." In CQ Almanac 1990, 46th ed., 319. Washington, DC: Congressional Quarterly, 1991. http://library.cqpress.com/cqalmanac/cqal90-1112687.
62. Ibid. 1991.
63. Isser, *The Economics and Politics of the United States Oil Industry, 1920–1990: Profits, Populism, and Petroleum*, 176
64. "Proposal to Drill in Arctic National Wildlife Refuge (ANWR) Kills Energy Bill." In CQ Almanac 1991, 47th ed., 195–208. Washington, DC: Congressional Quarterly, 1992. http://library.cqpress.com/cqalmanac/cqal91-1110326.
65. "ANWR Drilling Kills Energy Bill." In *Congressional Quarterly Almanac*, 1991, edited by Susan Kellam, 195-208. Washington, DC: Congressional Quarterly News Features, 1992.
66. Holly Idelson, "Energy Policy Filibuster in Senate . . . Fuel for Efficiency Standards Debate." *Congressional Quarterly Weekly Report*, November 2, 1991, 3192.
67. Ibid.
68. Holly Idelson, "Johnson Works to Clear Path for Revamped Energy Bill." *Congressional Quarterly Weekly*, February 8, 1992, 297–99.
69. Ibid.
70. Holly Idelson, "Senate Passes Energy Bill, 94-4; Arctic Refuge Issue Dropped." *Congressional Quarterly Weekly*, Feb 22, 1992, 397.
71. Holly Idelson, "Johnson Works to Clear Path for Revamped Energy Bill." .
72. Holly Idelson, "Energy Politics Emerges as Oil Crisis Subsides." *Congressional Quarterly Weekly*, June 15, 1991, 1573.
73. Ibid. 1574.

74. Keen and Neuborne, "The Oil War: Fight Hits the Home Front; Gas Price Hikes Well of Outrage; Oil Companies Reject Charge of 'Ripoff.' "
75. Press Conference: Chris Flavin, World Watch Institute, and Michael McCloskey, Sierra Club, et al., *Federal News Service*, August 23, 1990.
76. "An International Call to Action," *Earth Island Journal*, Winter 91/92, Vol. 7, Issue 1, p46.
77. Press Conference with Green Peace, *Federal News Service*, August 22, 1990.
78. Mark Potts, "Two Oil Companies Cut, Freeze Prices; Firms Respond to Bush's Plea for Restraint," *Washington Post*, August 9, 1990.
79. Holly Idelson, "Energy Policy Filibuster in Senate . . . Fuel for Efficiency Standards Debate." *Congressional Quarterly Weekly*, November 2, 1991, 3192.

Chapter 8

1. Crude oil prices quoted in this chapter refer to the spot price of West Texas Intermediate (WTI) except where stated otherwise. Source: US Energy Information Administration, http://www.eia.gov/dnav/pet/hist/LeafHandler.ashx?n=PET&s= RWTC&f=M.
2. James D. Hamilton, "Causes and Consequences of the Oil Shock of 2007–08," *Brookings Papers on Economic Activity* Vol. 2009 (Spring 2009): 215–61.
3. Weekly US retail gasoline price for all grades, all formulations. Source: US Energy Information Administration, http://www.eia.gov/dnav/pet/hist/LeafHandler.ashx?n=PET&s=EMM_ EPM0_PTE_NUS_DPG&f=W.
4. Hamilton, "Causes and Consequences of the Oil Shock of 2007–08."
5. In inflation-adjusted dollars.
6. Colin Campbell and Jean Laherrere, "The End of Cheap Oil," *Scientific American*, March 1998, 78–83.
7. Scott Carlson, "Local Drivers Feel Pinch at Pumps; Average Gas Prices are up 17 Cents from a Month Ago," *Saint Paul Pioneer Press*, April 21, 1999.
8. Sara Nathan, "Will Oil Prices Ruin Vacations?," *USA Today*, March 24, 1999.
9. Christian Berthelsen, "Sharpest Rise in the Prices for Gasoline is in California," *New York Times*, April 11, 1999.
10. Kaiser Family Foundation/Harvard University/NewsHour Survey, July 26–September 5, 2000; n = 850 adults nationwide; MoE = 2.4 percent. "In general, do you think oil companies make too much profit (75%), not enough profit (3%), or about the right amount of profit (16%)?" Accessed through the Roper Center iPOLL: http://ropercenter.cornell.edu/ ipoll-database/
11. Tim Weiner, "Battle Waged in the Senate over Royalties on Oil Firms," *New York Times*, September 21, 1999.
12. Juliet Eilperin, "GOP Environmental Riders Complicate Agency Funding," *Washington Post*, September 27, 1999.
13. Carey Goldberg, "The President's News Conference: The Main Issue; Government Was 'Napping' on Oil Cost, Energy Chief Says," *New York Times*, February 17, 2000.
14. Ibid.
15. Lisa Respers, "Truck Convoy to Protest Fuel Cost Rumbles to D.C.," *Baltimore Sun*, February 23, 2000, accessed at http://articles.baltimoresun.com/2000-02-23/business/0002240344_ 1_truckers-fuel-convoy.
16. H. Josef Hebert, "Worldwide Shortfall Forces Oil Prices to New High; Energy Secretary Richardson Says Congress Should not Overreact," *Contra Costa Times*, March 2, 2000.
17. Ibid.
18. The Associated Press, "House Calls on Clinton to Consider Restricting Aid to OPEC Countries Involved in Price Fixing," *St. Louis Post-Dispatch*, March 23, 2000.
19. Gallup Poll, October 25–28, 2000; n = 1,004; MoE = 3.1. "Suppose that on election day this year you could vote on key issues as well as candidates. Please tell me whether you would vote for (44%) or against (50%) opening up part of the Arctic National Wildlife Refuge in Alaska for oil exploration." Accessed through the Roper Center iPOLL: http://ropercenter.cornell. edu/ipoll-database/

20. Gallup Poll, March 30–April 2, 2000; n = 998, MoE = 3.2. "Would you favor (74%) or oppose (23%) a temporary reduction in the federal gas tax by 4.3 cents per gallon as a way of dealing with the increased price of oil?" Accessed through the Roper Center iPOLL: http://roper-center.cornell.edu/ipoll-database/

21. Tom Squitieri, "Clinton Considering Options on Fuel Costs," *USA Today*, March 17, 2000.

22. Ibid.

23. Chris Woodyard, "Profits Sky High for Oil Industry; Truckers, Others Scowl at Rich Gain," *USA Today*, April 26, 2000.

24. Ibid.

25. Sara Nathan, "Rising Gas Prices Spur Calls for National Boycott," *USA Today*, March 13, 2000.

26. Ibid.

27. Chris Woodyard, "Gas Price Gap Jars Travelers," *USA Today*, May 26, 2000..

28. Bloomberg News, "Gas Prices under Scrutiny," *New York Times*, June 28, 2000.

29. William Claiborne, "Clinton: Gas Prices Straining Economy; President Decries Impact on Consumers and Pledges Tough Probe of Oil Industry," *Washington Post*, June 23, 2000.

30. Sherri Day, "Schumer Calls for Action to Prevent Energy Crisis," *New York Times*, July 10, 2000.

31. Adam Shell, "Oil Giants Report Earnings Doubled; But Jump not from Gas Pump, Analysts Say," *USA Today*, July 26, 2000.

32. Richard Oppel, "Small Gas Stations Struggle as Big Oil Producers Profit," *New York Times*, July 13, 2000.

33. George Hager, "Texas Drillers Enjoy High Oil Prices, for Now; Memories of Hard Times Restrain Boom," *USA Today*, July 28, 2000.

34. Ibid.

35. David Fleischaker, "Oh, Sure, It's Easy toBlame Big Oil, but Consumers Point in the Wrong Direction," *USA Today*, July 5, 2000.

36. Shell, "Oil Giants Report Earnings Doubled; But Jump not from Gas Pump, Analysts Say."

37. "Gas Prices Fall in Time for Holiday; Midwest Vacationers Fill Up, Hit the Road," *Washington Post*, July 2, 2000.

38. George Hager, "Oil Prices Spike Back Up; Pump Prices May Follow," *USA Today*, August 15, 2000.

39. Ibid.

40. "Clinton Taps Emergency Oil Reserve," *St. Petersburg Times*, September 23, 2000.

41. Alison Mitchell, "The 2000 Campaign: The Texas Governor; Bush Criticizes Gore for Wanting to Use Petroleum Supply," *New York Times*, September 22, 2000.

42. International Energy Agency, *Monthly Oil Market Report*, December 11, 2000, 3.

43. Blake Clayton, *Market Madness: A Century of Oil Panics, Crises, and Crashes* (Oxford: Oxford University Press, 2015), chap. 5.

44. William McCall, "Physicist Warns Global Oil Production Peak Could Bring Economic Disaster," *Associated Press*, August 13, 2001.

45. Colin Campbell and Jean Laherrere, "The End of Cheap Oil," *Scientific American*, March 1998, 78–83.

46. Goldman Sachs, "Underinvestment in Commodities Means Markets Will Be Tighter, Sooner," *CEO Confidential*, April 2002, 5.

47. Clayton, *Market Madness: A Century of Oil Panics, Crises, and Crashes*,147.

48. Ibid.

49. Steven Mufson, "As Gas Prices Rise Again, Democrats Blame Big Oil," *Washington Post*, May 11, 2007.

50. Joe Carrol, "Exxon's Profit Surges to First-Quarter Record on Higher Gas Prices," *Washington Post*, April 27, 2007.

51. Associated Press, "Profits Climb 5.7% at Shell Despite Falling Oil Prices," *New York Times*, May 4, 2007..

52. Warren Brown, "A Gas Crisis 30 Years in the Making," *Washington Post*, May 27, 2007.

53. Barbara Hagenbaugh, "Gas Pump Gulps More of Family Pay; Average Household Spent $2,277 in '06," *USA Today*, May 17, 2007.

54. ABC/*Washington Post* Poll: "Have recent price increases in gasoline caused any financial hardship for you or others in your household, or not?" 67 percent yes (April 12 to April 15, 2007); 57 percent yes (May 11, 2006 to May 15, 2006). Accessed through the Roper Center iPOLL: http://ropercenter.cornell.edu/ipoll-database/

55. Gallup Poll, 5/21/07 to 5/24/07; n = 1,007 adults nationwide; MoE +/- 4: "Which of the following best describes how gas prices have affected you personally? Gas prices have created a hardship for you and your family (18%). Gas prices have caused you to adjust your usual spending and saving habits in significant ways, but have not caused a hardship (49%). OR, Gas prices haven't had much impact on your financial situation (33%)." Accessed through the Roper Center iPOLL: http://ropercenter.cornell.edu/ipoll-database/

56. Gallup Poll. May 21 to May 24, 2007; n = 1,007 adults nationwide; MoE +/- 4: "From what you have heard or read, why do you think the price of gasoline is so high right now?" Open-ended: oil/greedy gas companies gouging the public (34 percent), refinery problems/need maintenance/capacity (16 percent); due to the crisis in the Middle East (13 percent); increased supply and demand/not conserving (10 percent); politics/government involvement (9 percent). A June 2007 poll conducted by Quinnipiac University Poll (June 5 to June 11, 2007) found similar results: "Who do you blame the most for the recent increase in gasoline prices: oil producing countries (11%), oil companies (43%), President Bush (20%), Americans who drive vehicles that use a lot of gasoline (4%), or normal supply and demand pressures (13%)?" Accessed through the Roper Center iPOLL: http://ropercenter.cornell.edu/ipoll-database/

57. Steven Mufson, "Gas Prices Close to Historic Record; Regular Unleaded Just Shy of '81 mark," *Washington Post*, May 22, 2007.

58. Byron Dorgan, "Investigate Price Gouging," *USA Today*, May 25, 2007.

59. Bob Dart, "House Takes on Gas Pricing," *Atlanta Journal-Constitution*, May 23, 2007.

60. Mufson, "As Gas Prices Rise Again, Democrats Blame Big Oil."

61. Associated Press, "Metro Briefing New York: Manhattan: Call for Gas Investigation," *New York Times*, May 7, 2007.

62. The other energy-related executive order designated the ITER International Fusion Energy Organization as a Public International Organization.

63. It is worth noting that congressional action related to energy remained higher in the years following the 1999–2000 oil price shock than it had been in the years before that crisis.

64. Edmund Andrews, "Administration Proposes Expanded Energy Drilling Off Coasts," *New York Times*, May 1, 2007.

65. Clayton, *Market Madness: A Century of Oil Panics, Crises, and Crashes,* 157.

66. John Broder, "Industry Flexes Muscle, and a Weaker Energy Bill Passes," *New York Times*, December 14, 2007.

67. Jad Mouawad, "Oil Price Rise Fails to Open Tap," *New York Times*, April 29, 2008.

68. Jad Mouawad, "The Big Thirst," *New York Times*, April 20, 2008.

69. USA Today/Gallup Poll, May 2 to May 4, 2008; n = 1,017; MoE +/-3: "Have recent price increases in gasoline caused any financial hardship for your or your household?" 71 percent yes, 29 percent no.

70. Jad Mouawad and Mireya Navarro, "Teeth Gritted, Drivers Adjust to $4 Gasoline," *New York Times*, May 24, 2008.

71. Jad Mouawad, "Exxon Posts Its 2nd-Best Quarter, but It's not Enough for Wall St.," *New York Times*, May 2, 2008.

72. Mouawad and Navarro, "Teeth Gritted, Drivers Adjust to $4 Gasoline."

73. CNN/Opinion Research Corporation Poll, April 28–30, 2008; n = 1,008; MoE +/- 3. "Do you think oil companies as a whole are making too much profit (83%), a reasonable profit (13%), or not enough profit? (3%)?" Accessed through the Roper Center iPOLL: http://ropercenter.cornell.edu/ipoll-database/

74. *USA Today*/Gallup Poll, May 30–June 1, 2008; n = 514; MoE +/- 5: "Please tell me whether you think each of the following deserves a great deal of blame, some blame, not much blame, or no blame at all for the country's current energy problems: U.S. oil companies (60% great deal), the current Bush administration (49% great deal), foreign countries that produce oil (46% great deal), Congress (44% great deal), American consumers (31% great

deal), U.S. automobile companies (31% great deal), or environmental laws and regulations (25% great deal)." Quinnipiac University Poll, May 8–12, 2008; n = 1,745 registered voters; MoE +/−2.4: "Who do you blame the most for the recent increase in gasoline prices: oil companies (35 percent), President Bush (23 percent), oil producing countries (19 percent), normal supply and demand pressures (14 percent), or Americans who drive vehicles that use a lot of gasoline (3 percent)." Accessed through the Roper Center iPOLL: http://ropercenter. cornell.edu/ipoll-database/

75. Mouawad and Navarro, "Teeth Gritted, Drivers Adjust to $4 Gasoline.".

76. Damien Cave, "States Get in on the Calls for a Gas Tax Holiday," *New York Times*, May 6, 2008.

77. *USA Today*/Gallup Poll, May 2–4, 2008; n = 1,017; MoE +/− 3: "Thinking about the cost of gasoline, do you think the current rise in gas prices represents a temporary fluctuation in prices (19%), or a more permanent change in prices (78%)?" Accessed through the Roper Center iPOLL: http://ropercenter.cornell.edu/ipoll-database/

78. Quinnipiac University Poll, May 8–12, 2008; n = 1,745; MoE +/− 2.4: "Do you think that eliminating the federal gas tax for the summer months is a good idea (41%) or a bad idea (49%)?" Accessed through the Roper Center iPOLL: http://ropercenter.cornell.edu/ ipoll-database/

79. CBS News/*New York Times* Poll, May 2–8, 2008; n = 487; MoE +/− 4.5: "Do you think some candidates have proposed eliminating the gas tax this summer mainly because they think it is a sound proposal that will provide some relief to average Americans (21%) or mainly to help themselves politically (70%)?" Accessed through the Roper Center iPOLL: http://roper-center.cornell.edu/ipoll-database/

80. George W. Bush, "The President's News Conference," April 29, 2008, online by Gerhard Peters and John T. Woolley, American Presidency Project http:// http://www.presidency. ucsb.edu/ws/index.php?pid=77239.

81. Ibid.

82. David Herszenhorn, "Congress Adjourns, but Talks on Oil Persist," *New York Times*, August 2, 2008.

83. Associated Press, "Paulson: No Quick Fix for Oil Prices," *New York Times*, June 2, 2008.

84. Clayton, *Market Madness: A Century of Oil Panics, Crises, and Crashes*, 160.

85. Jad Mouawad, "OPEC Ponders Choices as Oil Prices Plummet; Seeking Stability as Demand Dwindles," *New York Times*, October 22, 2008.

86. The price of oil dropped below $50 per barrel at the end of 2008 for about four months during the financial crisis and again in January 2015 for about four months when OPEC members flooded the market with oil in order to undercut US oil producers.

Chapter 9

1. John W. Kingdon, *Agendas, Alternatives, and Public Policies* (New York: Longman, 2003); Frank R. Baumgartner and Bryan D. Jones, *Agendas and Instability in American Politics* (Chicago: University of Chicago Press, 1993); Bryan D. Jones and Frank R. Baumgartner, *The Politics of Attention* (Chicago: University of Chicago Press, 2005).

2. John W. Kingdon, *Agendas, Alternatives, and Public Policies* (Boston: Little, Brown, 1984).

3. E. E. Schattschneider, *The Semi-Sovereign People* (New York: Holt, Rinehart and Winston, 1960); Baumgartner and Jones, *Agendas and Instability in American Politics*.

4. Jones and Baumgartner, *The Politics of Attention*, 91.

5. Thomas E. Mann and Norman J. Ornstein, *It's Even Worse Than It Looks: How the American Constitutional System Collided With the New Politics of Extremism* (New York: Basic Books, 2012).

6. John W. Kingdon, *Congressmen's Voting Decisions*, 3rd ed. (Ann Arbor, MI: University of Michigan Press, 1989); R. Douglas Arnold, *The Logic of Congressional Action* (New Haven, CT: Yale University Press, 1990); Kristina Miler, *Constituency Representation in Congress* (New York: Cambridge University Press, 2014).

7. Paul Burstein, *American Public Opinion, Advocacy, and Policy in Congress* (New York: Cambridge University Press, 2014); Robert S. Erikson, Gerald C. Wright, and John P. McIver, *Statehouse Democracy* (New York: Cambridge University Press, 1993); Benjamin I. Page, "The

Semi-Sovereign People," in *Navigating Public Opinion*, ed. Jeff Manza, Fay Lomax Cook, and Benjamin I. Page (New York: Oxford University Press, 2002); Robert Y. Shapiro, "Public Opinion, Elites, and Democracy," *Critical Review* 12 (1998): 501–28; James Stimson, Michael B. MacKuen, and Robert S. Erikson, "Dynamic Representation," *American Political Science Review* 89 (1995): 543–65.

8. Burstein, *American Public Opinion, Advocacy, and Policy in Congress.*

INDEX